John Ball, William August Brevoort Coolidge

Hints and notes practical and scientific for travellers in the Alps

John Ball, William August Brevoort Coolidge

Hints and notes practical and scientific for travellers in the Alps

ISBN/EAN: 9783337206192

Printed in Europe, USA, Canada, Australia, Japan

Cover: Foto ©Andreas Hilbeck / pixelio.de

More available books at **www.hansebooks.com**

GENERAL INTRODUCTION
TO THE
'ALPINE GUIDE'

HINTS AND NOTES

PRACTICAL AND SCIENTIFIC
FOR
TRAVELLERS IN THE ALPS

BEING A REVISION OF THE
GENERAL INTRODUCTION TO THE 'ALPINE GUIDE'

BY THE LATE

JOHN BALL, F.R.S. &c.

PRESIDENT OF THE ALPINE CLUB

A NEW EDITION

PREPARED ON BEHALF OF THE ALPINE CLUB
BY

W. A. B. COOLIDGE

FELLOW OF MAGDALEN COLLEGE, OXFORD
AND FORMERLY EDITOR OF THE 'ALPINE JOURNAL'

LONGMANS, GREEN, AND CO.
39 PATERNOSTER ROW, LONDON
NEW YORK AND BOMBAY
1899

All rights reserved

PREFACE
TO
THE PRESENT EDITION.

—⋄—

IN this edition all the old articles that have been retained have been very carefully revised—that on the 'Geology of the Alps' having, indeed, been practically rewritten by Professor Bonney, while that on the 'Climate and Vegetation of the Alps' has been much expanded by Mr. Percy Groom. One article ('Hypsometry') of the old edition has been omitted, as the publication of the great Government Surveys has now rendered it superfluous. Two new articles have been added—'Photography in the High Alps,' by Mr. Sydney Spencer, and 'Life in an Alpine Valley,' by myself. Of the two appendices one ('List of Books and Maps relating to the Alps') is an extension and enlargement of a list previously given, while the other ('A Glossary of Alpine Terms') has been compiled by myself from many sources. It is hoped that both may be found of use, though neither makes any pretensions to exhaustive completeness.

The title of the book has been slightly altered, and the articles rearranged in what seems to be a better order.

I am greatly indebted to all those who have helped me, in various ways, in preparing this new edition.

The Preface to the first edition (and indeed to the whole work) is so interesting and characteristic that its historical importance warrants me in reprinting it with three slight omissions, while brackets indicate later alterations and additions, as they appear in the 1875 edition.

INTRODUCTION.

In the first edition (1863) of the first volume ('Western Alps') of the 'Alpine Guide' the 'General Introduction' was prefixed to the text, and immediately followed by 'Supplementary Notes' relating exclusively to the Western Alps. But in the first edition (1864) of the second volume ('Central Alps') the 'General Introduction' was omitted (being published in 1864 as a separate pamphlet), while the 'Preliminary Notes' relate to the Central Alps only. This plan of separating the general and special portions of the Introduction seems to have proved the more convenient. Hence, in the second edition (1866) of the first volume ('Western Alps'), the 'General Introduction' is omitted, a slip referring readers to the separate pamphlet in which it was then contained, while the 'Supplementary Notes' of 1863 have become 'Preliminary Notes to the Western Alps.' In this way the 'General Introduction' (now reissued in a revised form) and the special 'Preliminary Notes' relating to the great divisions of the Alps, though originally closely connected, have since 1864 been separate and distinct. In 1898 the new edition of the 'Western Alps' was prefaced by a new edition of its special 'Preliminary Notes,' and it is proposed to adopt a similar plan in the case of the new edition of the 'Central Alps,' now in preparation.

W. A. B. COOLIDGE.

GRINDELWALD: *April* 1899.

PREFACE

TO

THE FIRST EDITION (1863).

———◆◆———

A JUST distinction has been drawn between travellers who visit foreign countries with the object of gaining and communicating knowledge, and tourists who go from place to place seeking amusement and change of scene, but without any more definite scope than to gratify a superficial curiosity. The line of distinction between these two classes, which was easily drawn twenty or thirty years ago, is nowadays less definitely marked. The all but universal taste for travelling has spread at a time when increased knowledge and a more lively interest in physical science have become diffused throughout the educated classes in our own and other countries. Most men of cultivated minds occasionally seek relaxation in travelling, and a large proportion of tourists have sufficient knowledge to take an intelligent interest in some, or it may be in several, departments of science or art naturally connected with the country through which they pass.

These remarks especially apply to travellers in the Alps. The day is past when it could be thought necessary to apologise for or explain the prevalence of a love for mountain travelling. It is a simple fact that, especially in our own country, thousands of persons have learned to regard this as a sovereign medicine for mind and body, and to feel that the weeks or months devoted to it are the periods of life most full of true enjoyment, and those that leave the most abiding impressions. The fact that the scenery of the Alps is unsurpassed elsewhere in the world for the union of grandeur, beauty, and variety, and that it is accessible with a trifling expenditure of time and money, naturally accounts for the constantly increasing influx of strangers.

As high mountain countries, and the Alps in particular, abound with phenomena new and striking to the intelligent observer, there is a constant increase in the number of those who, without undertaking systematic research, are led to desire further information respecting the structure of the earth's surface, and the causes that have uplifted the mountain ranges, or the laws that regulate the circulation of heat and moisture, which maintain what may be called the inanimate life of our planet, or the animal and vegetable forms that exhibit in apparently inhospitable regions so rich a variety.

In addition to these objects of interest, there is a simpler branch of enquiry which especially recommends itself to many of our active and energetic countrymen. Many parts of the Alps are very difficult of access, and but a few years ago there were many considerable districts whose highest peaks had never been attained, which were not known to be traversed by practicable passes, and of which none but slight and imperfect information was anywhere accessible. To explore these little-known districts, to scale the higher summits, and to discover passes that should connect valleys that are separated by lofty ranges, have been the pursuits of the members of the Alpine Club.

Without exaggerating the importance of the work achieved, it is impossible to deny that a remarkable degree of enterprise and energy has been exhibited by many of the members of that association in accomplishing work which, if not actually scientific, is certainly conducive to the progress of science. They cannot indeed rival the men who, following the illustrious example of Saussure, have explored the Alps with the definite object of enlarging the bounds of science; but, in achieving the preparatory task of opening the way through many of the least accessible parts of the Alpine chain, they have undoubtedly surpassed the performances of all their predecessors. [Their example has not been without influence in other countries, and the formation of kindred associations in Switzerland, Austria, Italy, and France has given additional impulse to the spirit of Alpine exploration and enquiry.]

It has for some time been felt that the time had come for attempting to supply to Alpine travellers a guide-book differing in many respects from those hitherto in use, and the writer has been urged, by some of those most capable of contributing to such a work, to undertake the task. He has no claim to a brilliant share in the adventurous performances of his friends and fellow-members of the Alpine Club; his qualifications, such as they are, arise rather from a somewhat prolonged and extensive acquaintance with the greater portion of the Alps, in the course of which he has crossed the main chain more than sixty times by forty different passes, besides traversing more than one hundred and seventy of the lateral passes.

This work differs from most, if not all, of its predecessors in its plan, which is designed to include the entire region of the Alps. In regard to certain districts the available information is incomplete, but the arrangement is such, that the omissions may be easily supplied hereafter. Besides the preliminary matter contained in the Introduction, a variety of notes and indications connected with geology and botany are scattered through the body of the work, with a view to direct and guide those who feel an interest in those subjects. Detailed notices of the vegetation would occupy too much space, and the botanical indications have for the most part been confined to pointing out localities for the rarest species, chiefly from the writer's personal observation.

[In the arrangement of this work it soon became clear that it would not conduce to the convenience of travellers, nor to a clear understanding of the topography of the Alpine chain, that the writer should be guided by political boundaries. These, as very recent experience has shown, are subject to change, and they rarely follow the natural divisions suggested by the physical features of the country. Of the three main divisions of the work, that which appears] under the title 'Western Alps' includes the entire range that encircles the plain of Piedmont, from the Maritime Alps north of Nice to the Pass of the Simplon, along with the Dauphiné and Savoy Alps, and the portions of Switzerland connected with the Pennine range. This is the portion of the Alps in which the amount of new matter available through the activity of the members of the Alpine Club is most considerable, mainly because it includes the portions most difficult of access, and where, owing to the comparative neglect of their predecessors, most remained to be done. [The volume devoted to the Central Alps comprehends the greater part of Switzerland, with the portions of the Tyrol lying west of the Adige, along with the Lombard valleys to their natural boundary—the Lake of Garda. The third volume is devoted to the Eastern Alps, extending from the Adige nearly to Vienna, and from the plains of Venetia to the neighbourhood of Munich.]

[Although the activity of Swiss, Italian, Austrian, and German naturalists and mountaineers has left less scope for new explorations in the two latter volumes, the writer trusts that they will be found to contain a large amount of information, either new, or not easily accessible, derived from his own observations or those of his correspondents.]

It may be a satisfaction to future travellers if the writer here expresses his conviction that, in spite of all that has yet been done, no portion of the Alps can, in a topographical, and still less in a scientific sense, be said to be thoroughly explored. In districts supposed to be well known, an active mountaineer will constantly find scope for new expeditions; and if he has cultivated the habit of observation, he may, at the same time, make these subservient to the increase of knowledge.

It has been a matter of great difficulty to reconcile the necessity for compression with the abundance of materials at hand, and the writer cannot expect to escape criticism from readers who may find one or other subject imperfectly treated. Though it is hoped that the work will be found useful for reference, as containing a large body of topographical and other information, it is primarily intended for Alpine travellers, and the object kept in view has been to select the matter most likely to be of use and interest to that class. Had it been designed as a history of Alpine adventure, it would be open to the reproach that it does not adequately notice the labours of earlier explorers, such as Saussure, Hugi, Zumstein, and many other surviving travellers, nor often refer to the earlier authorities. The writer has perhaps more reason to fear that travellers may reproach him for having admitted too much matter, than for undue brevity.

In respect to expeditions which have been made but once, or very rarely, the writer has usually given the account in an abridged form, but in the actual words of the traveller whose initials are subscribed, the names being given in full in the annexed page of Explanations.

To the authors of these notes which have, for the most part, been communicated in MSS. to the writer, he begs hereby to express his cordial acknowledgments, and his hope that they will continue to furnish further information towards [future editions] of the work. At the risk of appearing to fail in more special acknowledgment to others who have contributed valuable matter, he feels bound to offer his especial thanks to Messrs. W. Mathews, jun., and F. F. Tuckett, and to [Colonel Karl v. Sonklar, of Innsbruck].* The two former gentlemen, in particular, have afforded invaluable assistance by the corrections and hints which they are each so well able to afford, and which were the more necessary as the work has been for the most part executed at a distance from England, and with but limited opportunities for consulting works of reference.

J. BALL.

1863.

* In the 1863 edition the third name mentioned was that of Chanoine Carrel of Aosta.

CONTENTS.

	PAGE
PREFACES (NEW AND OLD)	vii, ix
I. PRACTICAL HINTS	xv
Art. I. Preliminary Information	xv
,, II. Routes for Approaching the Alps from London	xviii
,, III. Modes of Travelling in the Alps	xxiv
,, IV. Plan of a Tour	xxvi
,, V. General Advice to Travellers in the Alps	xxvi
,, VI. Advice to Pedestrians	xxxii
,, VII. On Mountaineering	xxxvii
,, VIII. Guides and Porters	xliv
,, IX. Inns and Club Huts	xlviii
,, X. Life in an Alpine Valley. By W. A. B. Coolidge	lii
II. SCIENTIFIC NOTES	lxvi
Art. XI. Geology of the Alps. By Prof. Bonney	lxvi
,, XII. Alpine Zoology	xcviii
,, XIII. Climate and Vegetation of the Alps. By Percy Groom	ciii
,, XIV. The Snow Region of the Alps	cxxii
,, XV. Photography in the High Alps. By Sydney Spencer	cxxxiii
APPENDICES	cxli
a. List of Books and Maps relating to the Alps	cxli
b. A Glossary of Alpine Terms. By W. A. B. Coolidge	cliii
INDEX	clxi

INTRODUCTION.

I. PRACTICAL HINTS.

Art. I.—Preliminary Information.

PASSPORTS.—MONEY.—CUSTOM-HOUSE REGULATIONS.—LUGGAGE.—POST OFFICES.—TELEGRAPHS.—MEASURES.—TIME.

Passports.—English travellers are not now required, as a rule, to produce passports on entering France, Italy, Switzerland, Austria, or Germany. But if it is intended to visit the Franco-Italian frontier south of the Mont Blanc range it is prudent to have a passport, and also a *visa*, especially on the French side, where the spy mania is particularly prevalent. It is also often useful elsewhere to have a passport, which on the Continent is the legal mode of establishing the identity of the bearer, *e.g.* at Post Offices, and other public establishments.

Passports are issued at the Foreign Office, London, S.W., on a written application, accompanied by a recommendation from some one known to the Secretary of State (if the applicant is not personally known to him), or from a banker, or by a certificate of identity signed by the applicant, as well as by any Mayor, Magistrate, Justice of the Peace, Minister of Religion, Physician, Surgeon, Barrister, Solicitor, or Notary resident in the United Kingdom. The fee is 2s. The various members of a family *travelling together* may be included in a single passport, if the degrees of relationship are stated; names of male members of the family, and of any man-servant (if a British subject—otherwise he must procure a passport from his own Government), must be given in full. Friends travelling together, although not related, may be included in the same passport, but in this case each of their names should be stated in the application. Passports are issued between 11 A.M. and 4 P.M. on the day (but not on Sundays or public holidays) following that on which the application has been received at the Foreign Office. A passport cannot be granted in London to a person already abroad, who should apply to the nearest British Mission or Consulate. The bearer of every passport should sign his name clearly as soon as he receives it. A Foreign Office Passport is good for the life of the bearer.

There are several Passport Agencies in London where the whole business of obtaining a passport, and any needful *visa*, is transacted for a small fee, *e.g.* 1s. 6d. per passport, with 1s. per *visa*, in both cases *in addition* to the Foreign Office and Consulate charges.

Money.—The coinages of France, Italy, and Switzerland are the same, accounts being kept in francs and centimes. But Italian or Swiss coins below 5 francs pass in Italy or Switzerland only, while in Switzerland Swiss pieces of 1859–1863 (*sitting* figure of Helvetia) are no longer current. Papal coins are received in none of the three countries. French napoleons (there are but few Swiss 20-fr. pieces) are the most convenient coins to carry. Italian inconvertible notes pass in Italy only, while in Switzerland the notes of the Cantonal Banks are *not always* received in other Cantons, and French notes are generally taken only at a discount.

English sovereigns and Bank of England notes are accepted in all the villages frequented by travellers in Switzerland or Italy, but not always in France. Cheques, or Circular Notes (for sums of £10 and upwards) are cashed at most of the principal hôtels, or at the branch banks which are established in most of the chief tourist resorts during the summer. In the case of Circular Notes great care should be taken to keep the notes separate from the letter which accompanies them. In Austria the former coinage of silver florins (or gulden), each divided into 100 kreuzers, is being replaced by silver crowns, or 'kronen' (each worth about 10d., ½ florin, or a franc), divided into 100 'heller' (each worth ½ kreuzer), which thus roughly answers to the coinage of the three other countries. There are also 5 and 10 florin (or gulden) notes (besides higher denominations), which are current everywhere and are very convenient.

A little experience teaches the traveller the importance of being always provided with small coins of the country visited. It is often possible, before arriving at the frontier, to procure a supply at some Exchange Office, which is often more convenient and economical than doing so after arrival in the country. Of course the rates of exchange of the coinage of one country in another vary from day to day, and care should be taken to ascertain the actual current rate at the moment of application.

Custom-House Regulations.—The regulations affecting travellers are not usually very strict. Of the articles usually carried by travellers, cigars, spirits, and unworn wearing apparel are the principal liable to duty, and should be declared to avoid unpleasantness and inconvenience. A *small* number of cigars or a *small* amount of tobacco may be taken free, but the Italian officials are often very strict in this matter. Nowadays through travellers can generally register their heavy luggage from London direct to the more important towns in the country whither they are bound, *e.g.* Basel, Lucerne, Zürich, Bern (but only to the Italian frontier), where it will be examined, but not *en route*. If luggage is sent across the frontier without being accompanied by its owners, it will be examined, and the keys should be attached in such a way as to be easily accessible.

As a general rule officials in Switzerland, Italy, and Austria are civil and obliging when treated with the courtesy to which they are accustomed. In Prussia and at times in France the case is otherwise, and the temper of the traveller is tried by the rudeness of underlings. But unless the case be serious enough, and the facts sufficiently plain, to call for a complaint to the official superior, a wise traveller will disregard conduct which he cannot resent effectually, and which it is undignified to meet by an unavailing show of anger. These subordinate officials often have it in their power to cause great annoyance to a stranger, while he is powerless as regards them, and will do best to avoid an unequal encounter.

Luggage.—Travellers who register their luggage direct from London to their destination (but not beyond the Italian frontier) are entitled to a free allowance of 56 lbs. (25 kilogrammes). But within each country this privilege varies. In France the allowance is about 66 lbs. (30 kilos.) But in Switzerland (as in Italy) there is no free allowance at all on the railways, while on the diligences 22-33 lbs. (10-15 kilos.) are allowed, according as the road traversed is over a mountain pass or in the plains. On the other hand in Switzerland it is very easy and extremely cheap to forward luggage through any post office within the country.

Post Offices.—As a rule letters clearly addressed (especially if to an hôtel) rarely go astray within the four countries with which the traveller in the Alps is concerned. But the officials vary according to their nationality, as pointed out above, as well as the regulations which they are entitled to enforce. It is best to avoid all titles, prefixes, or affixes in addressing letters abroad, save the plain prefix 'Monsieur' or 'Madame.'

Letters to or from England in the case of Switzerland, Italy, France, and Austria cost $2\frac{1}{2}d.$ (25 cents., or 10 kreuzers) per $\frac{1}{2}$ oz., while post cards are $1d.$ (10 cents., or 5 kreuzers). Within the different countries the rates vary: in Switzerland a letter weighing $\frac{1}{2}$ lb. costs but $1d.$ (10 cents.), while a post card is $\frac{1}{2}d.$ (5 cents.); but in France a $\frac{1}{2}$-oz. letter costs $1\frac{1}{2}d.$ (15 cents.), while a post card is $1d.$ (10 cents.)

The convenience of forwarding luggage within Switzerland through the post office has been pointed out above.

Telegraphs and Telephones.—The telegraphic (and telephonic) network is now spread everywhere very widely, even (during the summer) extending to many of the high mountain inns. The charges are so low that it is an excellent plan, at least in the height of the season, to secure rooms in advance by a telegram. In Switzerland the rate for a telegram to Great Britain is a fixed charge of 50 cents., plus 29 cents. per word; while within the country itself the charges are 30 cents. and $2\frac{1}{4}$ cents. respectively. In France the rates are 20 cents. per word, 1 fr. minimum charge, and (inland) 50 cents. for 10 words, 5 cents. per additional word.

Measures.—In all four countries—Switzerland, France, Italy, and Austria—the metrical system is now adopted, which is extremely convenient. It is as follows:—

A Millimètre equals	·039 inch.
A Centimètre	,,	·39 inch.
A Mètre	,,	3·281 ft.
A Kilomètre	,,	·621 mile.
A Kilogramme	,,	2·20 lbs. av.

But old local measures linger here and there. A Swiss foot is 11·81 Engl. inches; a Swiss 'Stunde' is 2·98 Engl. miles; while a Swiss pound is 1·10 lb. av. In France a foot is 11·81 inches, a 'Toise' 70·86 inches, and a 'Livre' 1·10 lb. av. An old Austrian foot is 1·03 Engl. ft., a 'Klafter' is 2·87 yards, a post mile is 4·71 Engl. miles, while a pound is 1·23 lb. av.

Time.—In Belgium and Holland, like Great Britain, Greenwich (or *Western European*) time now prevails. This is just 1 hr. *later* than *Central European* time, which obtains in Switzerland, Italy, Germany, and Austria: but in France *Paris time* is 4–5 minutes faster than Greenwich time, or 55–56 minutes later than Central European time, while *French railway time* is 5 or 6 minutes later than Paris time. In some towns local time is still observed. Italian time is reckoned to 24 hours, from midnight to midnight.

Art. II.—Routes for Approaching the Alps from London.

It may be safely asserted that no class has profited more by the extension of railways than travellers in the Alps. To that large majority who are limited either as to time or as to money the means of crossing half Europe with the outlay of but 20 hours or so in time, and a trifling expenditure of money, very often makes a tour possible which otherwise would never have been undertaken. The extension of railways through and on both sides of the Alpine chain has not merely enabled strangers to approach all parts of the Alps with little loss of time, but has largely increased the facilities for passing from one part of the chain to another. Hence a traveller may now combine in a single tour visits to several different and distant districts, allotting to each of them a fair share of time, and expending but little on going from one to the other.

Some of the fast trains (especially in France) take only first-class passengers, and on a long journey, especially if time is limited, it is true economy to travel in such trains. The second-class carriages are now everywhere more comfortable than formerly, and should be used on shorter journeys. In Switzerland few, save through travellers, or very rich persons, make use of the luxurious first-class carriages.

In the following remarks an attempt is made to indicate the quickest and shortest route from London to each of the chief districts of the Alps. The traveller should take care to obtain the latest information as to the times of departure of the trains. The Continental 'Bradshaw' is very useful, but should be checked, when possible, by the Railway Time Tables issued by the various railway companies in the different countries visited. Return tickets, available for from 30 to 45 days, to all the chief tourist resorts, can now generally be procured, and can, like ordinary tickets, or special tickets for a Circular Tour, be bought beforehand at Cook's or Gaze's Tourist Agencies in London.

Roughly speaking, the fast routes for approaching the Alps from London may be classified under three main headings, according as the traveller wishes to visit the Western, the Central, or the Eastern Alps. If bound for any part of the **Western Alps** the traveller must go through

Paris; if bound for any part of the **Central Alps** (save the upper Rhône valley) he should make *Basel* his object; while for most parts of the **Eastern Alps** (some, as will be shown below, are best reached from Basel) he must go to *Innsbruck, Munich, Salzburg*, or *Vienna*. But naturally these routes occasionally overlap: *e.g.* the Bernese Oberland may be reached from London *via* Paris, as well as direct by Laon, while the Alpine districts on the W. of the Brenner line may be most conveniently gained without going quite to Innsbruck.

1. **WESTERN ALPS** (Paris to Nice, Grenoble, Gap, Briançon, Modane, Turin, Albertville, Geneva, Lausanne, or Brieg).—Paris may of course be reached from London by many routes with which we have not here to trouble ourselves. From Paris the various chief districts of the Western Alps may be best gained as follows:—

(*a*) **Maritime Alps** (§§ 1 and 2).—By Lyons and Marseilles to *Nice* (*c.* 18½ hrs.), and then by the Southern Railway (§ 2); or by the Mont Cenis line, to *Turin* (17½ hrs.), and on by Cuneo to Valdieri or Limone (§ 1).

(*b*) **Cottian Alps** (§§ 3, 4, 5, 6, and 7).—Much depends on which particular district of this very extensive mountain region it is desired to reach. The *Chambeyron* district may be best reached *via* Grenoble, Gap, and Prunières station, whence there is a diligence to Barcelonnette (§ 9. Rte. Q and § 3. Rte. A); or the Col de l'Argentière may be crossed from Cuneo to the same remote town (§ 3. Rte. A).

The *Viso* is most conveniently gained *via* Turin, Bricherasio, and Crissolo (§ 4. Rte. B).

The *Waldensian Valleys* are easily reached from Turin by rail to Torre Pellice past Pinerolo (§ 5. Rte. A). As on the southern sides of the Alps so many valleys open into the main valley of the Po, Turin is a natural centre, and is joined by railways to many towns in or at the opening of many different valleys—Cuneo, Saluzzo, Pinerolo, Oulx and Bardonnèche, Lanzo, Ivrea and Aosta, Biella, Varallo, Orta, and Domodossola—so that most spots on the Italian slope of the Western Alps may be best reached from Turin.

The *glens near the Mont Genèvre* are most accessible either on the French side from the railway stations of Montdauphin or Briançon (reached from Grenoble by Gap in 7–8 hrs. respectively, § 9. Rte. Q), or on the Italian side from Turin either by Pinerolo or by Oulx (§ 5. Rte. B and § 6. Rte. A).

The *Ambin* district is most easily visited from Modane, on the Mont Cenis line and 13 hrs. from Paris (§ 7. Rte. A).

(*c*) **Dauphiné Alps** (§§ 8, 9, and 10).—For nearly all parts of this district (save the Aiguilles d'Arves, most accessible from St. Michel de Maurienne, on the Mont Cenis line, and 12½ hrs. from Paris) the natural starting point is *Grenoble*. This may be reached from Paris either by Lyons (12 hrs.) or by Chambéry, the latter route offering the advantage of through carriages and quick trains as far as Chambéry (10 hrs.), which is only 2 hrs. by rail from Grenoble. From Grenoble there is a steam tramway to Bourg d'Oisans (§ 8. Rte. A), whence a high road leads up to La Grave (§ 8. Rte. A), a char road and a mule path up to La Bérarde (§ 9. Rte. A), and a char road and foot paths towards the Grandes Rousses either from Le Freney or from Allemont (§ 8. Rtes. D and E).

The S. portions of the Dauphiné Alps are best visited from Grenoble by way of La Mure and Corps (§ 9. Rtes. N and O) (so the Valgaudemar), or from the La Bessée station, on the railway from Grenoble by Gap to Briançon (so the Vallouise, § 9. Rte. G). Grenoble itself is the point of departure for the Grande Chartreuse (§ 10) and Belledonne ranges (§ 8. Rte. I).

(*d*) **Annecy and Albertville District** (§ 11).—A traveller bound direct for these parts should go by the Mont Cenis line (in 9½ hrs. from Paris) to Aix les Bains (whence there is a branch line in 1¼ hr. to Annecy, § 11. Rte. E), or a little further on to St. Pierre d'Albigny (branch line to Albertville, 35 min., and Moûtiers Tarentaise, 1 hr. on, § 12. Rte. A).

(*e*) **Graian Alps** (§§ 12, 13, 14, and 15).—Pralognan (§ 12. Rte. H) is accessible by road from Moûtiers Tarentaise, Val d'Isère (§ 12. Rte. B) by road from Moûtiers by Bourg St. Maurice, and Bonneval sur Arc (§ 7. Rte. B and § 12. Rte. B) by road from Modane. The Lanzo valleys on the Italian side are best approached from Lanzo, 1¼ hr. by rail from Turin (§ 13. Rte. B), while Cogne is most quickly reached by way of Turin, Ivrea and Aosta (4¼–5 hrs. by rail from Turin ; § 15. Rtes. A and B).

(*f*) **Mont Blanc and Sixt Districts** (§§ 16 and 17).—Most travellers wish to reach Chamonix, and that is most speedily gained (§ 16. Rte. A) from Geneva (which is 10½ hrs. by rail from Paris). From Geneva a steam tramway runs to Samoëns, whence there is a road on to Sixt (§ 17. Rte. A).

(*g*) **Champéry, Bourg St. Pierre, Evolena, Zinal, Zermatt, Saas, and the Simplon** (§§ 17, 18, 19, 20, and 21).—All these places are best reached from Lausanne, which may be gained in 11¾ hrs. from Paris by Pontarlier and Vallorbes. Then the line up the Rhône valley towards Brieg (§ 21. Rte. A ; 3¾ hrs. from Lausanne) is used, the Ollon St. Triphon, Martigny, Sion, Sierre, Visp, and Brieg stations giving access to the various spots. Zermatt is the only one which can be reached by railway throughout, 6½ hrs. being required from Lausanne in connection with the *fastest* night train from Paris.

2. **CENTRAL ALPS** (Basel to Bern, Interlaken, Grindelwald, Lauterbrunnen, Meiringen, Lucerne, Göschenen, Locarno, Lugano, Zürich, Glarus, Coire, Thusis, Davos, Landeck, Innsbruck, Appenzell, St. Gallen, Constance and Romanshorn).

(*a*) **Diablerets District** (§ 22).—Ormonts Dessus and Château d'Oex are best gained, indeed, by Paris, Lausanne, and (1 hr. on) Aigle, but there are beautiful routes from Thun direct to Saanen, Gsteig, Château d'Oex, and Bulle.

(*b*) **Gemmi District** (§ 23).—Thun (50 min. by rail from Bern) is ¼ hr. by rail from Spiez, which is the principal starting point for Kandersteg, Adelboden, and Lenk, but Leukerbad and Ried are most directly gained respectively from the Louèche (Leuk) and Gampel stations, on the Lausanne-Brieg railway.

(*c*) **Bernese Oberland** (§ 24).—Bern may be gained direct from Paris *viâ* Neuchâtel in 13 hrs., though it is far more convenient (no change of carriage from Calais) to reach it direct from London by Calais, Laon, Reims, and Delémont (22 hrs.); but, save in summer, when through carriages run by this route, it is better to go to Basel (18¾ hrs. from

London), and then round in 3 hrs. to Bern. From about July 10 to September 15 a 'train de luxe' has been run of late years direct from Calais to Interlaken; this leaves London at 11 A.M., like the ordinary service, but reaches Interlaken at 8.26 A.M. instead of at 12.45. But even by the ordinary train it is easy to gain (by rail) Grindelwald, Lauterbrunnen, Mürren, the Little Scheidegg, or (by rail and boat) Meiringen the same afternoon, while a traveller bound for Kandersteg or Adelboden should leave the train at Spiez ($\frac{1}{2}$ hr. beyond Thun) in order to attain those spots by road the same day. Ried, the Belalp and the Eggishorn are best reached from London by way of Paris, Lausanne, and Brieg (15$\frac{1}{2}$ hrs. from Paris), Gampel being the station for Ried and Brieg for the Belalp, while Viesch (for the Eggishorn) is 3 hrs. on by high road from Brieg.

The Emmenthal and the Entlebuch are traversed by the main railway from Bern to Lucerne.

(*d*) **Titlis and North Switzerland Districts** (§§ 25 and 26).—Lucerne (2 hrs. from Basel by quick train) is the best starting point for most spots included in these districts, whether they lie on the Brünig (*e.g.* Samen) or on the St. Gotthard (*e.g.* Brunnen, Altdorf, Wassen, Göschenen) railway lines, or on the shores of the Lake of Lucerne (Rigi and Pilatus). Engelberg is now connected with Stans (its harbour is Stansstad) by a light railway of its own (2$\frac{3}{4}$ hrs. from Lucerne to Engelberg). The Furka Pass is reached by quitting the St. Gotthard railway at Göschenen (2 hrs. from Lucerne), but the Grimsel Pass and the Gadmenthal are more directly gained from Meiringen by road.

(*e*) **Tödi District** (§ 27).—Zürich (2 hrs. from Basel by quick train) here takes the most prominent place. Thence Glarus (1$\frac{3}{4}$ hr.) and Linththal ($\frac{3}{4}$ hr. more) may be reached by rail, or Coire by Sargans in 3 hrs. Glarus is the starting point for Elm, and Coire for Disentis and the Oberalp Pass. The 'Engadine Express' (in connection with the 11 A.M. train from London) leaves Basel at 5.03 A.M. and Zürich at 7.12, reaching Coire at 9.48 A.M., in time to continue the journey a long way in any direction.

(*f*) **Säntis District** (§ 28).—Appenzell or Wildhaus are the best starting points for excursions in the Säntis range. The former is 3$\frac{1}{2}$ hrs. from Zürich by way of Winterthur and Winkeln; for the latter the station of Ebnat-Kappel, in the Toggenburg, is 2$\frac{1}{4}$ hrs. from Zürich by rail *via* Winterthur and Wyl, and thence it is a drive of 3$\frac{1}{2}$ hrs. to Wildhaus.

(*g*) **Lepontine and St. Gotthard Districts** (§§ 29 and 30).—The chief centres here are Binn (2$\frac{1}{2}$ hrs. from Viesch, in the Rhône valley, which is 3 hrs.' drive from Brieg), Airolo (on the St. Gotthard line, at the S. mouth of the great tunnel, and 6$\frac{3}{4}$ hrs. from Basel; quick trains do *not* stop at Airolo), and Disentis (best reached from Coire in 8$\frac{3}{4}$ hrs.' drive by the Vorder Rhein valley); Tosa Falls, Devero, and Veglia are all gained from Domodossola, at the Italian foot of the Simplon Pass, the first named also from Airolo by the easy San Giacomo Pass.

(*h*) **Adula District** (§ 31).—As this district is composed of the mountain mass lying between the Lukmanier, and Splügen-San Bernardino roads, it is most easily visited either from Biasca, on the St. Gotthard railway (8 hrs. from Basel) or from the various villages situated on those roads, all of which on the N. are accessible by road from Coire, the railway from Coire to Reichenau and Thusis shortening the distance to some extent.

(*i*) **Locarno and Como Districts** (§§ 32 and 33).—Locarno, Lugano, and Como are the principal resorts of travellers in these regions. Each may be reached direct from Basel by the St. Gotthard railway ($6\frac{1}{2}$ hrs., $6\frac{1}{4}$ hrs., and 7 hrs. respectively by quick trains). From them Bignasco, Bellagio, and other well known spots are accessible in a very short time.

(*k*) **Albula and Bernina Districts** (§§ 34 and 36).—Save the Avers glen (most easily reached by a drive from Andeer, on the Splügen road) these districts mainly comprise the Engadine and the ranges enclosing it on either side. That great valley may be reached by many passes, which start from several railway stations—the Julier and the Albula from Thusis, the Flüela from Davos, the Finstermünz from Landeck, on the Arlberg line, the Bernina from Sondrio, in the Valtellina, and the Maloja from Chiavenna. It is said that the last named route is on the whole the shortest and easiest, as Chiavenna may be reached in $3\frac{1}{2}$ hrs. by rail from Como, on the St. Gotthard line, which is 27 hrs. direct *viâ* Basel from London. But the proposed railway by the Albula Pass will (when completed) be by far the quickest way.

(*l*) **Silvretta District** (§ 35).—If this district is approached from the Swiss side the traveller should go direct to Klosters, below Davos ($7\frac{3}{4}$ hrs. by rail from Basel), while on the Austrian side Bludenz may be reached by the Arlberg line in 7 hrs. from Basel.

(*m*) **Ortler District** (§ 37).—The quickest way to reach either Trafoi or Sulden (the main tourist centres of this district) is by mail coach from Landeck, on the Arlberg line ($9\frac{1}{4}$ hrs. from Basel), over the Reschen Scheideck Pass ($12\frac{1}{2}$ hrs.' drive to Trafoi, and $16\frac{1}{4}$ hrs. to Sulden). But a less laborious route is to go from Zürich to Innsbruck by rail (11 hrs. from Zürich), and then by rail by Bozen to Meran (6 hrs.), whence the drive is not quite so long as by the first named route ($9\frac{3}{4}$–$12\frac{1}{2}$ hrs.)

(*n*) **Bergamasque Alps and Val Camonica District** (§§ 38 and 39).— From the N. these districts are best approached from the Valtellina, in which Sondrio may be gained in $1\frac{1}{4}$ hr. from Colico, easily reached by rail in $2\frac{3}{4}$ hrs. from Como, on the St. Gotthard line. But it is shorter to reach them on the S. from Bergamo, which is 3 hrs. by rail from Como. The valleys between the Val Camonica and the Chiese valley are best visited from Brescia (5 hrs. by rail from Como), which is also a centre for the more southerly valleys described in the next Section.

(*o*) **Adamello and Brenta Districts** (§ 40).—These regions are best reached from Bozen or Trent, on the Brenner line (respectively 5–$6\frac{1}{2}$ hrs. from Innsbruck), but only by means of a long drive either to Campiglio or Pinzolo for the former, or to Molveno for the latter district. On the W., Edolo may be easily gained from the Valtellina by the carriage road over the Aprica Pass, or by a longer route from Brescia or Bergamo by way of the Lake of Iseo, and the Val Camonica or Oglio valley.

3. **EASTERN ALPS** (Innsbruck, Munich, Salzburg, or Vienna).—As the present Editor (W. A. B. C.) has but a limited knowledge of the Eastern Alps, it is best for him to content himself here with a few general indications.

ROUTES FOR APPROACHING THE ALPS FROM LONDON. xxiii

Innsbruck is most quickly reached from London by way of Basel, Zürich, and the Arlberg line; a traveller leaving London at 11 A.M. may thus reach Basel at 5.45, and Zürich at 9.15 the next morning, and gain Innsbruck the same evening at 6.21 P.M., this being the direct Paris-Vienna express.

A traveller from Basel may join the Arlberg line at Feldkirch, after having taken one of the lines along the banks of the Rhine to Constance, and sailed down the lake of that name to Bregenz; this is a longer but a pleasanter route than the direct one *viâ* Zürich and Buchs.

Near Innsbruck the traveller may easily reach the Oetzthal and Pitzthal districts (from the *Oetzthal* or *Imst* stations, distant 28½ m. and 34 m. respectively on the Landeck line to the W.), or the Zillerthal group (from the Jenbach station, 24 m. off to the N.E. on the Munich line). There is an alternative entrance to the glaciers at the head of the Zillerthal from S. Jodok am Brenner (19 m. from Innsbruck). The Glockner and Venediger groups are best reached from Innsbruck by taking the Brenner line as far as *Franzensfeste* (52 m. from Innsbruck), whence it is 66 m. more by the Pusterthal railway to *Lienz*, the best starting point for these districts; there is an alternative approach by Jenbach and Zell. 38 m. from Franzensfeste, by the Pusterthal line, is *Toblach*, the station for Cortina and the Ampezzo Dolomites.

Further S. than Franzensfeste, on the Brenner line, are *Waidbruck* (69 m. from Innsbruck), the station for the Grödenerthal, and *Bozen* (83½ m. from Innsbruck), the station for the Rosengarten range, while still further S. (96¼ m. from Innsbruck, 13 m. S. of Bozen, or 22 m. N. of Trent) is *Neumarkt*, the station for Predazzo, S. Martino di Castrozza, and Primiero.

From Franzensfeste the Lienz line continues nearly due E. by *Villach* (64 m. from Lienz) and *Klagenfurt* (24 m. from Villach) to *Marburg* (233¼ m. from Franzensfeste). At Marburg (31 m. from Graz) the direct Semmering line from Vienna to Trieste (89½ m. from Laibach, or 366 m. from Vienna) by Bruck (106 m.), Graz (43 m.), and Laibach (96¼ m. from Marburg) (this line may be said throughout the greater part of its course to skirt the E. extremity of the Alps) is joined, so that this route from Innsbruck by Franzensfeste is probably now the quickest from London to Styria, Carinthia, and Carniola. At *Bruck* the Pontebba line leaves the Trieste line, and runs by Villach (128 m.) to Udine (82½ m.), whence either Venice or Trieste is easily reached.

Munich may be reached in 24 hrs. from London by way of Ostend, Cologne, Aschaffenburg, Würzburg, and Ingolstadt.

Vienna is most quickly gained from London (29½ hrs.) by branching off from the route to Munich at Würzburg, and then proceeding by Nürnberg, Regensburg (Ratisbon), and Passau. (The 'Oriental Express' makes the round by Paris, and employs 32¾ hrs. between London and Vienna.)

Salzburg is reached (54¼ m.) from the Rosenheim station, between Innsbruck (69 m. to Rosenheim) and Munich (40¾ m. to Rosenheim—3½ hrs. by quick train from Munich to Salzburg); it is 195 m. further from Salzburg to Vienna (6-6½ hrs. by quick trains).

Art. III.—Modes of Travelling in the Alps.

Of the various modes of conveyance to be enumerated in this Article none are more than imperfect substitutes for the only means of travelling which is completely satisfactory to the lover and student of nature. Walking is so peculiarly the suitable way of visiting the Alps that it is most conveniently discussed separately (Articles VI. and VII., below) under its two forms of pedestrianism and mountaineering. But there are times and occasions when even the most ardent walkers must have recourse to other means of conveyance.

1. **Railways.**—Apart from the facilities that railways afford for approaching the Alps from London (Art. II., above), they are of great service to mountain travellers, as they enable them, with the least possible expenditure of time and trouble, to transfer themselves from one centre of interest to another. Few persons will suppose that passing through a mountain country in a railway carriage can enable them to form any correct idea of its attractions, yet there are a few lines (such as those from Culoz by the Mont Cenis or Fréjus tunnel to Turin, from Lucerne to Milan by the St. Gotthard line and tunnel, and from Innsbruck to Verona by the Brenner) where a succession of beautiful pictures is unrolled before the traveller's eyes. But apart from the great lines that pierce the Alps by the Fréjus, St. Gotthard, and Arlberg Tunnels there are now a host of minor lines which run from the plains up into the mountains, whether in Switzerland, Italy, France, or Austria, and which thus enable a traveller to gain the very heart of the Alps below the snow line without trouble. Further, there are the light mountain railways (*e.g.* over the Wengern Alp, to Mürren, up the Rigi, Pilatus, &c.), which, however distasteful to the lover of quiet, are yet in their way convenient, even occasionally to ardent walkers. But those who have the strength and health required to gain acquaintance with the inmost recesses of the ice and snow world may be pardoned if they view with the greatest horror the modern schemes for taking railways up the Jungfrau, the Matterhorn, and Mont Blanc.

2. **Steamers.**—All the principal lakes of the Alps (though not always the minor lakes) are now traversed by steamers. Wherever they exist they offer an easy and economical mode of travelling (though not a speedy one), of which travellers will not be slow to avail themselves. One great advantage of travelling by steamer is that the noise and dust of the railway is avoided, while often the same ticket (as on the Lake of Thun) may be used indifferently for rail or steamer, thus enabling travellers to embark on the boat only when the weather is fine.

3. **Diligences.**—Nearly every year sees the opening of some new railway in the Alps, which means the disappearance of the diligences that formerly plied over that road. Yet every year too sees new carriage roads opened, so that a fresh service of diligences is required. All the great mountain roads which are as yet free from railways—*e.g.* the Col de Tenda, the Mont Genèvre, the Col du Lautaret, the Simplon, the Furka, the Grimsel, and in particular the passes leading to the Inn valley—are now well supplied with diligences. The carriages are usually

of modern make, and specially meant for travellers who desire to obtain views on the way, and form a great contrast to the heavy, lumbering vehicles that old travellers will recollect. The Swiss diligence service in particular is very well organised, as it is a Government monopoly. The prices in Switzerland vary slightly according to the seat occupied, but the maximum allowed by law is from 25 to 30 centimes per kilomètre (rather over ½ mile). Travellers have a free allowance of from 33 to 22 lbs. of luggage, according as the road is in the plains or traverses a mountain pass; but by a curious anomaly excess luggage is charged for *not* on the actual amount in excess, but on the *total weight* belonging to that particular traveller or party.

It should always be borne in mind that some of the great Alpine passes —*e.g.* the Mont Cenis and the St. Gotthard—are not now traversed by regular services of diligences, as there the railway through the mountain has practically supplanted the road over it. But the roads are still more or less kept up, though it is not always easy now to procure a private conveyance.

4. **Carriages.**—Save in the remoter parts of the Alps it may be said generally that where there is a road there will be found carriages for hire. But these vehicles vary much in size, shape, and convenience. Nearly everywhere, too, there is now an official tariff fixed by the Government authorities, so that it is only in certain corners of the Alps that travellers need bargain beforehand. This necessity in the better known parts of the Alps is practically confined to the wealthy traveller who desires to make a round over certain Alpine passes—*e.g.* from the Engadine and back by the Maloja, the Splügen, and the Albula. In that case it is most prudent to have a written agreement. But the old-fashioned vetturino has all but completely disappeared, save in such exceptional cases. At every railway station in the Alps of any importance one- and two-horse carriages are now certain to be found in waiting on the arrival of the principal trains; and the competition is then between the drivers, and not between the traveller and the driver. Sometimes a return carriage may be had at a reduced charge, but this means a special bargain made beforehand.

On many of the principal roads in Switzerland there is a convenient Government arrangement (with an official tariff) called 'Extrapost,' or posting, with the same carriage, but changes of horses.

5. **Riding.**—Railways and carriage roads have to a very considerable extent done away with the former usual practice of engaging horses or mules to cross mountain passes. This practice lingers mainly in certain great Alpine centres for one-day excursions, or small ascents in the immediate neighbourhood. Generally there is now an official tariff, but travellers should bear in mind that in remoter parts of the Alps, where no official tariffs exist, the prices given in guide books often depend on the experience of perhaps a single traveller, and should not fret when the next passer-by is asked a higher price. If a horse or mule be employed, it is well to abstain from interfering with the animal, which is probably used to carry loads only, and is not accustomed to being ridden in the proper sense.

6. **Chaises à Porteur** (Germ. *Tragsessel*).—This is a rough kind of

arm-chair, supported by two poles, and carried by two bearers. They are very rarely found now in the Alps, save for short excursions for those who dislike riding. Formerly they were very common in the Bernese Oberland, but nowadays they are hardly ever seen there, except for excursions, *e.g.* from Grindelwald to the two glaciers.

Art. IV.—Plan of a Tour.

The tastes of travellers in the Alps are too different, and the objects which they propose to themselves too various, to make it easy to offer useful advice respecting the plan of a tour. The desire to see as many remarkable places as possible within a given time is so natural in beginners, that it is useless to contend against it. Nothing but experience suffices to prove that to derive the fullest and most permanent satisfaction from natural scenery, even more than from other sources of æsthetic enjoyment, time is an essential element. When the impressions retained after a visit to some chosen district—where the same grand objects have been viewed repeatedly and in varied combination, under those changeful conditions of sky and colouring that constantly succeed each other in mountain countries—are compared with the imperfect recollections that remain after a hurried tour, most persons discover that they do not in truth make the most of their time when they arrange an expedition to the Alps with a view to do as much as possible within a given number of days and weeks. It is gradually ascertained that the true plan of a tour in the Alps is to select a succession of places combining the requisite attractions as head-quarters, and to arrange the journey so that as much time as possible shall be devoted to these, while as little as possible shall be given to travelling from one to the other. It is true that the advantages of such a plan are far more evident to those who are fortunate enough to have some pursuit, scientific or artistic, which connects itself naturally with their journey. The weather in mountain countries is subject to frequent change, and there are days when the scenery is hidden behind a veil of cloud, rain, or snow. To the unemployed tourist inaction is so irksome that he prefers to trudge doggedly along an Alpine track, seeing nothing of the country, rather than await fair weather in a mountain inn; while to the naturalist or geologist, or other traveller with an occupation, such days, if not too frequent, are acceptable as giving time to digest and put in order the materials accumulated during preceding mountain expeditions.

This work is designedly arranged so as to direct travellers to the most convenient centres in each district of the Alps, and those especially fitted to serve as head-quarters are pointed out in the remarks prefixed to each section. To these indications, and to the body of the work, travellers of some experience are referred.

Art. V.—General Advice to Travellers in the Alps.

Season for Travelling.—The higher parts of the Alps are most easily accessible during the height of summer; but it is not generally known that many districts, including much beautiful scenery, are seen to the best advantage in spring and autumn. In the month of May the neighbourhood of the Swiss lakes, and more especially the valleys of the Maritime, Lombard, and Venetian Alps, may be visited with full satisfaction. The vegetation of those districts is then seen in its full beauty, and many mountains of moderate height, commanding noble views, may be ascended without difficulty, though in some seasons a good deal of snow still remains on the secondary ridges. In June the rapid transition from winter to spring, and from spring to summer, is completed throughout all the inhabited valleys of the Alps. For the ordinary tourist who does not aim at difficult ascents, this would be the best season for travelling, were it not that the weather is usually more changeable than in the three succeeding months. Even for the aspiring mountaineer the second half of June possesses many advantages. The length of the day greatly facilitates long expeditions; the glaciers are more easily traversed, as the crevasses are narrower, and are more covered over by snow bridges; while slopes of ice, very difficult at other times, are made easy by a covering of snow that yields to the foot. On the other hand, it should be remembered that the snow at this season is ill consolidated, and that a slight disturbance very easily produces avalanches. Certain couloirs, and very steep slopes that are tolerably safe later in the year, are highly dangerous in the early season. The use of the rope, always expedient, is doubly so at a season when most of the crevasses are concealed by snow bridges of uncertain solidity. There is also the inconvenience that there is usually a greater extent of soft snow to be traversed than later in the season. Another slight drawback to mountaineering in June arises from the fact that the cattle have not yet been sent up to the higher pastures. The chalets to which the traveller resorts for milk, and sometimes for a night's rest, are not yet inhabited. But for the same reason nothing can then exceed the beauty of the Alpine pastures, in the full blaze of their brilliant colours, before the grass and flowers are eaten or trodden down by animals.

July and August are the months usually chosen by travellers in the higher parts of the Alps, and on an average of years the public is doubtless right in the selection. August is the season when the inns are most crowded; and a traveller who has moved from place to place in July does wisely to select comfortable and agreeable quarters for the succeeding month. One reason for passing this time in the higher valleys is the great heat that is then usually experienced in the low country at the foot of the Alps. The experience of many years has led the writer (J. B.) to believe that, on an average, the best chance of finding a continuous succession of fine weather, with the clearness of air favourable for distant views, is during the first half of September. During the summer it is rare to find more than three or four days together such as the mountaineer willingly chooses for an ascent, and even then the distant horizon is seldom clear of clouds. Eight or ten consecutive days of perfect weather are often to be had in September. About the middle of that month snow usually falls on the higher Alps, sometimes descending to the valleys. Those who do not take flight are often rewarded by a renewal of fine weather, extending into October. The fresh snow and the shortness of the days make that season unfit for high or difficult expeditions; but it is most enjoyable in the southern valleys, where the great heat of summer is a serious impediment to the pleasure of travelling in the earlier season. The Italian lakes may be visited with satisfaction until the end of October, save that in that month a week or ten days of heavy rain, extending through the entire N. of Italy, may usually be looked for.

Of late years winter climbing has become popular in the Alps, and many English flock thither for that purpose as well as to skate, toboggan, 'ski,' &c., Grindelwald being a favourite resort. November and February are the months during which the finest weather usually prevails.

Languages spoken in the Alps.—It may safely be said that half the pleasure of travelling is lost to a person who is unable to speak the language of the country through which he passes. Englishmen are more often prevented from speaking foreign languages by shyness and *mauvaise honte* than by indolence or incapacity. As there is little room for shyness in conversing, or attempting to converse, with a guide or waiter, a pedestrian expedition serves to help many persons over the first difficult step of beginning to exercise the tongue in the production of unaccustomed sounds. The region included in this work is pretty equally divided between the German, French, and Italian languages. German, which has rather the largest share, is spoken throughout nearly the whole of the Austrian and Bavarian Alps, and through three-quarters of Switzerland, the division between the French and German districts nearly corresponding with a line drawn from Porrentruy to Sierre in the Vallais. West of that line French is the language of the country, as it is throughout Savoy and Dauphiné, and in the Val d'Aosta (where it is the last relic of former Burgundian rule), and the Vaudois valleys of Piedmont. With those exceptions, and that of a few parishes at the S. and E. foot of Monte Rosa inhabited by a German population, Italian is spoken throughout the southern valleys of the Alps, including the Swiss Canton of Tessin. In the valley of the Adige, which may be said to cut through the dividing range of the Alps, the division between the Italian and German population lies rather S. of Bozen. Elsewhere it usually follows the watershed. But there are many exceptions to this general rule. It is a work of great interest to the philologist and to the historian to trace the surviving vestiges which alone show the former ethnological and linguistic fluctuations in the Alpine districts. Of especial interest are the fairly numerous German-speaking islands in the midst of an Italian sea. Chief of these are the thirteenth-century colonies from the Vallais to neighbouring glens, such as Val Formazza (above Domodossola), with its offshoot, Bosco, or even to distant valleys, such as the Rheinwald (at the chief sources of the Rhine), with the adjoining glens of Vals and Safien, and the settlement of Obersaxen, near Ilanz.* Davos itself was originally a thirteenth-century

---

* On Bosco see Dr. A. Baragiola's book entitled *Il Canto popolare a Bosco o Gurin* (Cividale, 1891); on the Val Formazza and the other Vallaisan colonies see the notes by the present Editor (W. A. B. C.) in the preliminary portion of the *Lepontine Alps* vol. (1892) of the *Climbers' Guides* Series, and the same writer's essay, 'Die deutschredenden Gemeinden im Grauen oder Oberen Bunde (Rhätien) der Schweiz,' in nos. 376-7 (1893) of the *Oesterreichische Alpen-Zeitung* of Vienna; on the colonies S. of Monte Rosa, particularly at Macugnaga, consult the notes given in the new edition of vol. i. of the *Alpine Guide*, pp. 493, 518, 521, 524-5, 535, 538, 542, as well as Julius Studer's *Walliser und Walser* (Zürich, 1886), Prof. H. Bresslau's excellent article 'Zur Geschichte der deutschen Gemeinden im Gebiet des Monte Rosa und im Ossolathal' (in vol. xvi. part 3 of Koner's *Zeitschrift der Gesellschaft für Erdkunde zu Berlin*

German-speaking colony from the Vallais planted amongst a Romance-speaking population. Further E. we have the most interesting region of the Sette Comuni, N. of Vicenza—a district of table-land and mountain pastures, enclosed between the Brenta and the Astico—which still speaks a mediæval Swabian dialect, locally called 'Cimbric,' besides (to pass over others) several German-speaking villages in the Fersina glen, E. of Trent, and those of Sauris in Friuli.*

With scarcely any exceptions the French, German, and Italian tongues are not to be heard in a state of purity in any part of the Alpine region. Dialects more or less uncouth prevail, though in many cases these patois preserve interesting forms and words which have dropped out from or have been discarded by the literary tongue. A stranger speaking the latter will, however, always be able to make himself understood, for the literary forms are now more or less taught in the schools, but he may find some trouble at first in understanding what is said to him.†

Besides these three principal languages there are at least two others which are spoken in different parts of the Alps, and which both possess very great historical interest. One is the old Rætian tongue, which is a backward sister (*not* descendant) of the other great Romance languages, being, like them, a form of the 'lingua rustica romana,' though it has lagged behind its fellows. It exists at present in two main dialects (there are many sub-dialects). One is the *Romonsch* (this is the proper spelling), spoken in the Vorder Rhein valley (Disentis, Ilanz, &c.); the other is properly known as *Ladin*, and is much more widely spread, being spoken throughout the Engadine and adjoining glens, as well as in certain parts of the Tyrol, such as the valleys of Gröden, Fassa, Ampezzo, and Buchenstein, as well as in far Friuli.‡

The second of the minor languages spoken in the Alps is the Slavonic

---

(Berlin, 1881), and A. Schott's older work, *Die deutschen Colonien in Piemont* (Stuttgart, 1842). A general view of the subject is to be found in Baron v. Czoernig's *Die deutschen Sprachinseln im Süden* (Klagenfurt, 1889).

* As regards the well known Sette Comuni, it may suffice to mention G. Nolli's *Ristretto di nozioni storiche ed economiche intorno ai Sette Comuni* (Asiago, 1880) and the accurate notice in Signor O. Brentari's *Guida Storico-Alpino di Bassano, Sette Comuni*, &c. (Bassano, 1885). As to Fersina, see a pamphlet by Hans Leck, entitled *Deutsche Sprachinseln in Wälschtirol* (Stuttgart, 1884), an article (without date or place) by Anton Zingerle, named *Die deutschen Gemeinden im Fersinathal*, and the careful notice in Signor Otto Brentari's *Guida del Trentino*, part i. (Bassano, 1891), pp. 272-85. For Sauris consult G. Marinelli's *Guida della Carnia* (Udine, 1898), pp. 121-6, 508-13, Baron v. Czoernig's article in the 1880 vol. of the *Zeitschrift* of the German and Austrian Alpine Club, his pamphlet mentioned in the preceding note, and another article by Herr J. Pock in the 1897 vol. of the *Zeitschrift*.

† For various French Alpine patois the following works may be consulted with advantage:—F. N. Nicollet's *Etudes sur les Patois du Midi de la France* (Gap, 1897); J. A. Chabrand and A. de Rochas d'Aiglun's *Patois des Alpes Cottiennes (Briançonnais et Vallées l'audoises), et en particulier du Queyras* (Grenoble and Paris, 1877); F. Brachet's *Dictionnaire du Patois Savoyard tel qu'il est parlé dans le Canton d'Albertville* (2nd edition, Albertville, 1889); and J. Gilliéron's *Patois de la Commune de Vionnaz (Bas-Valais)*, published in Paris in 1880 as no. 40 of the 'Bibliothèque de l'Ecole des Hautes Etudes;' a Dictionary of the Swiss-French patois of Switzerland is in preparation. The general subject of German Alpine patois may be studied in A. Socin's *Schriftsprache und Dialekte im Deutschen* (Heilbronn, 1888), while the magnificent Swiss-German Dialect Dictionary (the *Schweizerisches Idiotikon*), which has been in course of publication since 1881 (it has now reached the letter 'P'), and Stalder's older works, *Versuch eines Schweizerischen Idiotikons* (2 vols. Aarau, 1806-1812), and *Die Landessprachen der Schweiz* (Aarau, 1819), will be helpful for the Swiss side of the subject.

‡ The Romonsch may be best studied in Dr. C. Decurtins' *Rätoromanische Chrestomathie* (4 parts published at Erlangen between 1884 and 1896); while Z. Pallioppi's great *Dictionary of the Engadine Form of Ladin* (Samaden, 1895), and Prof. J. Alton's *Die Ladinischen Idiome in*

dialect, which extends through the Julic Alps, the Karawankas, and some other parts of Carinthia, Carniola, and Styria. German is, however, spoken by all the younger natives, so that a traveller need apprehend but little trouble from this cause. He should, nevertheless, bear in mind that each place in those regions has a German as well as a Slavonic name, and very often an Italian name also, so that, as these are sometimes quite unlike each other, care is needed to avoid mistakes, which may lead to considerable practical inconvenience.

For the mere purpose of living at hôtels an English traveller knowing only French or only German will, as a rule, save in very remote spots, meet with no serious difficulty, as almost everywhere in inns frequented by travellers the servants speak one or two, or sometimes even four, of the chief languages of Europe. In Switzerland, except in out of the way places, English is spoken in all large inns and most shops. Hence those enterprising Britons who travel on the Continent with no other medium of communication than their native tongue and a well filled purse should confine themselves to the beaten tracks in Switzerland or Italy, and avoid all but the chief places in France and Austria.

Expenses of Travelling.—The habits and wants of travellers are so various that nothing approaching a general estimate of the expenses of a tour can be given. To a considerable extent these vary also according to the district visited. It is not, however, difficult for a traveller to form an estimate for himself, so that in this place it is only necessary to mention some general considerations.

A pedestrian, carrying his own knapsack, and contenting himself with ordinary fare and accommodation, can get on for a few francs a day anywhere. But extra good food, wine, or rooms, or frequent hiring of carriages or guides, will, of course, raise the expenditure almost to any extent. If the party include ladies, further expenditure becomes desirable, while the mountaineer making many high ascents, retaining the services of good guides for some weeks, and often taking provisions up to Club huts, will spend most of all, though in his case the pleasure (at least in his belief) is worth the apparently high cost of his tour. It should always be borne in mind that the high charges of mountain hôtels, not accessible by railway, and open during a short period specially for the advantage of a comparatively small number of travellers, are justified, and should not be complained of. Most hôtels, even in the height of the season, receive at reduced fixed rates travellers who spend there at least five or seven days. This is the most convenient and most economical system for a traveller who is not in a hurry, and does not intend to absent himself from the valleys or mountain inns for several days in order to make high ascents. The rates of *pension* vary, of course, according to accommodation &c. In Switzerland there are many comfortable, clean inns where only 5 to 6 francs are charged a day in summer; the present writer (W.A.B.C.) is acquainted with many pleasant little Swiss inns, not on the beaten track, where the *pension* varies from $3\frac{1}{2}$ to 5 francs a day. In Switzerland the highest rates in the mountains do not exceed 12 to 15 francs. The

---

Ladinien, Gröden, Fassa, Buchenstein, Ampezzo (Innsbruck, 1879) will supply much information as to the Ladin branch of this curious survival, which is everywhere retiring before the encroachments of German and Italian.

most minute information as to the prices of Swiss inns is given in 'The Hôtels of Switzerland,' a work published annually at Basel by the 'Association of Swiss Hôtel Proprietors and Managers,' and to be obtained from their central office at Basel for 20 cents. (within Switzerland) or 40 cents. (Postal Union) post-free. It is an exceedingly useful and trustworthy compendium of information.

In some parts of France and Italy prices range higher than in Switzerland, the accommodation, too, not always being suited to the wants of English travellers. In the Eastern Alps the principal mountain hôtels are far from being as good as their Swiss rivals, while relatively more expensive; in the remoter districts of the Eastern Alps modest accommodation can be obtained at about the same prices as in Switzerland. When the traveller has made the best possible estimate of the sum he is likely to require for his Alpine tour, he should leave an ample margin for unforeseen expenses and for his fare from England and back. The worry of finding that he has expended the exact sum allowed for his whole journey, and of having no reserve in hand, seriously takes away from the pleasure of his trip, and may sometimes be extremely awkward. In Article I. some advice is given as to the best ways of carrying or procuring money during a journey. It is only necessary here once more to insist on the importance of being provided with small change, the want of which causes inconvenience and loss.

General Rules for Travelling.—Of these it would be easy to make a long list; a few only are here noted.

It is generally necessary to arrive at large foreign railway stations 20 or 30 minutes before the hour fixed for the departure of the train. Failing this, difficulties are made as to receiving luggage, and in the season there is a great bustle.

All arrangements for vehicles, mules, ordinary guides, or porters should be made overnight. He who waits till next morning will find inferior articles and higher prices.

Avoid sleeping with open windows in low valleys, especially those liable to inundation.

Advice as to dietary is little needed, as most people in good health can live on the food they find on their road. It may be noted that Alpine mutton is too often tough and stringy. Veal and fowls are usually the best meat. Chamois venison, when in good condition and kept long enough, is good, but is rarely eaten in perfection. Trout are delicate eating, but are sometimes rather dear. The same may be said of ptarmigan and *coq de bruyère*. The latter is excellent, but not often to be had.

For longer expeditions there is now a great variety of tinned provisions of more or less palatable kinds. In the principal tourist resorts many English articles of all kinds may now be purchased during the summer season.

Very fair wine is made in the Cantons of Neuchâtel, Vaud, and Vallais in Switzerland, in the neighbourhood of Chambéry in Savoy, in the Val d'Aosta, and in the Valtellina, round Meran and Bozen, and in the valleys near Verona; but the better qualities are rarely found in inns. Those who dislike the ordinary wine may best drink Beaujolais, a sound red wine found at most inns in Switzerland and Savoy. Some persons like Asti wine, a sweetish insipid liquor, usually to be had in Piedmont, and in many Swiss inns. Barbera is a strong and rough but sound Piedmontese wine, which is found in Italian towns; but, as a general rule, no wine but that of the district is to be had at Italian country inns. Many travellers like the effervescing lemonade, which, under the name *limonade gazeuse*, is found almost everywhere, as is also light and harmless beer.

Most of the requisites for travelling are enumerated in Art. VI. as especially important to pedestrians. A few universal requisites may be noted here.

Stationery, including writing-paper, pens, ink, pencils, and drawing materials for those who use them, are best obtained in London. Adhesive luggage-labels, and also those of parchment, and a strap for fastening together plaids and other loose articles should not be omitted. Many travellers carry a telescope; but except for chamois-hunting, where it is indispensable, this is rarely useful. An opera glass of moderate size is much lighter, and more useful. It also turns to account in visiting picture galleries, theatres, &c.

When all other requisites have been supplied, the most important of all must be found by the traveller himself. Good temper and good humour are the only things quite indispensable for the enjoyment of travelling. It is not wise to yield too easily to the demands that are pressed upon a stranger, and every now and then a show of anger may be requisite to defeat imposition; but a man who when travelling labours under the impression that all the world is combined in a conspiracy to maltreat and overreach him, and who loses his self-possession in a dispute about a franc, or because a waiter is slow to answer his summons, will consult his own peace and the convenience of others by staying at home.

Art. VI.—Advice to Pedestrians.

There are few men in tolerably good health who are not able to walk quite enough to enable them (and this applies also to more ladies than formerly) to enjoy nearly all the finest scenery in the Alps. The process of training is to some rather irksome, and it varies from a few days to two or three weeks, according to the constitution and previous habits; but this once accomplished, the unanimous testimony of all who have tried this manner of life declares that there is none other so enjoyable, and none so healthful for mind and body. Some patience and judicious preparation are needed to arrive at that delightful condition in which any reasonable amount of exertion is borne without fatigue, and a man, after a previous day's walk of 30 miles over mountain and glacier, rises with the sun, refreshed and ready for fresh enterprise. Assuming that, on reaching the Alps, a traveller is not already in good training, he must carefully avoid overworking himself at first. He cannot begin better (if his time allows) than by making the ascent of some one of those minor summits that are placed round the outer margin of the great chain, and command views that often rival in beauty the panoramas from the higher peaks. Such are the Moucherotte, the Mont Revard, Dent du Chat, Mont

Granier, and Grand Som, in the French Alps; the Dôle, Weissenstein, Chaumont, Rigi, Pilatus, Niesen, Säntis, and Hohenkasten, in Switzerland; the Besimauda, Mottarone, Monte Generoso, Sasso del Ferro, Corno di Canzo, and Ritten, more to the S. and E.; and very many others that might be added to the list. On arriving at some place that serves for headquarters, it becomes easy for a man to graduate the length and difficulty of his excursions to his increasing powers, being careful, whenever he feels somewhat overtired, to make the following a day of comparative rest.

If his design be to carry his pack himself, he will do wisely to begin with very short journeys. For the first few days it is felt as a decided encumbrance, and somewhat increases the labour of the day's work; but after a short time the muscles become adapted to the effort, and it is scarcely found to make any difference, except to persons with tender feet, who are apt to feel the effects of the additional weight. For travellers who have not the instinctive faculty of finding their way without a guide, there is no inducement to take the trouble of carrying their own packs; but quite apart from the saving, which to many may be a matter of indifference, the keen sense of absolute freedom and independence, and the intense enjoyment of nature, unbroken by the presence of even the most satisfactory guide, are motives enough to tempt many a man to rely on himself for his means of conveyance in the Alps. The writer (J. B.) warmly admires and sympathises with the feelings of those who have developed the ardent and aspiring style of mountaineering that has so largely increased our knowledge of the Alps, and all but 'effaced the word "inaccessible" from the Alpine dictionary;' but, for the sake of the next generation, he would think it a matter for regret if the life of Alpine travellers were to be always one of struggle and warfare. There is a keen pleasure in storming some citadel of nature, hewing the way axe in hand, or clambering up some precipitous outwork; but the recollections of days of solitary enjoyment amid more accessible and not less sublime scenery leave an impression no less deep and abiding.

Equipment of a Pedestrian.—It need hardly be said that temperaments are variable, and that what suits many travellers does not necessarily suit all. The inexperienced will do well to try, in the first place, what has been found useful by others. The following hints are chiefly meant for those who undertake minor Alpine expeditions, though some notes are added (especially under 3) which may be useful to those meditating high and difficult climbs. The latter class of travellers will, of course, consult the Report of a Special Committee of the Alpine Club on 'Equipment for Mountaineers,' issued with the 'Alpine Journal' for May, 1892, and to be had as a separate pamphlet from the Assistant Secretary of the Alpine Club, 23 Savile Row, W., post free for 7*d*.

1. **Clothing.**—An Alpine traveller is occasionally exposed to cold and piercing winds, but also to great heat, as the rays of the sun in clear weather have a force which is quite unknown in England. A shooting coat or Norfolk jacket is the best pattern for a *coat*. It may be made entirely of wool, though there is much to be said for Swiss (especially Oberland) homespun, its extra weight being compensated by the fact that it is very warm and practically waterproof. It is tempting to have

many pockets in the coat, but this means that it becomes weighted down with many articles, and cannot well be taken off in very hot weather. In any case there should be at least one inside pocket large enough to hold a folded map, while every pocket should be made to fasten tight outside by means of tabs or buttons. The *waistcoat* too should be woollen, and should contain inside pockets for money and other valuables. *Knickerbockers* are now almost universally worn, even by some Swiss guides, and by all guides in the Tyrol. In that case *stockings* become of great importance. These (or *socks*) should be hand-knitted, and very stout—they are best obtained in Switzerland or other parts of the Alps. *Gaiters* too are important for those who propose to be much in the snow region. By far the best kind are those of ordinary stout homespun, worn among the mountains in summer and all through the winter by the men of the Bernese Oberland—they are fastened by a chain that passes under the hollow of the boot, and are made to fasten with hooks and eyes, which are much handier than buttons or straps when the gaiters are wet.

The *shirt* should be of thick flannel (grey best), thoroughly shrunk. A collar is not always convenient when walking, but the change shirt for evenings in hôtels should certainly have one attached. A watch pocket in the shirt is often convenient. Some climbers prefer to a shirt a woollen combination garment.

The *hat* should be of felt, broad in the brim, and soft, so that in case of necessity it may be folded down and tied about the ears, and grey in colour, as that attracts the sun's rays less than any other colour. For protection against extreme cold or high wind a *woollen knitted helmet*, such as is sometimes used for skating, is useful. It should cover the whole head, save the face, and be made to pull on. Some prefer a tweed cap, with flaps for the neck and ears, but this does not afford so much protection as a woollen helmet. In fine weather, however, the wearers of either are very much exposed to the pitiless rays of the sun.

Mittens are better than gloves. They should be hand-knitted, and have but two pods, one for the thumb, the other for all the fingers together, which thus better retain their heat than when each has its own pod.

A silk or woollen *muffler* or large handkerchief is indispensable.

Many consider a *waterproof coat* a necessity. It should not be very long, and should be made of some stout waterproof material. In the Tyrol light short cloaks (*Wettermantel*) of a loose homespun (weighing about 3 lbs.) and long enough to cover the rucksack, carried on the back, are very popular. But if the suit worn is really good (especially the Oberland homespun) any waterproof coat is quite unnecessary. Beginners should be warned that long thin caoutchouc coats, coming down to the feet, are very inconvenient while walking, do not really protect the legs from wet, and are extremely liable to be soon torn and so completely ruined.

Mr. Ball recommended a *Scotch plaid*; but, though useful in certain cases, it is much too heavy to be carried on a long expedition, save, of course, for use at a camp.

The covering and protection of the feet is to the pedestrian a matter of the first importance. The *boots* cannot be too strong, solid, and durable in workmanship. They should come up to the ankles, and be fastened by leather laces. (Elastic sides have many drawbacks.) The tongue should be let into the uppers on both sides of the opening, so as to be water-tight up to the top of the boot. The heels should be large and rather low. One most important point is that the soles (not necessarily the heel) shall project all round the uppers. The nails should be so arranged as to clamp over the lower edge of this projecting rim, in order to afford protection from stones, &c. It is best not to have nails in the centre of the sole, but both edges of the sole and the heel should be well supplied with them. The front part of the boot should be long and broad, while the boot should fit easily, as otherwise a steep descent of many thousands of feet will be found most trying. An easy, comfortable fit is extremely important, and if the boot be found here and there too loose it is easy to put on a second pair of socks, or one extra thick pair. A supply of spare laces should never be forgotten. By far the most suitable boots for the purpose are to be purchased in the Alps, as the shoemakers there know by practical experience what is required, and what will best stand rough wear and tear. Some like an iron cap to protect the toes of the boot. Every one with the least experience knows that it is rash to commence walking in new boots. They should be worn for three or four weeks beforehand.

Slippers are essential. They should be of leather (with elastic sides) and strong enough for wear in the neighbourhood of a Club hut or hôtel. A lighter pair of slippers for use exclusively in the house is convenient.

2. **Knapsack or Rucksack.**—Formerly knapsacks of various patterns, though all having a stiff back, were universally employed. But of recent years they have been largely superseded by 'rucksacks,' a bag of strong canvas, closed at the top by a cord, and carried by broad straps, so placed that the pack lies in the hollow of the wearer's back in a very comfortable and easy fashion. Originally brought from the Tyrol, they may now be found in most parts of Switzerland, and rucksacks of local manufacture are used by all the Grindelwald guides. If the canvas is stout enough there is practically no danger of rain or snow working through it. But if it is desired to use special precautions it is best not to have the bag lined with waterproof, but to have a movable light waterproof bag which, after being packed, can be slipped bodily into the rucksack. The rucksack should have two inside pockets and two outside pockets, as well as a pair of straps on top for carrying coat or gaiters when not in use, while it is convenient to have a canvas partition dividing the bag into two compartments.

3. **Ice Axes and other Articles for Mountaineers.**—*Ice axes* are very important articles to Alpine travellers, even to those who do not propose to cut steps themselves. If they do, the axe must be extra heavy and strong. Otherwise a lighter weapon is advisable. The handle of the axe should be of such length as to reach up to the armpit of its owner. Great care should be taken in securing the head on to the handle. By far the best axes are made in Switzerland, and may be purchased there in all the chief Alpine centres. Those used by the Grindelwald guides (who are at the very head of their profession) are manufactured by Christian Schenk, blacksmith, of Grindelwald.

Next to the ice axe comes in point of importance the **rope**. A few prefer silk ropes, which are light indeed, but liable to snap under a great strain, and very unpleasant to handle when wet. The best rope is made of Manilla hemp, and is supplied under the name of 'Alpine Club rope,' by Messrs. Beale and Cloves (late John Buckingham), 194 Shaftesbury Avenue, W.C. A length of fifty feet suffices for a party of three. Of course the rope must be carefully examined from time to time to see if it shows sign of wear, but as a rule a rope will not be worth much after it has been through *one* hard summer's climbing.

Crampons, or **Steigeisen,** are irons (with several points turned downwards) a little wider than the sole of the boot, and attached to it by leather straps. They are convenient on a slope of hard snow, when the points pierce the snow, and so do away with the necessity of cutting steps. But it is dangerous to attempt to use them on ice slopes, while on rocks they are an encumbrance and must be taken off. They have never come into favour with English mountaineers, but are very much used in the Tyrol, where they can best be purchased. A somewhat analogous artificial aid is that of the four sharp iron spikes (an inch or more in length) which in the Swiss Alps, especially in the Bernese Oberland, are driven into the heel of the boot at the corners or edges: they are designed to enable the men coming down in winter with heavy wood sledges to get a grip in the ice or snow in the track, and will be found very handy by travellers wishing to make winter excursions, though not suited for high ascents.

Wine is best carried in long tin rounded *bottles*, made to fit into the inner or outer pockets of the rucksack. India rubber should be carefully avoided for bottles as well as for *drinking cups*, leather being the best material for the latter. *Spectacles* with smoked glasses (*not* blue) and with velvet round the edge of the wire network are most to be recommended, while for *lanterns* the Italian pattern known as 'Excelsior' is the most suitable in every way.

Among minor articles are a strong knife (with corkscrew), a field glass, some spare bits of strong twine, spare boot laces, vaseline for sun-burn, and lip salve to prevent cracked lips; but every traveller will of course make, and always carefully consult, a 'Rucksack List' for himself.

4. **Sundries.**—Washing materials may be most compactly carried in a small sheet of mackintosh, with pockets for soap, or in a small bag of the same material. A little arnica, adhesive plaster, and lint are useful in the case of wounds or bruises. Maps should never be forgotten (it is best to carry them in a transparent oiled silk case), nor the guide-book and the compass. Smokers will not forget to carry all materials for their favourite indulgence, while botanists will add a quire of soft thick paper, and a sheet of light pasteboard of the same size. There will generally be a few maps and guide-books not in actual use, while some (especially if they do not carry the bag themselves) will add a favourite book or two to while away weary hours when storm-bound in a Club hut.

It is not necessary to say anything here about tents and other elaborate arrangements required by a party making a camp high up in the mountains. Much useful information on that subject, as well as regards the various kinds of tinned provisions, may be found in the Report of the Special Committee of the Alpine Club referred to at the opening of this Article.

Art. VII.—On Mountaineering.*

ITS DIFFICULTIES AND DANGERS.—NEEDFUL PRECAUTIONS.

All active exercises and athletic sports require a certain amount of training, in order that the muscles and senses may be used to act together. Most Englishmen acquire in early life habits of bodily activity that make mountaineering come easy to them, and what more is required must be gained by experience. A few hints may, however, not be thrown away upon beginners. The quality of sure-footedness—a mountaineer's first *desideratum*—depends upon two habits, both easily acquired: first, that of lifting the foot well from the ground, and bringing it down at once; secondly, that of observing the spot on which the foot is to rest. It is not mainly in order to choose the ground for each footstep that this is useful, though in some places it is requisite to do so; the chief advantage is that the muscles, being warned by the eye, are prepared for the precise exertion that is wanted at the moment. If aware that the next step is to be on rock worn smooth, an instinctive movement of the body is made to maintain the hold of the ground, when otherwise a slip would be inevitable. In the same way a suitable slight effort often prevents débris from slipping, but here the choice of the particular stone on which the foot is to rest becomes important. With habit, the slightest glance at the ground is sufficient, and the process is an almost unconscious one.

One of the chief uses of the ice axe or alpenstock is in descending over steep and rough ground. Grasping the pole in both hands, the whole weight of the body may be safely thrown back upon the point, and in a

---

* On the general subject of Mountaineering the reader should consult the vol. (by Mr. C. T. Dent and others) in the 'Badminton' Series entitled *Mountaineering* (1892—revised German translation at Leipzig in 1893), or Dr. Claude Wilson's smaller work with the same title (1893) in the 'All-England' Series, or Herr J. Meurer's *Handbuch des Alpinen Sport* (1882).

On the dangers of mountaineering the best works are Herr Emil Zsigmondy's *Die Gefahren der Alpen* (1885: French translation published at Neuchâtel in 1886), and Signori Fiorio and Ratti's *I Pericoli dell' Alpinismo* (published at Turin in 1889 with no. 55 of the *Bollettino* of the Italian Alpine Club. The English reader will not fail to study carefully Mr. Leslie Stephen's essay on the subject in his *Playground of Europe* (1871: but unluckily *not* reprinted in the editions of 1894 and 1899).

The following are the dates at which the principal European Alpine Clubs were founded (see a full account in the *Bollettino* of the Italian Alpine Club for 1880 and 1884):—

- 1857. The Alpine Club (A.C.)
- 1862. Austrian Alpine Club, which in 1873 was fused with the German Alpine Club (founded in 1869) under the name of the 'German and Austrian Alpine Club' (D. und Oe.A.V.)
- 1863. Swiss Alpine Club (S.A.C.)
- ,,   Italian Alpine Club (C.A.I.)
- 1869. Austrian Touristen-Club (Oe.T.C.)
- 1872. Tridentine Alpine Society (S.A.T.)
- 1874. French Alpine Club (C.A.F.)
- 1875. Société des Touristes du Dauphiné (S.T.D.)
- 1878. Austrian Alpine Club (Oe.A.C.)
- 1882. Belgian Alpine Club (C.A.B.)

There are many other Alpine Societies of a more purely local character.

few minutes it is easy to clear by a succession of leaps a distance which otherwise would require thrice the time. It is often necessary to pass at a level along the face of a very steep slope. The beginner, involuntarily shrinking from the apparent danger, is apt to lean in the opposite direction. This is a mistake, as by causing an outward thrust of the foot the risk of slipping is much increased. In all such places the body should be kept perfectly upright, and the ice axe or alpenstock held in both hands ready to steady the balance, or by a bold thrust at the ascending slope to stay the movement if the foot should begin to slip. It must be recollected that wherever the ice axe or alpenstock is really wanted, it must be held in both hands. On very steep ground it is sometimes extremely difficult to avoid detaching loose fragments of rock, which may be a source of real danger to the traveller's companions. When possible, especially in a descent, it is best to take slightly different lines, so that the foremost shall not be in the way of stones sent down by the next comer. When this is not possible, the best plan is for the party to keep close together. The risk of harm is much less when the detached stone has not acquired a dangerous velocity.

The preceding hints apply to travelling over rocks and rough ground, such as may be found in all high mountain districts. The peculiar difficulties of Alpine travelling depend upon the extent of ice and snow that cover the upper region. The ice is chiefly in the form of glaciers, whose origin and constitution are described in Art. XIV.: the snow, except after a recent fall, is in that peculiar condition called *névé*. In ascending the Alps, the traveller usually begins his acquaintance with the ice region by traversing a greater or less extent of glacier ice; if he continue to ascend, he will reach the névé, and it may easily happen that, at a still greater height, he will find the surface covered with a layer of fresh snow. The surface of a glacier is sometimes very even and slightly inclined, sometimes steep and irregular, being cut up by deep rents called crevasses, which may vary from a few inches to many yards in width. When the sun has shone for even a short time upon the glacier, the upper layer of ice partially melts, leaving a crisp and crumbling surface, on which the foot holds very well; but after rain, and before sunrise, the ice generally shows a hard and very slippery surface; the foot, though shod with steel points, makes scarcely any impression, and it is necessary to cut steps with much labour on slopes that a few hours later may be crossed with ease. The lower portion of a glacier, below the point where the névé begins, is quite as easy and safe to traverse as if it were formed of rock instead of ice. Reasonable caution is needed in jumping over crevasses, but there is no more reason why a traveller should fall into them than that he should walk over the edge of a chalk cliff on the South Downs.

Above the limit of the névé the obstacles that stand in the way of the mountaineer may properly be called dangers rather than difficulties, and are discussed below under that head.

In the ascent of the higher peaks of the Alps, the pleasure and excitement are not unalloyed by some inconveniences. The first of these is *thirst*, painfully felt by those who are not used to such expeditions, for but few find by experience that they can drink cold or ice water with impunity. In this, as in other matters, prevention is better than cure.

The practice of carrying a small quartz pebble in the mouth has been ridiculed, but it rests upon a rational foundation. By causing an involuntary movement of the jaws, it stimulates the salivary glands, and keeps the mouth moist. In cases where this means of prevention is insufficient, dried prunes or raisins are to be recommended; they are far more serviceable than drinking. The fruit should be kept in the mouth as long as possible, and chewed very slowly during the ascent. As a drink along with food, cold tea diluted is the best remedy for thirst. Snow and ice relieve thirst for the moment, but generally remove the skin from the inside of the mouth, a result which is extremely painful.

Another source of inconvenience is the *heat of the sun* upon the head, which may partially be obviated by wearing a grey hat, as that attracts the sun far less than black or white.

More serious than either of the above is the risk of *frost-bites*. Numbness in the feet or hands is the first symptom. Vigorous clenching of the toes or fingers usually prevents mischief. When this has actually commenced, violent rubbing with snow, and beating the parts affected, are the proper means for restoring circulation.

The painful affection called *mountain sickness* is due to the combined effects of unusual exertion or privation and the diminished density of the air at great heights. It shows itself by difficulty of breathing, indisposition to exertion, headache, drowsiness, loss of appetite, and, if continued, by nausea. It is felt mostly by persons unused to the attenuated air of the high region; while those accustomed to exertion at a height of 10,000 or 11,000 ft. rarely suffer in ascending the higher peaks of the Alps. As it seldom attacks travellers till they are near the goal of their exertions, it may usually be overcome by patience and perseverance. The patient should halt every twenty paces, or even oftener, and resort rather to food than to strong liquor as a restorative. The best proof that unusual exertion or privation is the chief cause of the symptoms is the fact that they are rarely felt in descending, even from the highest summits. Although habit diminishes very much the evil effects, there is little doubt that all mountaineers are more or less affected by the mechanical and physiological disadvantages that attend muscular exertion at a great height. If the time be noted that is required to ascend two snow slopes of equal height and steepness, but at very different elevations, it will be seen that more is consumed at an elevation exceeding 13,000 ft. than is required at 9,000 or 10,000.

Long exposure to the glare of the snow, especially in sunshine, is very apt to cause *inflammation* either *of the eyes* themselves or of the surrounding membranes. The precaution of wearing smoked spectacles should be adopted in time, without waiting till disagreeable sensations are felt. These show that the inflammatory action has begun. The consequences of neglecting these precautions are sometimes extremely painful. The best remedy is to apply a cloth or handkerchief, steeped in water, closely pressed upon the inflamed eyelids, and retained as long as possible. Tepid water should be preferred.

This list of minor miseries of mountaineering may be closed with one which is often felt for some days after an ascent, though but little at the moment. This is the *blistering and peeling off of the skin*, caused by the direct rays of the sun, or the reflection from the snow, aided by the sharp wind which often blows at great heights. After a long day's exposure at a great height it often happens that every portion of the outer skin exposed to the air peels off, leaving the surface raw and uncomfortable for several days. Cold cream or vaseline, and especially 'Crème Simon,' applied beforehand is a preventive. The lips are the part that most frequently suffers from this cause, being sometimes split in a painful manner, if not protected by lip salve. Collodion, although a disagreeable application, is sometimes useful by forming a pellicle over the surface which excludes the air.

Blisters in the soles of the feet should not be cut, but pierced with a needle near the edge, and the contents pressed out. Rubbing the inside of the sock with yellow soap is a preventive, and it is a good plan to rub the feet with tallow and brandy. Some persons are apt to lose the skin of the toes during a long and steep descent. It is easily replaced by good adhesive plaster.

Precautions for Health.—Few of these are required; for the combination of active exercise, pure air, and freedom from care is better for the health than all the prescriptions yet framed by doctors. A few hints, however, may not be useless.

Avoid overworking yourself at first.

When fatigued after an unusually hard day's work, avoid wine, and drink very weak tea or mineral waters in the evening. You will sleep soundly and awake refreshed.

Should you still feel the effects of over-fatigue, make the following day one of rest.

Make it an invariable rule (if possible) to wash extensively with cold or tepid water, and to change your inner clothing immediately on your arrival after a day's walk.

Dietary.—In the frequented parts of the Alps it is now quite safe to rely on obtaining food at the places where a traveller puts up for the night. In other districts, where provisions are poor and scanty, it is necessary to carry supplies, more or less extensive according to the wants of each traveller. The writer (J. B.) has found 1 lb. of rice per day, thoroughly boiled in the excellent milk which is always to be had at the upper chalets, quite sufficient to give two good meals to two travellers. Chocolate may be used for one meal, but in that case bread should also be taken. Hard-boiled eggs contain much nourishment in small space, but are disliked by some. They are usually boiled too hard; five minutes is quite enough, but even so they are not very attractive food. The bread commonly found in chalets is a hard black bread, baked once or twice a year, and not agreeable to unaccustomed palates. On the Italian side of the Alps (and in many parts of Switzerland) a substitute for bread is often found in the shape of *polenta*, made of maize flour. When the flour is good and thoroughly cooked, this, eaten with milk or fresh butter, is wholesome and palatable food. The *brousse* made in the cheese chalets in many parts of the Alps is highly recommended by some, but does not suit all stomachs.

The **dangers of Alpine travelling** have been often exaggerated, but they are real, and no rational man will disregard them. The best proof that these dangers are not greater than those attending many other active exercises, such as fox-hunting and yachting, is the fact that, in spite of inexperience and the neglect of the best known precautions, the fatal accidents in the Alps have been relatively so few. The loss of many lives within the last fifty years, and a much larger number of very narrow escapes, some of them happening to first-rate guides and mountaineers, ought, however, to operate as a salutary warning. The wives and mothers of Alpine travellers, who are disquieted by the reports of accidents, should know that very few have as yet occurred that could not have been prevented by ordinary caution, and adherence to well known rules; and, instead of endeavouring to withhold their husbands and sons from a healthful and invigorating pursuit, should simply urge them to observe the precautions which afford security against all its ordinary dangers.

The following remarks are condensed, with slight alterations, from a paper by Mr. Ball, in the First Series of 'Peaks, Passes, and Glaciers.'

The dangers of Alpine expeditions may be divided into two classes—the real and the imaginary. Where a ridge or slope of rock or ice is such that it could be traversed without difficulty if it lay but a few feet above the level of a garden, the substitution on either side of a precipice some thousands of feet in depth, or of a glacier crevasse, makes no real difference in the work to be done, though it may have a formidable effect on the traveller's imagination. Those who cannot remove this source of danger by accustoming themselves to look unmoved down vertical precipices, and, in cases of real difficulty, to fix their attention exclusively on the ledge or jutting crag to which they must cling with foot or hand, should avoid expeditions on which a moment's nervousness may endanger their own lives or those of others.

The real dangers of the High Alps may, under ordinary circumstances, be reduced to three—first, the *yielding of the snow bridges that cover glacier crevasses*; second, the risk of slipping upon steep slopes of hard ice or of snow on ice; third, the fall of ice or rocks from above.

(1) From the first and most frequent source of danger absolute security is obtained by a precaution generally known but often neglected. In the higher region of the glaciers, crevasses, even of considerable width, are often completely bridged over by a covering of snow or névé, so that no indication of their existence is seen on the surface of the glacier. The bridges, especially when formed of fresh snow, often yield under the weight of a man's footsteps; in such a case an active man whose attention is on the alert may sometimes extricate himself at once, but it more commonly happens that he falls into the chasm beneath, in which case his chance of life is very uncertain. But if several travellers are tied together with a stout rope, at intervals of about 15 feet, and keep their distance, as it is most unlikely that more than one should fall at the same time into the same crevasse, no appreciable danger from this cause need be incurred. Even two men tied together may with proper attention diminish this risk, but greater security is obtained when they are three or more in number. It is mainly because he cannot be protected from this danger that a man who goes alone over the higher regions of the great glaciers incurs a risk that must be called unjustifiable.

As it is hard to persuade a landsman that a well-found yacht has more danger to fear in a fog, with a smooth sea around, than when a stiff breeze is blowing, so inexperienced mountaineers are slow to admit that there is more real chance of accident in traversing some wide expanse of névé, unbroken by a single ruffle, than in crossing a broken glacier with wide crevasses opening on every side. A very moderate amount of practice enables a man to make sure of his footing and to avoid seen dangers, but unseen perils call forth no caution, and though the rope offers complete security, many travellers, and even some guides, are disposed to neglect it. At the risk of being thought over-cautious, the writer (J. B.) will not cease to urge upon his fellow-travellers in the Alps the enactment, as a fixed rule in mountaineering, that on reaching the névé (if not before) the members of a party should all be roped together. He is perfectly aware that there are many places where the risk is very slight: a practised mountaineer might cross the St. Théodule Pass 500 times without accident, but the 501st time he might be lost in a crevasse, as has happened twice on or near the pass since the writer first knew it. With a sufficient inducement, and if it were impossible to find a companion, he would not hesitate to cross that or some other high passes alone; but if he were in company, he would insist on the use of the rope.

It would seem scarcely necessary to insist that the rope should be sound and strong, if it did not sometimes happen that untrustworthy articles are taken by guides; and it is not less important to note that it should be fastened round the body of each member of the party, *guides included*, leaving both hands free to use the ice axe or alpenstock in case of a slip. A neglect of the first precaution led to a fatal accident in 1859, and to another in 1863, and a breach of the second to the loss of three English travellers, and one of their guides, in 1860, in the descent from the Col du Géant to Courmayeur.

When it is a matter of importance to cross a snow bridge of doubtful solidity, it is a good plan to let each person in succession crawl across on hands and knees, with the alpenstock in one hand laid flat upon the snow, so as to distribute the weight over as large a surface as possible. It is needless to say that, as a matter of course, the whole party should be well roped together.

(2) The ascent and descent of *steep ice-slopes, or of snow on ice*, are amongst the most difficult operations that commonly fall in the way of the mountaineer, but when properly conducted there should be little or no danger to those concerned. It should be explained that the term ice slope is commonly applied to slopes of névé on which, after a certain amount of exposure, a crust is formed, too hard to yield to the foot, yet very different from compact glacier ice. This icy crust yields easily to the axe, and a couple of well directed blows suffice to make a step on which the foot may take secure hold. When we read of ascents in which several hundred steps have been cut, it must usually (though not always) be understood that these have been made on slopes of frozen névé. Though the operation is rather tedious, and fatiguing to those engaged in cutting the steps, such ascents seldom involve any risk, for the steps are usually very easily enlarged so as to give good standing-ground. On slopes exposed to the sun, where a thin layer of snow has lain over rocks, the whole mass is sometimes so saturated by the

melting of the surface that when refrozen at night it is converted into a continuous mass of nearly compact solid ice. Such a slope, especially if it be steep, is far more troublesome than those above described ; to cut steps is a much more laborious operation, and these are generally shallower, and give but precarious footing. In such situations some experience and perfect steadiness are indispensable, and it is essential that the rope should be kept tightly stretched.

In spite of every precaution, a traveller may slip on an ice slope where, if unchecked, a fall would lead to certain destruction. Against this danger the rope is usually an effectual preservative. Cases are said to occur where the footing is so precarious that a party cannot be tied together, as, if one were to slip, he would inevitably drag all his companions along with him to destruction. It is for those concerned to consider whether in such instances the object in view is such as to justify the inevitable peril of the ascent. The writer (J. B.) believes, however, that such cases are extremely rare, and that very few slopes have yet been surmounted where two men, with well-stretched rope, could not hold up a third who should slip, especially if the latter be not wanting in steadiness and presence of mind.

There is one description of slope which usually involves serious risk. That is when a layer of fresh snow lies upon a surface of hard ice, or even well-compacted névé. For some days there is little adhesion between the upper and the under layer, and if the slope be steep the disturbance caused by the pressure of a foot may easily produce an avalanche capable of carrying away and burying an entire party. Practical experience is needed to determine whether the ascent can be safely attempted. Several fatal accidents that have occurred in the numerous ascents of Mont Blanc should serve as warnings against attempting an ascent when the snow is in this condition.

(3) The dangers arising from *masses of ice or rock falling across the track* are at the moment beyond the skill of the traveller, but they may, to a great extent, be avoided by a judicious choice of route. Experienced mountaineers learn to recognise the positions where ice detached from a higher level descends over a precipice or steep slope of rock. They either avoid such spots altogether, or are careful to pass them either early in the morning, before the sun has loosened the impending masses, or late in the day, after his rays have been withdrawn.

During bad weather the ordinary risks of Alpine travelling are much increased, and serious dangers from other causes may assail the traveller. Masses of rock are detached from their previously firm resting-places, and come thundering down across the track. Falling snow obscures the view and effaces the footprints, so that it becomes equally difficult to advance or to retreat. Most formidable of all, the *tourmente*, or snow whirlwind—when the wind begins to blow in violent gusts—bewilders the traveller, half blinded by the fine dust-like snow of the higher regions, and benumbs his limbs with its biting breath if he be unable to keep up rapid exercise. A reasonable man will not attempt expeditions in the higher regions of the Alps during bad weather, and will resort to an immediate retreat when unexpectedly attacked by it. Attention to the bearings of the compass and to landmarks will in most cases enable travellers to retrace their steps. In attempting to traverse an unknown glacier, it is prudent to gain a height overlooking the projected route, and examine the surface carefully through a glass.

Very serious danger is incurred when inexperienced men take part in difficult expeditions.

Of recent years mountaineering without guides has come into fashion, and in some cases has been carried to an excess. Few (if any) amateurs, having but five or six weeks at their disposal annually, can hope to become as good all round as even a second-class professional glacier guide. But to many amateurs there is a keen pleasure in overcoming obstacles by their own unaided efforts, and nothing can be more justified in the case of those qualified by experience and physical capacities for such feats. Solitary mountaineering in the High Alps is unreservedly condemned by all competent judges.

Art. VIII.—Guides and Porters.

The inducements to the natives to adopt the profession of guide have constantly increased during the last half-century, in the same proportion as the number of strangers annually resorting to the Alps. The large majority of tourists do no more than follow a frequented path, where one native of the district is as competent as another. The increased desire to explore the less accessible parts of the Alps, and to undertake difficult and dangerous expeditions, has led to a demand for the services of a superior class of men, who possess in a high degree the special qualities of the mountaineer. Although there is no recognised distinction between the two classes, and the best guide, when not otherwise engaged, is ready to carry a lady's shawl over the easiest Alpine pass, there is in fact as wide a difference between them as between the most eminent and the inferior men in any other profession. The practice of taking the same guide throughout an entire tour, which has become very common among Alpine travellers, has led to another distinction, better defined than the last, between general and local guides. While the latter have no pretension to go beyond the bounds of their own immediate district, the others are men who have acquired a tolerably wide acquaintance with many or even most parts of the Alps, who speak French and German, and sometimes English, and have a sufficient knowledge of the dialects used in different parts of the chain to serve as interpreters, and as useful travelling servants. The men who unite the qualities of the mountaineer with a wide range of local knowledge are naturally the most valuable to the Alpine traveller, but their number is very limited. The best men are usually engaged weeks, or months, beforehand, mainly by members of the Alpine Club. An ordinary tourist has no occasion to seek for men of this class, but he may find it an excellent plan to secure the services of a steady respectable man who will accompany him throughout his tour.

The early travellers in the Alps found that the natives most likely to possess a knowledge of the mountains of their district, and therefore most familiar with what was then largely a *terra incognita*, were the herdsmen and goatherds, the smugglers (if the district was near the frontier), and particularly (if it was intended to make difficult ascents or explorations) the local chamois hunters, though it did not prove that any but a few of the men belonging to one or other of these classes were really fitted to permanently become guides to strangers. Little by little the more enterprising and bolder men in each district found that it was profitable to devote themselves to guiding as a profession, especially as the number of visitors to their valleys increased ; for there was thus a chance of more or less constant employment during the summer, and so of earning ready money, the stock of which in most Alpine valleys is otherwise far from large. Soon it was found desirable to place the members of this new profession under rules and regulations. At Chamonix the first set of regulations dates back as far as 1821, but ceased to have force in 1848, the later codes dating from 1851 and especially 1856. The Bernese Oberland guides do not seem to have been organised till 1856 (these regulations were modified in 1874), while the Pontresina men did not form a society till 1861. Other districts followed suit at a still more recent period, and it may now be said that, with the exception of some very little frequented spots, the guides in each district form a sort of corporation, with strict rules and regulations.

The system is best organised in Switzerland, where it is under the control of the Cantonal (*not* communal) authorities, assisted by the Swiss Alpine Club. In other districts matters are managed more or less exclusively by the local branch of the national Alpine Society, which issues licenses, &c., and exercises a general supervision over its men. The following remarks refer mainly to the Swiss system (particularly that of the Bernese Oberland), which is followed in its general outlines by those of other Alpine lands.

In Switzerland any strong man, of good reputation and 18 years of age, may apply for a license as 'porter :' his pay (7-9 francs—including food—per day of 8 hrs.) and other rights and obligations are very similar to those of a 'guide,' save that he is bound to carry 50 pounds weight (the guides only 20), while a 'porter' has no responsibility for the safety of the party, being under the orders of the guide, and practically occupying the position of an apprentice. He cannot become a 'guide' till he has attained the age of 20 years, and has successfully passed an examination in the topography, &c., of his valley and Switzerland in general, and other practical subjects, before a Commission appointed for that purpose in each district. Then his responsibilities increase, and he becomes something more than a beast of burden.

Each porter or guide on being licensed receives (like every other workman on the Continent) a book, containing the printed regulations by which he is bound, &c., together with a number of blank leaves whereon his employers enter their remarks and recommendations. Each man, of whichever class, is *bound* to offer his book to his employer at the beginning and at the end of his engagement, while it has to be inspected by the licensing authority annually, when the license is renewed. In many cases the records in these books, if carefully preserved, come in the course of time to possess great interest, and even considerable historical value.

Where the guides and porters are numerous the Cantonal authorities appoint a 'Chief Guide,' who is charged with the general supervision of the men, and with settling the minor disputes that may arise between them and their employers, though a serious complaint against a man should be addressed to the Cantonal authorities, in the person of the nearest 'Prefect.' Grave misconduct may be punished by fine or even by withdrawal of the license, but such cases are luckily rare, and are generally made known in the various Alpine periodicals.

Most of the Oberland guides, and some of those in other districts, effect, with the aid of the Swiss Alpine Club, insurances on their lives (mainly for the summer) against injuries received by them in the exercise of their profession. (See an article by Pfarrer Strasser in vol. xxxi. of the S.A.C. 'Jahrbuch').

Though all guides are on the same legal footing, in practice there is a great distinction between those who may be called ordinary guides and those who are strictly glacier guides.

The *ordinary guides* are respectable men, ready and willing to show the way, and to perform small services for their employers; but, except here and there, they confine themselves to the minor excursions, rarely venturing beyond, say, the Mer de Glace at Chamonix, or the Grindelwald Eismeer. They are generally engaged for a single excursion, though the traveller may sometimes decide to take a pleasant-spoken man with him for a few days. But, save in special cases, they are not acquainted with anything beyond their own immediate district.

The *glacier guides*, on the other hand, are those who devote their energies, save for a day or two now and then, to making high and difficult mountain expeditions in any part of the Alps. This higher class of guide possesses the strength and activity, combined with the courage, coolness, and skill, that make the accomplished mountaineer, and is formed only by the union of training and experience with the requisite natural faculties. To a certain extent the raw material may be said to exist wherever chamois-hunting is a favourite pursuit of the young and active men. But this of itself does not suffice. The most skilful Pyrenean *chasseur*, placed on the summit of the Strahlegg Pass, would probably be overpowered with terror, and if unaided would be little likely to reach Grindelwald or the Grimsel; while many good Oberland guides might hesitate before trusting themselves on the face of a dizzy limestone precipice that is traversed with ease by the Aragonese cragsman with his *alpargatas* (shoes with hempen soles). Active men and bold climbers may now be found in most parts of the Alps, but it is mainly in the Bernese Oberland and in the Vallais (for Chamonix has fallen in this respect from its high estate) that the degree of experience and skill requisite for contending with the difficulties of the snow and ice region of the Alps is to be acquired. With a few brilliant exceptions, however, the Vallais guides are inferior to their rivals of Grindelwald, but these two sets may be classed together in point of icecraft *and* rockcraft as against their comrades in other Alpine districts, E. and W., who are often excellent cragsmen, but rarely know much (if anything) about ice and snow.

A glacier guide is expected to carry a sack (though not a *very* heavy one), and to find himself in the articles requisite for his profession (such as rope and ice axe). In strictness he is bound to feed himself out of his pay, but save in Switzerland (where the prices for guides are very low) it is usual for the employer to pay part or the whole of his guide's ordinary hôtel expenses. Of course, when food has to be carried up to some Club hut far from an hôtel, the traveller is bound to take sufficient provisions, wood, &c., for his guides as well as for himself.

In pretty well every district of the Alps the sum to be paid for any glacier ascent or pass is now fixed by an official printed tariff, which can be seen in the inns of the district. The Swiss Alpine Club has just rendered a very great service, to mountaineers by collecting into two small volumes, and to a certain extent in codifying, the fees due for all the chief high expeditions in Switzerland (save in the Bernese Alps). Of course a traveller who is content with the services rendered by his guide after a few days, or it may be weeks, of companionship will add to the sum legally due (including, if necessary, the 6 francs per day of 8 hrs. payable for the expense of the return to a man discharged at a distance from his home) a gratuity proportional to the work done.

While it may be said with truth that every glacier guide still on the active list may be trusted to safely lead his employer on any of the ordinary glacier expeditions, it is only a select minority which is capable of achieving the more difficult peaks and passes. This class of men is, of course, extremely limited in point of numbers (it has, indeed, been reckoned that at present there are perhaps not more than 25 guides of the first class in the whole range of the Alps), while such men are engaged long in advance, often for year after year by the same mountaineer, so that ordinary travellers have no chance of picking one up, unless by accident between two engagements. In such cases of extended tours it is usual that the pay should be settled not by the official tariff, but by some private arrangement between the parties concerned. Sometimes it is agreed that the guide shall receive so much per day (wet or fine), save when a high expedition is made, when so much will be deducted from the tariff for that climb, since it is evident that being sure of even some pay in bad weather, it is to the interest of the guide to smooth matters for his employer. Another plan is to promise a guide a lump sum down for an engagement of so many weeks, the employer here taking the chance of fine weather, health, &c., while the guide is bound to make as many ascents in the given time as his employer's legs and the weather may enable the party to achieve. Yet a third plan (in some ways the simplest and fairest of all) is that the guide shall receive so much per day (wet or fine), but that if a high pass is made he shall *in lieu* of his day's pay receive a fixed sum, and if a high peak be climbed a still higher fixed sum, always *in lieu* of the ordinary day's pay.

It often happens that a guide may travel with the same employer for a series of years, and in many different districts of the Alps. In that case a strong bond is formed between the two who have so often been in danger and undergone exciting adventures together. This bond not unfrequently gets stronger and stronger as years roll by, and it sometimes becomes a lasting friendship between two men who, by being constantly thrown together in moments of danger and anxiety, have their good qualities brought out. No one who does not know it by personal experience can form any idea of the devotion and loyalty displayed by the picked men of this class towards travellers who treat them with proper consideration and respect, so that a real affection springs up between men who might be thought at first sight to have but little in common. The writer of these lines (W. A. B. C.) can bear witness on this point, as he has enjoyed the great privilege of having had different members of the same family as his guides for the last thirty years. In his opinion the nature of this tie has never been better set forth than in the following sentences penned by a brilliant writer (Sir F. Pollock, Bart.) in memory of an Oberlander who had been his faithful guide and companion for several seasons :—

'There are travellers to the Alps, I believe, who, having made one or more excursions for which a guide is necessary, still regard their guide as a sort of hired servant a little above the lowest degree. To such persons these words are not addressed, for to them I should be speaking an unknown language. But those will understand me who have known what it is to share day after day the smiles or anger of the high air, and break bread among the perennial snows, with a chosen faithful companion— Oberlander, or Walliser, or Chamoniard ; nor these only, but all who have learned the worth of true and simple manhood in times and places where the refinements of our artificial life are of no account. Therefore it will seem nothing strange to Englishmen of the right sort who use their eyes and their limbs, whether they be Alpine climbers or not, that one should not esteem lightly the loss of a valiant and courteous guide who will never wield ice-axe more. These, I know, are the terms of old romance, associated with pageants and great solemnities, and companies of stately men and fair women. It may seem incongruous to apply them to people who wear hob-nailed boots and clothes of the roughest homespun, and talk in an uncouth highland dialect of German. But if valour and courtesy are not the fitting words for the character of the best Swiss guides, I know not what other to find. They are ever ready to perform what they have undertaken, or at least carry the attempt to the uttermost of man's power, not as the bare fulfilment of a bargain, but joyfully and as an honourable achievement ; they are ever watchful not merely for the safety of the travellers they have taken in their charge, but for their ease and comfort in everything ; and all this they do as if it were pure pleasure to them and the most natural thing in the world.' *

Art. IX.—Inns and Club Huts.

So much does the comfort of travellers depend upon the goodness or badness of the accommodation found at **inns**, that it is not surprising if they exact a degree of accuracy on this point from a guide-book that, from the nature of the case, it is impossible fully to attain. Assuming that the information at the Editor's disposal were always very recent, there is a great degree of uncertainty about the impression left upon a passing traveller by an inn where he remains for one or two nights. One traveller happens

* *Alpine Journal*, vol. x. p. 78.

to arrive when the house is crowded, the larder ill-provided, and servants and the master tired. He is ill-lodged, ill-fed, and ill-attended, and as a natural consequence his report is highly unfavourable. A few days later another traveller is lodged in the best rooms, finds abundant supplies, and is treated with attention. The second report is, as it ought to be, entirely different from the first. There are but a few hôtels of the best class so well arranged, and under such skilful and active management, as not to be liable to such vicissitudes. In truth, however, the information obtainable dates back at least several months, perhaps even two or three years, and in that time very many changes can occur. The management of an inn, especially a large one, requires constant activity and watchfulness on the part of some one directly interested in its success ; and it constantly happens that a change of management, or a mere relaxation of the innkeeper's activity, caused by over-prosperity or by engaging in other pursuits, reduces an hôtel from the first to an inferior rank. At the same time new houses are every year opened in the frequented parts of the Alps ; so that between the falling off of old and the rise of new inns it is impossible to achieve invariable accuracy. Those who use this book will, therefore, confer a favour on the Editor, and on future travellers, if they will note down the inns at which they stop in the course of their tour, with such observations as they consider due, and communicate the same to him for use in a future edition. Such information is useful even in respect to the most frequented places, whether the traveller's judgment agree with that here expressed or not.

It is generally known that no country in Europe is so well provided with inns as Switzerland. The hôtels in the more frequented places leave very little to be desired by the most fastidious, and in country places they are much superior to similar establishments in our own country. In the principal inns great attention is paid to the requirements of English guests in every respect. There is always a late dinner as well as a 1 o'clock lunch, while there is generally a resident English chaplain during the summer, a small English church being often built close by the inn. The smaller inns are, of course, more simple, but clean and good, while the prices fall in proportion to their distance from frequented tourist centres. Great improvements as regards inns have been made of late years in the French and Italian Alps, though as a rule these are not yet quite up to the Swiss standard. The smaller inns in the Tyrolese, Lombard, and Venetian Alps are perhaps no longer so primitive and unsophisticated as they formerly were, though, as in all other parts of the Alps, exceptions may be found here and there. In the first edition of this 'Introduction' Mr. Ball stated that he was in the habit of stopping in remote villages and hamlets in the Lombard and Venetian Alps wherever convenience dictated, without caring to make previous enquiry as to the accommodation to be found there, and that he rarely failed to obtain tolerable food and a clean bed. The present Editor (W. A. B. C.) has long followed the same plan in all parts of the Western and Central Alps, and his experience is similar to that of Mr. Ball. In a previous Article (Art. V., above) some remarks were made as to the prices of mountain inns, whether for passers-by or for those remaining some days *en pension*. It is only necessary to repeat here the warning there given that the appa-

INTRODUCTION.

rently excessive charges of high mountain inns should not be complained of, since the expenses of transport (often of even water and wood) are very great, and the season for which they are open (and that for the benefit of a limited number of travellers and subject to all the chances of the weather) is often extremely short.

In justice to themselves and the public, travellers should take the trouble to look over their bills, and to point out for reduction any items that appear unreasonable. Should a simple remonstrance fail, there is generally no use in further resistance. The extortion must be gross indeed that will not be sanctioned by the local authorities, should a traveller lose time by resorting to them. There is but one effective threat to which innkeepers are usually very susceptible—that of exposure in English newspapers and guide-books, and this, in gross cases, should always be enforced. Cases of shameless extortion are usually confined to the meaner class of inns, or to those which have been opened expressly for tourists on some Alpine route. No reasonable person will object to pay somewhat more than the usual rate of accommodation at an inn set up expressly for the convenience of a limited class, but it is well to make the owners understand that by unreasonably high charges they defeat their own object.

One of the chief matters which occupy the attention of the great Continental Alpine Clubs is the construction and maintenance of **Club huts** in suitable spots on the way to the principal peaks and passes of their respective districts. Formerly these were but rough shelters, but every year sees a steady advance and improvement in this point, so that high expeditions are very much facilitated thereby.

In the *Swiss Alps* the huts are not large or luxurious, but are generally open, and nothing is charged for accommodation; one of the guides in the nearest Alpine centre is entrusted with the general care of the hut, while the section of the Club to which it belongs sends annually a representative to inspect and to report on the actual condition of the hut and its fittings. In a few cases there is a man or woman resident during the summer, who supplies provisions, wood, &c., at a fixed rate; here and there wood for fuel is placed in the hut, and may be used on a small payment, while in one or two cases the hut (or part of it) is closed by means of a key.

The *French* and *Italian* Club huts are almost always locked, and the key must be brought up either from the nearest village or by one of the local guides; the inconveniences of this practice are obvious, and it is to be hoped that it will gradually give way to the plan usual in the *Austrian* huts. Very many of these latter are really small (or even large) mountain inns (with resident managers), having separate bedrooms, dining-rooms, &c. In these cases a regular charge is made for staying a few hours or sleeping there, members of any of the great Alpine Clubs generally paying half-price. But in many other Austrian huts the door is secured by a Club key. One of these Club keys may be purchased (on signing a formal document) by any member of the Club to which the hut belongs, and opens all the huts. This is a very convenient and practical method of solving a real difficulty. Most of the Austrian huts (not being inns, *i.e.* not 'bewirthschaftet') contain a stock of tinned provisions, wine, spirits, &c., according to Dr. Pott's excellent system: these are packed in large baskets, and all a traveller has to do is to enter what he has taken on one of the printed lists provided for that purpose and giving the price of each article, and then (after signing it) to drop it with the sum due into a box placed in the hut for the purpose. Recently in several huts in the Austrian Alps the money in these boxes has been robbed, but the abuse of an excellent system will not (it is to be hoped) lead to its abolition, since by this plan of provisioning huts the necessity of descending to the valleys between two expeditions is done away with. A man appointed by the section owning it visits each of these huts periodically in order to renew the stock of provisions and to empty the money boxes.

The German and Austrian Alpine Club publishes annually a more or less complete list of all the Club huts and small mountain inns in the Alps; this is very convenient, though the information as to the Western and Central Alps is not always quite up to date. The same society issued in 1897 a most useful map, showing precisely the exact position of every Club hut (to whatever society it belongs) and small mountain inn in the Eastern Alps; by a system of elaborate signs it is possible to tell at once whether a Club hut is inhabited by a manager during the summer, or whether it is only 'provisioned,' or whether it is a mere shelter hut.

The Swiss Alpine Club published in 1896 a very handy and detailed pamphlet (with map) describing each of its Club huts, mentioning what expeditions may be made from it, &c., though unluckily without a minute account of the path up from the nearest village. 'This booklet was supplemented in 1898 by a set of views of all the Swiss Club huts, old and new. The same Club also publishes in its monthly organ, 'Alpina,' from time to time reports as to the precise *actual* condition of each of its Club huts, a plan which cannot be too highly recommended for adoption by other Alpine societies.

The Dauphiné Société des Touristes also issues an account of all the Club huts in that district, together with the tariff for the guides and porters there (latest issue in 1896).

The French Alpine Club in 1898 put forth a short notice of its huts in the Alps and in the Pyrenees.

But as far as the present writer (W. A. B. C.) is aware there is no recent and full account of the Club huts of the Italian Alpine Club, the list given in its 'Cronaca' (1888) being naturally rather out of date.

It would be an enormous practical advantage to mountaineers of all nationalities if the great Clubs would combine to issue *each spring* a small pamphlet, stating the exact state of each Club hut (for some are ruined, more or less permanently, every winter), with a clear account of the route thither (something like those in the later volumes of the 'Climbers' Guides'), for nothing is harder to ascertain than whether a hut still exists, and if so, where it is situated precisely, and how to reach it. Possibly, though this would almost be too good, in the course of time it might be arranged that all locked Club huts should be made to open with similar keys, due restrictions of course being placed on the sale of such keys, as is now done by the German and Austrian Club.

Art. X.—Life in an Alpine Valley.*

The traveller in the Alps who really takes an interest in the lands through which he is making a holiday trip can scarcely fail to desire to know more about their inhabitants than he can gain from those with whom he comes into contact in what may be called their official capacity, *e.g.* innkeepers, postal, railway, and diligence officials. At first he is apt to believe that the inhabitants of Alpine lands have no other care or occupation than attending to the wants of passing travellers. But gradually he realises (especially if he visits his favourite haunts in winter) that the state of things to which he is accustomed in summer is really extraordinary and abnormal. This feverish period lasts but two or three months in the year, while for the rest of the time the inhabitants are living quite a different life, and that the life which they led all the year round previous to the comparatively recent fashion on the part of the dwellers in the plains of visiting the Alps in summer. Few travellers, however, have either the leisure or opportunities for studying the home life of the Alpine folk for themselves, while the abundant printed materials on this subject are widely scattered, and are generally in a foreign tongue. Hence the following outline sketch of the real conditions of life prevailing among the Alpine folk may be welcome to some readers, for whose convenience, should they care to fill up the scanty outline which alone space allows us to give here, some of the more important printed sources are indicated in the notes. But by far the best way of getting information is by personal conversation with some of the natives, *e.g.* the guides, often very intelligent men, who will be surprised and delighted to find that their travellers consider them as something better than mere path-finders, and who will readily describe their everyday life, amid conditions very unlike those subsisting in the plains.

1. The question of *origins* is always fascinating, though the available materials rarely allow of a final and definite solution of the problem. In Article V. something was said of the distribution throughout the Alps of the various races which represent either tribes that remained there when others descended into the plains, or sometimes tribes that have been driven up into the hills by the pressure of strangers coming from distant lands, who either absorb or expel those whom they find in possession of the lands they covet. But, to whatever race the inhabitants of the Alps belong, the manner in which they occupied the Alpine valleys seems to have been very similar. In the case of the *lower* Alpine valleys it is a well ascertained fact that the early settlers took up their abode on the slopes high above the valley stream, thus securing at once pastures for their herds and flocks, wood for fuel and building, much sunshine, and freedom from the evils of the marshy banks of the

---

* This Article is new and has been written by Mr. Coolidge, who, towards the end, has included the substance of the page devoted by Mr. Ball (in the 'Climate and Vegetation' article of the old edition) to *Chalet Life in the Alps*. The present writer has kept chiefly in view the German-speaking parts of Switzerland, which are both better known and better organised than the Alpine districts of the French, Italian, or Tyrolese Alps. Many illustrations have been drawn from the past and existing state of things in Grindelwald, as the residence of the author in that valley enables him to command much local information as regards it.

stream : only little by little did the increasing population descend to the river bank, and from sheer necessity clear away the reeds and brushwood, and even undertake an elementary kind of drainage. In the *upper* Alpine valleys, or the side valleys, the early settlers pushed along the mountain slopes in the same fashion, above the often narrow and rocky bed of the stream, thus avoiding too the swampy flats at the junction of this stream with a mightier torrent, and finally occupied the pasture hollow or basin at the upper end of the glen, immediately under the great mountain peaks. In many cases doubtless the higher regions were originally only inhabited in summer for purposes of pasture. Now and then a few daring spirits or very poor men did not descend to the lower regions in winter, and so little by little the upper regions became permanently inhabited, while summer pastures had to be sought still higher up. It must, too, be always borne in mind that each of these early settlers in the Alps (as now in the wilder parts of the earth) brought with him his family, so that each little settlement was 'self-sufficing,' depending solely on its own exertions for obtaining food, fuel, clothing, and other necessaries : each household would have its own meadows, pastures, woods, &c., and but scanty communication with its neighbours, who were perhaps many leagues distant. As the population increased of course this complete isolation became a thing of the past, and rules and regulations were adopted by common accord as to various weighty points regarding pastures, forest, rotation of crops, &c. But it was only very slowly that what originally were mere customs hardened into fixed rules and regulations. Again, with increased population, and residence all the year round in these high regions, came the necessity of having a permanent chapel for common religious worship, and this became the centre of the life of the valley : meetings to discuss common matters of interest would be held after service on Sundays or holy days near or even in the chapel, for at those times it was easiest to gather together the scattered dwellers in the valley. In course of time the humble chapel would be replaced by a more or less stately parish church, which would be in an even greater degree the centre of the common life of the community : thither they were bound to come for baptisms, marriages, burials, &c. ; near by dwelt the priest, who represented education and the outer world, and would be the natural adviser and counsellor of his rustic parishioners ; and there would be the warning bell to tell of sudden calamity, or to gather together the inhabitants in haste for any urgent cause. But it was only at a comparatively late period that buildings, other than the priest's house (in which was the school), and the inn, clustered round the church or were erected in its neighbourhood. In short, the origin of Alpine *villages* is usually quite modern, though from very early days the church stood on a knoll visible far and wide, and was practically the nucleus of the future hamlet. Even now in many Alpine valleys there is often no one considerable village, but many more or less isolated homesteads, with perchance a few small hamlets ; but the 'church town' (as they call it in Cornwall) is always the most important of these hamlets (though by no means always the largest), for it is the natural centre of the life of the inhabitants, and so bears *par éminence* the name of the valley or commune of which it is, so to speak, the tiny capital. The church hamlet may also have its own special name, and travellers in the Alps soon discover (sometimes by painful experience) that in a remote valley they must first ascertain where the church hamlet is, and there they may be certain is the valley inn, not unfrequently in former days kept by the priest or *pasteur* himself.*

The early history of Grindelwald illustrates most of the points indicated above. By local tradition the earliest settlements were high above the right bank of the Lütschine, and most probably the valley was first visited for the sake of pasture in summer only. Various great lords settled their serfs there in widely scattered homesteads, which only later crept down towards the river bed (even now there are but few houses here), while in the course of time these lords were gradually bought out by the great house of Austin Canons at Interlaken. The original chapel of S. Petronella, high up in a cave under the cliffs of the Eiger (the cave is still shown), gave way to a wooden church (dedicated to our Lady of Interlaken), built and consecrated (*c.* 1146) on the present site by the diocesan, the Bishop of Lausanne, this being replaced *c.* 1180 by a stone church, which subsisted till 1793. It was not till the suppression of the religious house of Interlaken in 1528-1532, at the time of the Bernese Reformation, that the men of Grindelwald passed from the condition of serfs of the convent to that of subjects of the ambitious and encroaching town of Bern. The valley then, too, first became a separate parish, having previously been only a chapelry of the religious house, and served by one or other of the Canons. To this day the traveller can see for himself that the population live in widely scattered homesteads, or in one or two small hamlets (each bearing its own name). He will also soon discover that there is only a valley of Grindelwald, but no village of that name, the church hamlet, with its few houses, being properly known as 'Gydisdorf,' a name which is found in the documents relating to the valley as early as 1275, while later we hear of a meeting of the men of the valley held on 'the hillock at Gydisdorf.'

2. The simplicity which, as we have seen, characterises the occupation and gradual settlement of an Alpine valley is even nowadays maintained in the *daily manner of life* of its inhabitants. Not much money circulates, for, save those connected in some way with the reception, &c., of foreign visitors, little money is to be found there, and most transactions are made in kind. There are few industries in the mountain valleys, except in such cases as the wood-carving industry at Brienz and in the Grödenerthal. Each household is chiefly occupied in supplying its own wants, though of course there are a few necessary artisans, such as bakers, cobblers, blacksmiths, carpenters, and the like. It is cheaper now to import corn from the lowlands than to grow it at considerable heights (where, as at La Bérarde, in the Dauphiné Alps, the seed must remain two winters in the earth, and yet the corn is cut while still but half ripe), so that in such a valley there is not much arable land, and that little mainly devoted to potatoes and other vegetables. Meat and wine

---

* On the origin of Alpine villages see Herr von Inama-Sternegg's excellent essay 'Die Entwickelung der deutschen Alpendörfer,' in series v. vol. 4 of Riehl's *Historisches Taschenbuch* (Leipzig, 1874), and also part 2 (and particularly the notes) of Prof. A. von Miaskowski's *Die Verfassung der Land-, Alpen- und Forstwirthschaft d. deutschen Schweiz* (Basel, 1878).

are rare luxuries in a mountain valley, though occasionally a pig may be salted down, and half a bottle of wine drunk on some special occasion of rejoicing. Spinning and weaving have almost disappeared, as cloth can be purchased at low prices, and then made up at home. The young and active men in many cases take naturally to hunting (especially chamois-hunting), though more for pleasure than as a regular business. But although such conditions of life may seem poor and cramped to townsmen, the mountain dwellers lead a free and healthy life, having but few wants, and those mainly supplied on the spot, though at the price of much labour and fatigue. Of these wants food and wood are the principal. The former want is satisfied by the milk, cheese, butter, &c., all due to the cherished kine, and the latter (whether wood for fuel or for house-building) by the forests which clothe the upper slopes of most mountain valleys, though a few communities have recklessly sold their woods, and now bitterly regret it. The care of the cattle and the procuring of wood from the forests (especially in winter) thus constitute the greater part of the real life of the inhabitants of mountain valleys. It is thus practically an exclusively pastoral one, so that the ownership and use of the land, whether meadow, pasture, or forest, is the foundation on which rests the welfare, and indeed the very existence, of an Alpine community. Hence we find that as soon as the first colonising process is over fixed arrangements must be made, by custom or by law, as to the land in any particular valley. Private property, indeed, exists in the case of the homestead, and perhaps a field or two, but the rest of the land in a mountain valley is held as common property, not to be used at any man's will, but subject to the rights of each man in this property belonging to all and maintained for the common benefit according to strict customs and rules. Hence we find that in each mountain valley there comes a time when such customs or rules obtain force of law, which regulates the use of the land owned in common. It is this common ownership of land, subject to the rights of user on the part of each male inhabitant, that constitutes the special characteristic institution of the Alpine folk, the *Commune* or *Gemeinde* being the name given to the common owners, each of whom is a burgher, and as such entitled to special rights of user. All through the Middle Ages the Communes were purely pastoral associations, resting on the regulated user of the common lands (*Allmend*, originally written 'Allmeind,' and related to the word 'Gemeinde'). The original settlers, and those who came soon after, were alone both owners and users of the land, and in their Common Meetings settled all matters relating to the common land in the valley and rights of user over it. Hence, save in very rare cases, all the inhabitants were burghers, and there were but few who came to live in the valley without being born in it. The latter class was known as 'Beisässen' or 'Hintersässen' (in English municipal history 'foreigners'), for though residents they were not burghers. It was not till about the middle of the sixteenth century that this class became important in point of numbers, partly from easier means of travel, partly for other reasons. It was the necessity of replacing the old system of Poor Relief by a new system which completely altered the character of these pastoral associations. Formerly it would rarely happen that any 'burgher' could, with his rights of user of the common land, fall into great need and distress, save in the case of illness and old age, when the alms of the faithful in the valley sufficed to support a brother in need. But when at the time of the Reformation, in the Alpine districts as elsewhere, the increasing number of 'residents' taxed that charity heavily, a special provision had to be made (in Switzerland it is dated 1551) by which each Commune was bound to support, in case of need, not merely its full members, but also those who were merely 'residents.' Hence for the first time there arose a distinction, which gradually became more and more important, between the old 'Burgergemeinden' (or associations of full 'burghers') * and the new 'Einwohnergemeinden' (or the communes consisting of all residents in the valley, whether burghers or not). The former were exclusively pastoral; the latter became more and more political, and it is obvious that great difficulties would arise as to the sources whence to procure funds to meet these new calls, whether by imposing rates or by accumulating funds for the special purposes of poor relief. The story is long and complicated, and here it need only be said that in the Swiss Alps the two kinds of Communes still subsist side by side, save in glens (*e.g.* Grindelwald) where there are practically only 'burghers,' or where the 'burghers' have more or less freely made over all or part of their common property to the new political associations. Yet both kinds of Communes have one very important feature in common—that Swiss citizenship, or even Cantonal citizenship, can only be obtained by a person who has previously become, whether by purchase or in any other manner, a member of a Commune. The Commune is the unit out of which first the Canton, and then the Swiss Confederation itself, has been built up. And the Commune in its original sense is simply the association of the inhabitants of a valley, based on the common ownership of land, which is subject to certain well defined rights of user on the part of each of the male burghers of full age. This pastoral community is thus the basis of the institutions by which the Alpine folk have been ruled in the past, and are still ruled in the present. Its importance, therefore, in considering their manner of life cannot be over-estimated.†

Space does not allow us to illustrate the above sketch by even a brief notice of the development of the Commune in the valley of Grindelwald, though existing documents allow us to form a very fair idea of the course of events. It may, however, be stated that while the valley (which technically includes the hamlet of Burglauenen, the first railway station on the way down towards Interlaken) forms a single 'Einwohnergemeinde' from a political, ecclesiastical, and educational point of view,

---

* An exact parallel to these 'Burgergemeinden' still exists in Oxford, where the 'freemen' of the city (*i.e.* the 'burghers') still have the right of pasturing their cattle on the common pasture ground known as 'Port Meadow.'

† The clearest account of this very intricate subject that is known to the present writer is contained in Professor A. von Orelli's admirable work *Das Staatsrecht der schweizerischen Eidgenossenschaft* (Freiburg i. B., 1885), p. 121 *sqq*. Those who desire to go more deeply into the subject may consult for the history of the development of the Communes Prof. F. von Wyss's elaborate essay entitled 'Die schweizerischen Landgemeinden in ihrer historischen Entwickelung,' in his *Abhandlungen zur Geschichte des schweizerischen öffentlichen Rechts* (Zürich, 1892), while for the actual state of the Communes in different Cantons the student should refer to vol. ii. (Zürich, 1873) of Max Wirth's *Allgemeine Beschreibung und Statistik der Schweiz*.

yet it is composed of no fewer than seven Communes from the point of view of the common pastures, of which we must now speak.

3. *The Alps or Common Pastures.*—Stress has been laid in the preceding remarks on the position of an inhabitant of a Swiss mountain valley, as member of a sort of corporation with common lands, subject to certain limited though well defined rights of user. But though it may be said generally that this membership is of vital importance to a peasant, yet it should never be forgotten that private property also prevails to a considerable extent. A fairly well to do Swiss peasant (*e.g.* in the valley of Grindelwald) is therefore the owner of two different sets of rights :—

i. **Private Property.**—This includes, or may include, three items—

(*a*) The *Homestead*, *i.e.* the dwelling-house, with the land (arable or meadow) surrounding it, this, of course, varying in extent and in value.

(*b*) A 'Vorsass' ('Maiensäss,' 'Mayen,' or 'Voralp'), *i.e.* a plot (larger or smaller, as the case may be) of land on the lower mountain slopes immediately above the village, or the scattered homesteads of which the valley is made up; this land may be used at the free will of the owner for arable purposes (*e.g.* potatoes), or as pastures for the cattle in spring or autumn, or as meadow land, the hay being cut and stored for the use of the owner's cattle in the winter. A house, with one or more dwelling-rooms, is usually found on each 'Vorsass.'

In the case of both items the owner has the fullest rights of private ownership as to the use he may choose to make of any part of his land, rotation of crops, &c. Naturally these bits of land first received special names, so that in the valley of Grindelwald we hear already in 1146 of 'Schonegg' (N. of the parish church, and the former home of the famous guide Christian Almer), while the still surviving name of 'auf der Herrschaft' (applied to certain lands with houses at the N.W. end of the valley) recalls the former owners, the lords of the castle of Unspunnen, near Interlaken, who in 1432 parted with them (and also with the 'Buss Alp' above) to the Canons of Interlaken. In fact the number of local names in the valley of Grindelwald which are preserved in old documents, and are still in daily use, is quite extraordinary when one considers that the valley is of no very great size, and is and always has been an Alpine valley.

(*c*) A bit of *forest*, as to which the owner is tied down by various regulations, intended to prevent undue thinning and felling in general, though (as in the case of communal forests) these regulations are generally of recent date.

ii. **Rights of User over Land held in Common.**—It is a matter of no surprise to find that very early indeed, if not from the time of the first colonists, the bits of land in our Alpine valley best suited for use as arable or meadow land passed into private ownership, originally, no doubt, that of some great religious house or feudal lord, and later, as feudalism dissolved, that of the former serfs, who stepped into the position of their late feudal superiors. But the mountain pastures to a very large extent (and the forests also in some degree) remained in the possession of the Commune, subject to the rights of user to which each member of that commune was entitled. These mountain pastures are in Switzerland called 'Alps,' and we must now proceed to give some account of them, reminding our readers of the immense importance of these 'Alps' to the Alpine folk, who are, as shown above, pre-eminently a pastoral race.*

It seems most convenient to treat this subject (which is but little known to the generality of English travellers) under three heads—

What is meant precisely by an 'Alp.'
Who are entitled to rights of user on an 'Alp.'
What is the manner of life on an 'Alp.'

(a) *What is an 'Alp.'*—An 'Alp' may be generally described as 'a mountain pasture, specially fitted for pasturing cows in milk,' so that cheese can be made on the spot (there are also special 'Alpen' for heifers, sheep, and goats). This is the original meaning of the word, which is now frequently used also of the lofty peaks that overhang the mountain pastures. The term used in the Tyrol is 'Alm,' which some consider a shortened form of 'Allmend' (common land), though it is probably but a mutilated form of 'Alp.' †

It is obvious that 'alps' in this sense are of immemorial antiquity. In 739 Abbo by his will gave his 'alpes in Cenisio' to the monastery of Novalesa, which he had founded in 726.‡ In the Appenzell Inner Rhoden vol. (Soleure, 1899) of the 'Schweizerische Alpstatistik' (p. 1) it is stated that the Sämbtiser alp, on the Säntis, was given by its owner to the great abbey of St. Gallen as early as 868, while in the charter of foundation (dated 1061) of the parish church of Appenzell the Megglis alp,

* In the following remarks we have mainly in view the 'Alps' of the German-speaking parts of the Swiss Alps; comparatively little has been published or is known as to those of the 'Suisse Romande' (which is, too, largely non-Alpine), that little agreeing in its main lines with the system prevailing in the German-speaking districts. In the French, South Swiss, and Italian Alps the pastures, unless (as in the Tarentaise) managed by Swiss herdsmen on Swiss principles, are in a very bad and backward state, largely owing to the almost incredible ravages committed (as in the Dauphiné Alps, Ticino, Graubünden) by the sheep from the plains of Provence or the Bergamasca, to whose owners these pastures are often let. As to the French Alps and their present generally wretched condition, M. Briot's *Etudes sur l'Economie Alpestre* (Nancy, 1896) supplies much authentic information. In the Tyrolese Alps the pastures are as a rule badly managed and little cared for: see on these in particular the work by Dr. Martin Wilckens entitled *Die Alpenwirthschaft der Schweiz, des Algäus und der westösterreichischen Alpenländer* (Vienna, 1874).

Amid the multitude of excellent works relating to the 'Alps' of German-speaking Switzerland the most recent and most comprehensive is that (nearly 1,000 pages) by Prof. Felix Anderegg, *Illustriertes Lehrbuch für die gesamte schweizerische Alpwirthschaft* (3 parts, Bern, 1897-8). For statistics (which are, however, not unfrequently corrected by Prof. Anderegg's book) the official work, *Die Alpenwirthschaft der Schweiz im Jahre 1864* (Bern, 1868), must be consulted. In the series called 'Schweizerische Alpstatistik' (Solothurn) a set of monographs on the 'Alps' of the Swiss cantons is being published—rural Basel, Solothurn, St. Gallen, Nidwalden, Uri, Glarus, Schwyz, and Appenzell Inner Rhoden have as yet been treated. The history is best set forth in two books by Prof. A. von Miaskowski, *Die schweizerische Allmend in ihrer geschichtlichen Entwickelung* (Leipzig, 1879), and *Die Verfassung der Land-, Alpen- und Forstwirthschaft der deutschen Schweiz* (Basel, 1878). Many technical details may be found in Dr. Schatzmann's *Alpwirthschaftliche Volksschriften* (new edition, 2 vols., 1887), and the same writer's article 'Alpwirthschaft' in vol. i. of Furrer's *Volkswirthschafts-Lexikon der Schweiz* (Bern, 1885). More general accounts are given in Berlepsch's *Die Alpen und Schweizerkunde*. The history of the 'Alps' in the valley of Grindelwald must be worked out from the documents (down to 1353) in the *Fontes Rerum Bernensium* (8 vols., Bern, 1883-1893), and in the muniments of the Austin house of Interlaken (calendar published by Fr. Stettler in 1849 at Coire in vol. ii. of the *Regesten der Archive der schweizerischen Eidgenossenschaft*), while many local details are contained in the periodical called *Der Gletschermann*, which Herr Strasser (the pastor of Grindelwald) put forth at Grindelwald in 1888-1890.

† *Schweizerisches Idiotikon*, vol. i. p. 190; *Jahrbuch des österr. Alpenvereins*, 1866, p. 403, 1867, p. 374; *Zeitschrift* of the same society, 1873, p. 130.

‡ See Vaccarone's *Le Vie delle Alpi Occidentali*, p. 29, and Ménabréa, *Des Origines Féodales dans les Alpes Occidentales*, p. 107.

higher up the same peak, is mentioned, as well as several other 'alps.' The first distinct mention of lofty 'alps' that the present writer has come across dates from the year 999, when the Archbishop of Milan (as trustee for the church of Brebia, in the Val d'Ossola) exchanged certain lands, &c., with the monastery of San Salvatore, at Arona; among the lands received by the monastery are four 'alpicellæ,' situated at the head of the Val Anzasca, two of which bear the familiar names of Macugnaga and Rofel.* Thus even over 900 years ago 'alps' existed. In the valley of Grindelwald the first distinct mention of an 'alp' as such is that of the Scheidegg Alp in 1238.†

No doubt originally, when there were few cows as compared with the extent of available mountain pasture, the right of grazing was unlimited and unfettered by any regulations, but as the population, and therefore the number of cows, increased, it became necessary to make regulations. Hence there arose a rather complicated system, which is found in full vigour in the fourteenth century, and is no doubt considerably older. In its main outlines it was that which still obtains. Its leading principle was that only cows that had wintered in that particular valley should be allowed to graze in summer on the 'alps' of that valley, a regulation obviously designed to limit the enjoyment of the 'alps' to the cows of the burghers, to the exclusion of 'foreign cattle.' Within the valley there was also a restriction introduced which was intended to prevent the over-use of the 'alps,' which might thereby become exhausted in point of fertility. This restriction consisted in limiting the number of the cows, even of the burghers, which could be pastured on each 'alp.' Each 'alp' was thus divided into 'Kuhstösse,' *i.e.* cow-shares, each share being a plot of ground which would suffice for the maintenance of one cow during the summer. These shares were carefully recorded in the 'Alp Register' ('Seybuch,' 'Alpbuch,' or 'Alpenrodel'), and in view of the overwhelming importance of the pastures for the inhabitants it was each man's natural interest to keep a sharp look-out on his neighbour, so as to make sure that he did not transgress these regulations. Alienation of these shares in any way to non-burghers was prohibited under stringent penalties. The first 'Alp Regulations' in the valley of Grindelwald (for the six alps of the monastery—as the Buss Alp was not purchased by the monastery of Interlaken till 1432—and the 'Gletscher Alp,' or Zäsenberg) date from 1404, and contain the provision as to the wintering of the cattle which can be sent up to the 'alp,' each burgher being allowed to send his cows only to that 'alp' on which he had rights owing to his possession of a particular bit of land in the valley (see also under *b*, below). Both provisions are found in the existing 'Regulations' of 1883. Already in 1404 there were seven 'Alpen,' and now, therefore, 'Alp Communes,' in the valley of Grindelwald —Scheidegg (Grosse S., of course), Grindel, Holzmatten, Bach, and Buss, all on the N. slope of the valley, while Itramen is on the way up to the Männlichen, and Wärgisthal on the way up to the Wengern Alp. (The Wengern Alp belongs to the commune of Lauterbrunnen, is mentioned as early as 1268, and in 1318 passed into the possession of the monastery

* See Bianchetti's *L' Ossola Inferiore*, i. p. 97 and ii. p. 25.
† *Fontes Rerum Bernensium*, ii. p. 176

of Interlaken. The Canons too from 1335 onwards acquired bit by bit all the 'Kuhrechte' on the 'alp' of Mürren).

It may interest our readers to learn that those who have rights of user on an 'alp' may send thither other animals instead of cows, the proportion being thus reckoned (at Grindelwald) to one cow or 'Kuhstoss:' 2 heifers, 3 calves or sheep, 4 pigs, or 8 goats. As to horses, the regulations of the different 'alps' vary. The sheep and goats go to the highest pastures, whither heavy cows cannot climb; the pigs remain with the cows, and the heifers have 'alps' to themselves.

The following tables may be of interest to our readers; the first is taken from Professor Anderegg's book (pp. 135 and 661), that corrects the 'Alpwirthschaft' in 1864, from which the other special tables are extracted.*

I. THE 'ALPS' IN THE SWISS MOUNTAIN CANTONS.

Canton	No. of 'Alps'	No. of 'Kuhstösse'	Capital Value of the 'Alps'
1. Bern	836 (597)	39,965	12,707,000 frcs.
2. Grisons	646 (596)	63,317	7,429,000
3. Tessin	435 (400)	24,473	2,218,000
4. Vallais	422 (272)	20,171	4,431,000
5. Vaud	409 (385)	23,005	9,816,000
6. Obwalden . . .	281 (202)	8,534	3,537,500
7. St. Gallen . . .	274 (234)	24,907	7,809,600
8. Neuchâtel . . .	245 (776)	7,382	3,675,000
9. Lucerne . . .	214 (176)	6,258	3,815,000
10. Schwyz	208 (177)	12,945	6,968,000
11. Freiburg . . .	192 (178)	9,901	6,520,000
12. Appenzell (Inn. Rhod.) .	124 (112)	3,282	768,800
13. Glarus	102 (90)	8,813	5,202,000
14. Nidwalden . . .	99 (81)	4,436	1,821,600
15. Appenzell (Auss. Rhod.)	93 (93)	1,832	827,700
16. Uri	89 (81)	8,527	2,187,200
17. Solothurn . . .	68 (68)	1,632	836,400
18. Basel (rural) . . .	38 (38)	889	629,800
19. Zug	3 (3)	120	144,300
—	4,778 (4,559)	270,389	81,573,300

* Prof. Anderegg adopts a different reckoning of 'Alps' from that of the 1864 *Alpenwirthschaft*, so that the numbers in the latter are given in brackets in col. 1. There are, therefore, some discrepancies, partly owing also to omissions in the 1864 book; the greatest is the case of Neuchâtel, in which the 1864 book counts the shares of individual users, instead of (as Prof. Anderegg) the actual number of independent 'alps.' The *Schweizerische Alpstatistik* furnishes more local corrections for the cantons that have as yet been described in that series; *e.g.* Uri (5,036,400 frcs. capital value) has 10,354 'Kuhstösse,' divided among 102 'alps;' Nidwalden (3,673,025 frcs.), 5,207 on 166 'alps;' Glarus (6,159,280 frcs.), 8,054 on 87; St. Gallen (13,986,700 frcs.), 21,744 on 304; Solothurn (2,395,215 frcs.), 4,179 on 209; rural Basel (690,620 frcs.), 1,026 on 60; Schwyz (11,280,000 frcs.), 17,492 on 417; and Appenzell Inner Rhoden (2,682,955 frcs.), 4,008 on 168. Unluckily Prof. Anderegg does not give the number of 'Kuhstösse' per canton, so that the 1864 number is given in col. 2, but he reckons (p. 665) that the actual *total* of 'Kuhstösse' is now 318,792, an increase of 48,403 on the census of 1864. The capital value (in col. 3) is taken from Prof. Anderegg, the total amount of that of 1864 being 77,186,103 frcs.

II. Some well known Swiss 'Alp Communes.'

Name	No. of 'Alps'	No. of 'Kuhstösse'	Capital Value
Grindelwald	7	2,176	352,512 frcs.
Lauterbrunnen	6	1,093	165,650
Meiringen	5	742	123,665
Zermatt	7	483	24,429
Saas	6	647	30,192
Pontresina	7	415	55,195

III. Some well known Swiss 'Alps.'

Name	Name of Owner	No. of 'Kuhstösse'
Grindelwald:—		
Grindel	Same Alp commune	475
Bussalp	,,	430
Scheidegg	,,	360
Itramen	,,	346
Bachalp	,,	260
Wärgisthal	,,	205
Holzmatten	,,	100
Wengernalp	Lauterbrunnen	300
Engstlenalp	Innertkirchen	449½
Belalp	Mund	451
Fee	Fee	46¼

As the result of old quarrels, and probably deeds of violence, some of the Swiss 'alps' extend beyond what might seem to be their natural limits—*e.g.* Scheidegg (Grindelwald) extends across the Gr. Scheidegg nearly to where the Schwarzwald inn now stands, while the Blackenalp (near Engelberg) belongs (since the thirteenth century) to Attinghausen, near Altdorf (Uri), on the other side of the Surenen Pass, and the Ennetmärchtalp, on the Urnerboden (since at least the twelfth century), to Spiringen, in the Schächenthal, above Altdorf, though on the other side of the Klausen Pass. The last named alp is said to be the most considerable in Switzerland, having a summer population of 350 souls, 1,300 'Kuhstösse' and 154 milk huts (besides 145 stables and 30 cheese storehouses), while its capital value is put at about a million francs. It would, no doubt, be possible and very interesting to trace out from old documents these gradual encroachments, which introduce quaint variations into the geography of some of the Cantons.

(*b*) *Who are Entitled to Rights of User on an 'Alp.'*—From what has been said previously it will be clear to the reader that neither 'residents' in an Alp Commune nor foreigners (unless in either case by virtue of a lease) can have any rights over the 'alps' in that Alpine valley. Those rights are strictly limited to the 'burghers.' But here comes in a difference, for these rights can be enjoyed by the burghers in one of two capacities—

(1) *As Owner of a Particular Bit of Land.*—*I.e.* the right of pasture ('Kuhrecht' for one, two, or more cows) is annexed to the possession of a plot of land in the valley, and cannot be alienated from it. The rights here are 'real,' and thus belong not to each burgher as such, but to a burgher who happens to possess one of the bits of land (of course carefully registered in an official book) to which are annexed one or more 'Kuhrechte.'

This is the system which obtains (and existed already in 1404) in the valley of Grindelwald, so that of course the value of a piece of land there depends on how many, if any, cow-rights are annexed to it.

(2) *As Burgher of that Particular Alp Commune or 'Alpgemeinde.'*— *I.e.* each male burgher of full age has the right of pasturing his cows (as far as the 'alp' will suffice) on that particular 'alp' which belongs to his own Commune.

These rights are thus 'personal,' *e.g.* at Hasleberg and in the Emmenthal.

Hitherto under this head we have spoken only of 'alps' which belong to Communes, since these alone are of importance for the purpose of this paper; but there are very many 'alps' in Switzerland which belong either to private individuals exclusively, to the State or to monasteries, or to ancient corporations existing within a Commune. The following table (extracted from Professor Anderegg's book, pp. 660 and 665) will show the exact state of things as regards the 4,778 'alps' in Switzerland:—

—	'Kuhstösse'	Capital Value
1. Owned by Communes, 1,577 (33 p.c.)	105,201	26,918,169 frcs.
2. Owned by Communes and individuals jointly, 95 (2 p.c.)	6,376	1,631,466
3. Owned by Communes and 'corporations' jointly, 478 (10 p.c.)	31,879	8,157,330
4. Owned solely by individuals, 2,580 (54 p.c.)	172,146	44,783,762
5. Owned by State or monasteries, 48 (1 p.c.)	3,190	81,573

If we refer to Tables II. and III., above, the following is the state of things with regard to the special 'alps' there mentioned. All are owned by Communes, save the Meiringen 'alps' (in the hand of 'corporations') and the Engstlen Alp (joint ownership of Commune and individuals). Of the 'alps' which belong exclusively to individuals a well known instance is that of the Stein Alp, in the Gadmen valley, which belongs (like the best house—now the inn,—the mill, and the best land) to the heiress of the old lords, the Von Weissenfluh family, so that travellers will there discover the lady of the manor in their obliging hostess. The great monastery of Einsiedeln still owns several 'alps,' while the wide Sand Alp, under the Tödi, belongs half to some Linththal men and half to the Commune of Betschwanden.

Even where there is no proper 'alp' there are often scanty pastures (*e.g.* on high slopes of the Wetterhorn and the Mettenberg), and these may be visited by any one, and the grass cut by the first comer. This is what is called 'Wildheu' (wild hay), and stirring tales are told of the dangers and perils to which a poor burgher may be exposed if he has no 'Kuhrechte' of his own, and so depends entirely on 'Wildheu.'

(*c*) *What is the manner of Life on an 'Alp.'*—Subject to the general regulations prevailing for the 'alps' in any particular Swiss valley, the owners of any of these 'alps' (*i.e.* the members of the 'Alp' Commune) have a right to determine various minor details. A day (varying according to the more or less advanced season) is fixed by them on which (but not before which) the cows may be driven up to the 'Alps,' this being called the 'Alpfahrt.' The cows may be separately driven up, but many go together with the men who are to take charge of them during the summer, and who have been previously busy in transporting to the lowest huts on the 'alp' the great kettles, &c., required for cheese-making. The cows, after their long winter imprisonment in their stables in the valley, are frantic with joy at regaining their freedom and liberty of eating as much fresh grass as they desire, though in the spring they have in many cases had a foretaste of these joys on the 'Vorsassen' belonging to their several owners.

The 'Alpfahrt' takes place usually in the first half of June, and the average time during which the cows are on the 'alp' each summer may be reckoned at about 100 days. But, of course, an early autumn may drive them down sooner. By the end of September at latest they are all on the 'Vorsassen' again, and there in some cases they spend the winter (in stables), instead of being brought down to the valley; but in that case milk porters descend daily to the homestead.

On each 'alp' there are always at least two sets of huts, sometimes three (on the Scheidegg Alp, in the Grindelwald valley, there are no less than five), from one to another of which the cattle and their attendants shift as the grass is gradually consumed. A fortnight or three weeks are spent at the highest huts, and then a second halt made at the middle and at the lowest huts, so as to profit by the new-grown grass. These successive tiers of pasture are known as 'Staffel' or 'Läger,' and are distinguished by the epithets of 'Unter,' 'Mittel,' and 'Ober.' (The French equivalents are, 'd'en bas,' 'du milieu,' and 'd'en haut,' while 'di sotto,' 'di mezzo,' and 'di sopra' are the Italian terms.) The goats and sheep are sent up to the very highest Alpine pastures, whither cows cannot mount; sometimes, indeed, the sheep and goats have remote pastures of their own, such as those near the Gleckstein, on the Wetterhorn, and on the Zäsenberg, beyond the Eismeer, at Grindelwald. (The latter alp, the 'Gletscher Alp,' was grazed in 1898 by small Vallais cows, who are said to have thriven exceedingly, but is said never to have been used by cows previously.) The huts which form the summer hamlets on an 'alp' are properly known as 'chalets,' this word having only in recent times been applied also to the dwelling-houses in the valley. But it cannot be too carefully borne in mind that every hut on an 'alp' is not a 'milk' hut, for near the milk huts are other huts, in which the cheeses are stored, while here and there, especially on the lower slopes (and very often on the 'Vorsassen'), there are huts used for storing hay.

In a milk chalet the chief man is the 'Senn' or 'fruitier,' who is in charge of all the milking, cheese-making, &c., arrangements. He is a very important personage in his way, and the same man often spends thirty or forty summers or more on perhaps the same 'alp.' A general superintendence is, however, exercised by two officials on each 'alp,' who are called 'Pfander' (the name occurs already in 1404) at Grindelwald. As (we give the usual arrangements at Grindelwald) several cow-owners join together in employing the same 'Senn,' it is obvious that considerable difficulties might arise as to the amount of milk actually drawn from each cow, and consequently the precise amount of cheese due at the end of the season to each cow-owner. Hence twice a year, once soon after the 'Alpfahrt' and again in August, it is usual for each cow-owner (or his representative) on one evening to milk some one else's cow, in order to prevent any cheating by not fully milking the cow. The amount of milk given by each cow (the owner then milking) in the morning and evening of the next day ('Messtag') is added together, and the mean taken for the day. This operation is repeated in autumn, and the two means are added together, so as to arrive at the definitive mean. As this is done in the case of each cow it is easy to calculate in the case of the owner of several cows how much cheese is due to him at the end of the season. The 'Senn' and his assistants are allowed sufficient cheese, milk, &c., for their maintenance, as well as a fixed payment per cow for their trouble. But of course there is nothing paid by the cow-owners for the use of the pastures, though a rent is due when the 'Kuhrechte' are taken on lease; sometimes a particular man may temporarily exchange his 'Kuhrechte' on one 'alp' in the valley with a friend for others on another 'alp,' this being an arrangement for mutual convenience, each then taking the other's place for that season.

It is in these milk chalets that Alpine travellers have often sought and found hospitality, especially in the days when 'Club huts' were still unknown; even now it is occasionally necessary to have recourse to the courtesy of the 'Senn,' which is very rarely at fault, though, unfortunately, it sometimes happens that travellers abuse it. It should always be borne in mind that the 'Senn' is not *bound* in any way to take in wandering tourists, and that a suitable payment should be made for the milk, &c., consumed, as well as for the rough bed, or accommodation in a neighbouring hay barn. If treated properly the inhabitants of these milk chalets will readily give much interesting information, for though rough in outward appearance they are often well-to-do peasants, who take to this free, healthy life in summer for the sheer pleasure of it.

It does not enter into the scope of the present paper to describe the daily life of a 'Senn' (beyond warning our readers that the best *exported* Swiss cheese comes from the lower-placed 'alps'—*e.g.* those in the Emmenthal and the Gruyère—the rest being kept for local consumption in the valley where it is made), or his diversions, such as wrestling, hurling boulders, dances, &c., of which the two well known works by Berlepsch, besides many others, give full accounts. But when possible a traveller should try to visit one of these festivals (but *not* one of those specially got up for the edification of travellers), so as to realise for himself the rough, but simple and brave, life led by the 'Aelpler' on their mountain pastures. On the better class of Alps the cheese-makers make a fine show in their old-fashioned Sunday best of short breeches, velvet or satin jackets, with embroideries, and short sleeves puffed at the shoulders, and a ribbon-decorated hat. It is often hard to recognise in a gaily attired young fellow the hard-working and roughly clad cheese-maker who may have been seen on the same 'alp' the day before.

A word must suffice for the cow songs ('Ranz des Vaches' or 'Kuh-reihen') which are sung *to* the cows, whose names are often enumerated one after the other, and for the falsetto method of singing called 'Jodeln.'* But it is difficult to part from the 'Aelpler' without making some mention of the ' Prayers on the Alps,' sung in the evening after sun-down. The text generally consists of a thrice-repeated 'Ave Maria,' followed by appeals to various saints to watch over the herds, and to preserve them from all harm during the coming night : in these appeals the name of ·St. ·Wendelin, the patron of herdsmen, is generally prominent. These metrical prayers or litanies are now used only on a few 'alps,' particularly on those in the Calfeisenthal, and on the Lasa, and other. 'alps,' all above Ragatz, as well as on the Ober Lavtina alp, in the Weisstannenthal.† Naturally these litanies are chiefly preserved in the Roman Catholic Cantons, but it is said that the 'Senn' who sings them on the Brändlisberg Alp (Calfeisenthal) is a Protestant.‡

---

* For the subject of music and songs in the Alps generally consult two articles by Herr Szadrowsky in the 1st and 4th vols. of the *Jahrbuch* of the Swiss Alpine Club, and two essays by Prof. Ritter and Dr. Pommer in vols. xx. and xxvii. of the *Zeitschrift* of the German and Austrian Alpine Club : they contain many musical illustrations.

† Several texts of these Prayers (as well as of the various forms of the ' Ranz des Vaches ') are given by Prof. Anderegg, pp. 705-10 and 730-53, and in Herr L. Tobler's *Schweizerische Volks-lieder* (Frauenfeld, 1882). A litany from Schwyz is printed in vol. i. p. 240 of the *Schweizer-isches Archiv für Volkskunde*, and several from the Upper Vallais (sometimes the opening verses of St. John's Gospel are recited) in the same periodical, vol. ii. pp. 295-6, while in the *Alpina* of the Swiss Alpine Club, 1895, p. 136, that used in the Melchthal (Obwalden) is given.

‡ *Jahrb. d. S.A.C.* xxiv. p. 481 n.

II. SCIENTIFIC NOTES.

Art. XI.—Geology of the Alps.*

CONTENTS.
		PAGE
1. Crystalline Rocks occurring in the Alps	. . . .	lxvii
2. History of the Genesis of the Alps	. . . .	lxix
3. Constituent Rocks of the Alps	. . . .	lxxiii
4. The Growth and Sculpture of the Alps	. . . .	lxxxv
5. The Glacial Period	. . . .	xciii
6. Geological Literature and Maps	. . . .	xcvi

On turning his eyes along the horizon from any commanding position in the valley of the Po, the spectator sees himself surrounded by a vast rampart of mountains, open only on the eastern side, but elsewhere enclosing the plain of Piedmont within a continuous wall. The impression conveyed to the mind is that this great chain, known under the collective name of the Alps, forms but a single system, and has a common origin. The same impression is derived from the examination of a general map of Europe. It is apparent that the ranges which enclose the plain of Piedmont, and extend eastward to the neighbourhood of Vienna, constitute but one chain, whose members are linked together by the action of causes common to them all.

In this vast mountain mass there are some portions which at first sight are distinguishable as separate groups, the limits of which are more or less accurately definable, and it thus happens that denominations, such as Maritime Alps, Graian Alps, Pennine Alps, &c., have from an early period been affixed to certain portions of the chain. These denominations, most of which were admitted by the ancient geographers, arose from the desire to recognise certain obvious facts in the orography of the country, without reference to its geological structure; but in several cases the divisions adopted by the physical geographer are the same that are suggested to the geologist by the study of the rocks of which the mountains are composed. Thus, the Maritime Alps, with a central granitic ridge limited by the valleys of the Stura and the Tinea, the Col de l'Argentière, and the Col de Tenda, form a group which is as

---

* The article in the former editions was mainly from the pen of the late Monsieur E. Desor, of Neuchâtel. Portions have been retained in the present edition, but the greater part, more especially that dealing with the petrology and stratigraphy of the Alps, has been rewritten by Professor T. G. Bonney, F.R.S., past President of the Geological Society and of the Alpine Club.

well defined to the eye of the geologist as to that of the common observer. The same may be said of the Finsteraarhorn group, the Pelvoux group, the Carnic Alps, and generally of all the groups which have a well defined crystalline nucleus. The case is otherwise when several crystalline nuclei approach each other so nearly that there is no depression or trough apparent between the neighbouring centres, and nothing in the form of the surface to indicate a separation between them.

These observations apply to the Central Pennine, Simplon, and Monte Rosa groups, also to the Noric, and in some measure to the Rætian Alps. The physical features of the surface do not here conform to the geological structure. Geographers have necessarily followed the former as their guide, and as it was necessary to fix some limits to the separate groups, they have usually adopted a valley or gorge, which affords to the eye the external evidence of a separation between adjoining mountain masses. In this way the Pennine Alps have been held to extend from the Dora Baltea to the Tosa, and the Noric Alps from the Adige to Vienna.

The geologist is forced to look for some more positive bases of classification than the mere contour of the surface. He endeavours, amid the irregularities and disturbances of the strata, to trace the causes which have operated in upraising the mountains and have given them their present form, as the comparative anatomist strives to trace the essential elements of the organic structure amidst the varied forms assumed by the different species.

The general shapes and aspect of mountains depend upon the nature of the rocks of which they are composed, and on the intensity of forces that have upraised them. It is evident that peaks so bold in outline as the Matterhorn or Monte Viso could not be formed of strata such as the molasse or the flysch. Their shape implies a great degree of hardness in the rocks from which they are fashioned. In the same manner it may be affirmed that the reservoirs in which the greater glaciers are accumulated, and the narrow gorges through which they now advance—or did once flow, between faces of rock that still bear the traces of their passage—demonstrate a high degree of resistance in the materials.

1. *Crystalline Rocks occurring in the Alps.*

The following is a brief *résumé* of the more typical crystalline rocks which occur in the Alps.

Granite is a crystalline granular rock, composed essentially of quartz, felspar (mostly orthoclase), and mica ; hornblende is a not infrequent accessory.

Syenite is a similar rock, composed essentially of felspar (mostly orthoclase) and hornblende ; the latter mineral may be more or less replaced by mica (biotite) or augite ; the rock is then called a mica-syenite, or augite-syenite.

Diorite differs from syenite in that the felspar is a plagioclase.

Tonalite is a variety of Diorite, which contains quartz as an essential constituent. Biotite also occurs. The Adamello consists of this rock, the name being taken from the Tonale Pass.

Felstone is the name given to a large group of rocks, having a rather compact felspathic matrix, in which not seldom distinct crystals of felspar (orthoclase or plagioclase), quartz, hornblende, augite, mica, &c., are scattered about, and are sometimes very conspicuous. These varieties are called by many authors *porphyry*. Where the felspar is orthoclase the rock is termed *felspar-porphyry* or *felsite*; if quartz be also present, *quartz-porphyry* or *quartz-felsite*; if the felspar be plagioclase the rock is called either *porphyrite* or *quartz-porphyrite*, according as quartz be absent or present. Rocks consisting essentially of a species of plagioclase felspar (generally less rich in silica than in the cases just mentioned), augite, iron oxide, and (often) olivine, if rather coarsely crystalline are called *dolerite*; if finely crystalline or compact, *basalt*. In varieties of the latter rock augite occurs in conspicuous crystals, and the rock has been named by some *augite-porphyry*. When the rock is very coarse and the augite commonly is the variety called diallage, the rock is termed *gabbro*. Some authors use the word *euphotide* as an equivalent, others apply this term to gabbro in which certain mineral changes have occurred, the felspar being replaced by a mineral akin to saussurite, and the diallage by a green hornblende (often the kind called smaragdite).

Melaphyre is only a name given to rather old basalts. *Diabase* is applied to members of the same group which have undergone a greater amount of secondary change; these, with the finer-grained diorites, which can hardly be distinguished one from another without microscopic examination, are often grouped together for descriptive purposes under the name *Greenstone*.

Serpentine results from the alteration of a group of rocks which consist mainly of olivine; these in their unaltered condition are called *peridotites*. Serpentine commonly also contains a variety of enstatite, which occurs in flaky crystals with a lustre something like that of brass. The rock is rather easily scratched with a knife, has a slightly 'soapy' feeling, and is generally, in the Alps, of a dark colour, commonly dark-green. Some varieties, in chemical composition, approach rather nearer to the basalts; these are generally harder than the rest. The mineral serpentine (for the rock and its chief constituent bear the same name) may be produced from ferro-magnesian minerals other than olivine, but the rock of which the well known serpentine near the Lizard, in Cornwall, is a good type was originally a peridotite. The name, however, has been used by earlier writers with considerable laxity, and this has given rise to much confusion.

Of the rocks more or less foliated, *Gneiss* has practically the same composition as granite. *Protogine* is only a granite modified by pressure. It was formerly asserted to contain talc instead of mica; this, however, is a mistake; the mineral so named is only a somewhat altered biotite. *Hornblende-schist* is, in composition, nearly identical with a diorite, and in many cases is only a modified form of that rock or of a dolerite. *Chlorite-schist*, *Talc-schist*, *Mica-schist*, are foliated rocks in which the minerals named are dominant. *Potstone* is, as a rule, a variety of the first rock without foliation. Mica-schist commonly also contains a fair proportion of quartz, and sometimes of calcite, and thus graduates, on the one hand, into *quartz-schist*, a foliated rock consisting mainly of quartz, and, on the other, into *calc-schist*, which has the same structure, and consists mainly of calcite. If the rock is without foliation, and is practically pure calcite, it is called *marble*, the difference between this and limestone being that all the constituents of the former have crystallised *in situ*. *Dolomite* is a mineral composed of carbonate of both lime and magnesia. The name is also applied to the rock which mainly consists of this mineral. This sometimes is thoroughly crystalline, as in the Binnenthal; sometimes it is imperfectly crystalline, like many limestones, as in the case of the 'Dolomites' of South Tyrol.

2. *History of the Genesis of the Alps.*

In the study of a mountain chain two sets of questions are raised, the one relating to its growth and development, the other to the history of its constituent rocks. These cannot be wholly separated, because the effects of one may be recorded in the other, but nothing is gained, and sometimes much is lost, by failing to keep in mind the fact that they are generally distinct. Both have led to much controversy, which in neither case can be regarded as closed, though one may venture to predict what will be the leading outlines of the ultimate conclusions.

The Alpine chain, as it now exists, is the product of a series of movements which, in the main, occurred in the Tertiary era. Mountains, indeed, there were at an epoch, geologically speaking, much earlier, which, however, in all probability differed widely as to both trend and outline from the present Alps. These will presently be mentioned, but by the time (approximately) when the Bagshot sands of England were deposited they had wholly, or almost wholly, disappeared. The end of a long period of subsidence was now approaching. Here and there, it is true, this already had been locally interrupted, but, as yet, neither the Alps nor any other mountain chain in connection with them had been developed. About the end, however, of the Eocene period long folds began to form in the crust of the earth on the site of the Alps. The cause of these movements is still a subject of dispute. The effect, however, seems to be beyond question; the strata forming this crust, to a depth below what can now be examined, were bent and folded into a series of huge parallel wrinkles. These movements, apparently, gave rise not only to the Western, Central, and Eastern Alps, but also to the Appennines on the one side and the Julian and Dinaric Alps on the other. The outline of the Italian peninsula, as every child knows, resembles a boot, but a similar form, though in the reverse position, is enclosed by these mountains from the south end of the Adriatic northward. Whether the development of a series of associate ranges on a plan so complicated was the result of a single group of movements, or of a succession of movements, is a point on which different opinions are entertained, to which reference will later be made; but at any rate it must be admitted that any attempt to break up the Alps into two or more distinct mountain masses involves very serious difficulties. We may be content in these pages to avoid abstruse theoretical questions, and to speak of the Alpine chain as a whole. .

The earth's crust, as has been said, began to be folded, and the result of the process was to raise it above the sea in long strips or shoals. Then by degrees the banks became hills, and the hills became mountains. All this time the retiring waves were beating upon the coast line; the rain, as now, fell on the rising ground, and was discharged seawards in streams and torrents; the rocks were expanded by heat and contracted by cold; they cracked, and they were shattered by the strains. In a word, no sooner did the land appear than the processes of denudation began. The detritus, hurried down from the highlands, was deposited as beds of sand and conglomerate on either side of the growing mountain chain. Then after a long interval of time, an epoch of comparative quiescence during which this process of mountain sculpture and marginal deposit continued, not only the Alps themselves but also the latter area were subjected to renewed disturbances like the former; but these appear to have acted with greatest intensity in the region of the Central Alps, roughly speaking, and to have produced more effect on the northern than on the southern side of the chain. By them the folds already existing were intensified and complicated, the beds of sandstone (molasse) and puddingstone (nagelfluh) were uptilted and uplifted, till in some cases, as in the Rigi and the Speer, they rise about 6,000 feet above the sea level.

Without entering into details, it will suffice to say that the crust thus folded consisted of a thick mass of sedimentary rocks—limestones, shales, and sandstones, the majority being of Secondary or early Tertiary age. This rested upon a floor of crystalline rocks—granites, gneisses, and schists: these, whatever may have been their origin, are much more ancient. When the crust was bent into folds the latter rocks, being the harder, may have been occasionally forced through the former; their masses, at any rate, have better resisted denudation, so that they, or the remnants of them, project in bold peaks and lofty ridges, while the softer sedimentaries sometimes form valley-like troughs between them. The rock masses which now compose the Alps were greatly compressed during this process of crumpling: shales were thus converted into slates; limestones and sandstones not seldom assumed a rude cleavage. In certain cases secondary minerals were developed, though generally only on a microscopic scale, so that the new divisional surfaces assume a peculiar sheen, and the slate, for instance, becomes a phyllite. But, besides the sedimentaries, the crystalline rocks themselves were affected, and in them also similar structures were developed. Schists assumed, so to say, a new schistosity; foliated rocks a new foliation, which rendered them fissile in directions quite different from those along which they could formerly be split. In the case of the more massive rocks, serpentines sometimes are slaty: even granites have yielded to the pressures, have assumed a foliated structure, and have been converted into gneiss; for in the crystalline rocks this mechanical change has been followed by a more marked mineral change than in the sedimentaries, and the powdered mineral constituents, when acted upon by water, have entered into new combinations: thus mica, black and white, secondary hornblende, quartz, and other minerals can be found, which either have been developed along the divisional planes, produced by crushing, or at least have had their direction of growth affected by these. To take, for example, the case of granite : from the powder of the felspar, under the action of water, white mica and free quartz have been produced. Of these the former is developed upon the divisional surfaces, which are, so to say, veneered, or varnished, with the new mineral; the rock assumes a foliation, and answers to the definition of a gneiss. When crushing has been carried still further, the felspar may be practically destroyed and a kind of mica-schist produced. It is then strictly true that, as the older school of geologists affirmed, a granite may be found passing into a gneiss, or a gneiss into a mica-schist; only, instead of a granite representing, as they supposed, the ultimate result of metamorphism in materials which, in a less advanced stage of alteration, had made a mica-schist, and, in a greater, a gneiss, exactly the reverse had happened, for the mica-schist and the gneiss have been, as it were, manufactured from the granite, and represent stages of a certain kind of metamorphism, the mica-schist answering to the most extreme one. Foliation, therefore, may be a result of pressure, but it is by no means proved, and probably is not true, that all foliation is due to the action of pressure, as described above, or, in other words, to a process which is later in date than the solidification of the rock. There are gneisses, for instance, in which a mineral banding is conspicuous; mica, or some such constituent dominating in occasional layers, which sometimes exceed half an inch in thickness. This structure, in the writer's opinion, cannot be shown to be the result of pressure subsequent to solidification. In some cases it may be the record of an original stratification, but in not a few it is probably produced by differentiation in the constituents of the mass, previous to its complete solidification, and is analogous to the 'flow structure,' which is exhibited by certain lavas, and is common in artificial slags. But that many schists, possibly also some gneisses, were originally sediments, clayey, sandy, or calcareous, cannot be doubted; the first and second being the detritus of older rocks, while the third sometimes may have been formed by the accumulation of organisms; the materials of these, under the combined action of heat, pressure, and water, have entered into crystalline combination; producing new minerals, and, in most cases, obliterating the records of their previous history. It is impossible, in the present state of knowledge, to separate these various classes of so called metamorphic rocks by hard and fast lines, or to pronounce, in every case, upon the origin of a specimen, but we may assert with confidence that the crystalline rocks of the Alps are partly igneous, partly sedimentary, in their origin, and that both groups have been modified by pressure, followed by mineral change; these modifications, in the case of the former group, being subsequent to the assumption of a crystalline structure.

In the Alps, at any rate, when due allowance is made for the result of subsequent pressure, the crystalline rocks which were sedimentary in origin commonly overlie those for which an igneous origin seems more probable. But at this stage a distinction must be made, for we find here, as in other mountain chains, two kinds of igneous rocks, the one underlying, and apparently older than, the altered sedimentaries, the other clearly later in date than the rocks with which they are associated, whatever these may be : in other words, igneous rocks of the latter kind are obviously intrusive, while those of the former, though igneous in origin, may have been covered up by the materials which have since become crystalline. The intrusive rocks, of course, even if mainly lower in position than another group of rocks, send off veins into it, or occasionally break through it. Thus, in the Alps, there are certain gneissoid granites, which are intrusive and comparatively late in date ; such, for instance, as the porphyritic gneissoid granite of the Lukmanier Pass, the so called Fibbia gneiss at the top of the St. Gotthard Pass, and the Protogine of Mont Blanc—indeed, so far as the writer has observed, all the porphyritic (gneissoid) granites. Other granites, like the 'core' of the Central Oberland, Dauphiné, and the Central Tyrol, may be also intrusive, but the evidence, so far as it goes, suggests that they must be referred to a very remote period. In the Alps, then, the amount of granite is much greater than was originally supposed ; only its appearance is somewhat illusory, as it has been modified by pressure, has assumed a foliated structure, and is now petrographically a gneiss. The same may be said of many other schistose rocks in the Alps. Some of the mica-schists (though by no means all) are also modified igneous rocks, allied to granite ; the serpentinous schists are often only serpentine or rocks closely allied to it, which have been rendered fissile by pressure ; while very many of the hornblende schists certainly are modified dolerites, or basalts ; some of the chlorite schists also may have had a like origin.

It is very difficult to determine the age of the above named intrusive rocks. As will be presently mentioned, there is evidence of volcanic activity in the Vicentine district in Tertiary times, and of the same, on a much grander scale, on the Southern side of the Alps, in Permian or early Secondary times. But in the Alps, as a rule, intrusive igneous rocks are rare among the Secondary and Tertiary sedimentary deposits, and the above named gneissoid granites, foliated diorites (hornblende schists), and similar pressure-modified rocks are associated with other crystalline schists ; hence they are later than these, and earlier than the great earth movements which upraised the present chain, but, as nothing more can be affirmed, that leaves a very wide margin of time. There are, however, some granites and allied rocks, thus situated, which still retain their normal aspects, and appear, as a rule, to have escaped uncrushed ; such are the granite of Biella, extending N.E. towards Varallo, and that of Baveno, Mont' Orfano, and the vicinity. The red granite of the second locality and the grey granite of the third are extensively worked. To these may be added the granite of the Cima d'Asta, with some smaller masses in various localities, and the Tonalite or quartz-diorite of the Adamello. The 'protogine' of the Meije and other neighbouring peaks of the Central Dauphiné Alps is also a granite, which is but little modified ; and the Bernina group affords examples of granitic rocks, indubitably igneous, which generally have escaped with but slight damage.

3. *Constituent Rocks of the Alps.*

We pass on to give a brief sketch of the rock masses which constitute the *present Alpine chain*, leaving for a while the details of its growth and development.

The Foundation Stones.—These, as stated above, are crystalline rocks ; if we put aside those obviously of igneous origin, they may be roughly grouped under three heads :—

(1) *Rocks rather Granitoid in Aspect*, which appear, as a rule, to occupy the lowest position, and to constitute generally the 'core' of a range. Such are the granitoid gneisses common in the 'Laurentian' region of Canada, or beneath the Torridon sandstone in the N.W. of Scotland. Rocks of this character occur, as mentioned above, in various districts of the Alps.

(2) *Rocks more Variable in Character and often more Stratified in Aspect.*—Among these rather thick masses of mica-schists and various gneisses, often markedly banded, are common, in which garnets, hornblende, and various accessory minerals frequently occur ; the gneisses often have a rather saccharoidal aspect, and are somewhat friable when hammered. These are well developed on the N. and S. sides of the St. Gotthard Pass, *e.g.* about the Val Tremola. This group is not infrequently poorly developed, and is sometimes missing : it must be regarded as of only provisional value, and its origin an open question ; probably some of its members will be found ultimately to have been sedimentary, others igneous.

(3) *Rocks mainly of Sedimentary Origin.*—This group consists chiefly of micaceous schists, varying from dark or lead-coloured, often calcareous, and sometimes passing into pure crystalline limestones or dolomites, with occasional quartz-schists, brown and white, besides actinolitic, talcose, and chloritic schists. Many of the last named schists may be modified igneous rocks; sometimes they may have been originally volcanic tuffs. The dark micaceous schists not seldom contain garnets of considerable size; smaller garnets of lighter colour, cyanite, and staurolite are not uncommon minerals. This group has a great development. It may be traced along the chain practically from one end to the other. It appears sometimes to succeed the second group by a gradual transition ; sometimes its rests, with a rather marked indication of unconformity, on the rocks of the first group. The mass at a distance has a thoroughly stratified aspect, as may be seen, for instance, on the S. side of the Rhône valley from above Brieg to Obergestelen. In its members the more quartzose and more micaceous layers are often interstratified, precisely as are the sandy and clayey bands in an ordinary sedimentary rock. The geological age of the group is, however, a more difficult question than that of its origin, and has been the subject of much dispute. In the Cottian Alps these rocks have been called 'schistes lustrées,' in the more E. part of Switzerland ' Bündner Schiefer,' and in both they have been regarded as altered rocks of Secondary age—in the former case as mainly Triassic, in the latter as Triassic or Jurassic, or both. In the Lepontine Alps also the schists, which include the beds bearing black

garnets, have been referred to the Jurassic age. The controversy on the subject, which has attracted considerable attention, still continues. The writer, who has taken some part in it, has a very distinct opinion that in some cases the disputants have been regarding different sides of the shield, and that the terms 'schistes lustrées' and 'Bündner Schiefer' will be found to cover rocks of more than one geological age, some being crystalline schists of very great antiquity, others only comparatively unaltered rocks of Primary (probably Carboniferous) and of Secondary age. He is, however, convinced, after careful examination, that the group of schists in which the black garnet bands of the Lepontine Alps occur had already become schists in Triassic times, for some members of this group are represented by fragments in the basement beds of the Trias. The statement also that garnets and staurolites are associated with belemnites* in rocks of Jurassic age is incorrect, for the 'knoten' and 'prismen' of the schistose Jurassic rocks of Scopi, and of the region about the Nufenen Pass, are neither garnets nor staurolites, but, as can be proved by a microscopic examination, totally different minerals, the occurrence of which proves little with regard to the history of the rock. He ventures, therefore, to affirm that none of the crystalline schists in the Alps have been proved to be the equivalents of either Primary or Secondary rocks, and many of them have been demonstrated to be much more ancient than any strata to which a date can be assigned. It is accordingly his opinion that all the true crystalline schists of the Alps are older than the Cambrian rocks, and so belong to the 'dawn period' of geological history, or, in other words, to the great series, now termed Archæan, and commonly not to the very latest epoch of this era.†

If then we regard these upper schists of the Alpine chain as Archæan, and pass on to the rocks which, as a rule, have undergone mineral change only on a minute scale, and in which fossils can be still distinguished, more or less readily, we find that, as yet, Cambrian rocks have not been identified in the Alps, and even those which have been assigned to earlier Palæozoic ages are restricted to a comparatively limited district.

Silurian and Devonian.—Rocks which can be thus identified (by the presence of fossils, or by conformity with beds containing them) occur only in the extreme E. and N.E. of the Alpine chain, as, for instance, in the Carnic Alps (forming a long strip south of the Upper Gailthal, where Upper Silurian, and a fairly complete section of the Devonian system, have been identified), in the Karawankas, and on either side of the Mur for some considerable distance to the N. of Graz, where Devonian fossils occur, and, in the lower part, some contemporaneous igneous rocks. Devonian and Upper Silurian rocks have also been identified on the N. side of the Central range in a long strip, which extends from E. of Radstadt to the neighbourhood of Schwaz, in the Innthal. The Devonian system, as a rule, seems to be well represented; the Silurian fossils more

---

* *Quart. Journ. Geol. Soc.* 1890, p. 236.
† It must be remembered that the Archæan is no more marked off by a hard and fast universal line from the Palæozoic (Primary) than this is from the Secondary, or the latter from the Tertiary.

often indicate the upper part of the system, though probably the whole of that, as distinguished from the Ordovician (Lower Silurian of many geologists), is represented in some places. How far the latter can be identified seems to be more questionable. The occurrence of either Silurian or Devonian rocks in the Central or Western Alps at present is not established.

Carboniferous.—Strata belonging to this system are more widely distributed in the Alps, though they generally occur in rather restricted areas, and often form comparatively narrow strips, enfolded among crystalline rocks of much greater antiquity. Commonly they are obviously detrital in origin—conglomerates, sandstones and shales. The first are frequently full of fragments of the crystalline rocks; when these are small and the rock is a kind of grit, made of quartz, felspar, and mica, which has been modified by subsequent pressure, it is locally difficult to distinguish from a crushed crystalline rock—gneiss or schist. The sandy rocks are sometimes, as to the N. of Briançon, of considerable thickness. But the clayey rocks are more common, and usually have been converted into slates by subsequent pressure. These very often are black from carbonaceous materials, and thin beds of anthracite occur, which have been worked at different points, as at Chandolin, near Sion, Les Coupeaux, near Chamonix, and in the valleys of the Arc, Isère, and upper Romanche. Fossil plants are found abundantly in certain localities, such as the upper valley of the Diosaz, N. of the Brévent. Limestones are rare; they occur, however (containing *Fusulina* and marine fossils), at the Ofen Alp, in the Gailthal (where they belong to the upper part of the system), and in the Stang Alp district, at the junction of the frontiers of Salzburg, Styria, and Carinthia (where, however, no fossils have been found in the limestone, which is assigned to the lower part of the system).

Permian.—During the last thirty years this system in the Alps has been much augmented in extent, chiefly at the expense of the Trias. It is, however, only developed on a large scale in the Eastern Alps. In the Central and Western Alps it is often missing, or is merely represented by a grit, conglomerate, or sandstone, generally of no great thickness, which forms a base to the Secondary rocks, is unconformable with and composed of the ruins of the underlying crystalline rocks, and is often called *Verrucano*. So far as the writer knows, the rock does not contain fossils, and, as it is sometimes followed directly by Jurassic rocks, may represent more than one geological period. Still some of the Verrucano in all probability is rightly referred to the Permian. To this age also the red 'porphyry' of the Windgälle is assigned by some geologists. In the Eastern Alps, however, more especially on the S. side, a most interesting series of rocks (as explained below) is now referred to the Permian period. In the Karawankas district some marine deposits, with *Fusulina*, have been observed; these are followed by sandstone, and this again by calcareous beds, containing *Bellerophon* and other marine fossils. The upper and lower deposits are rather limited in area, but the sandstone extends, with some interruption, in a long strip from the valley of the Save, S.E. of Villach, to near the E. bank of the Eisack. From a well known locality on the W. side of the district it receives the name of 'Grödner' sandstone, which occasionally much resembles the red Triassic sandstone of England and parts of Germany. Beneath this, over a large area, on both sides of the Eisack, near Bozen, is a great eruptive series, consisting mainly of quartziferous felstones, commonly called quartz-porphyries, with some associated tuffs; these prove the group to be eruptive, and to indicate an ancient volcanic district. Where it is most completely developed, two thick masses of quartz-porphyries, separated by tuffs, occur, and beneath the lower are more tuffs and a basement conglomerate. All this district has been made classic ground by the labours of Von Richthofen, Mojsisovics, and many other geologists of the present and previous generations. The area more or less covered by the great lava-flows measures hardly less than forty miles from N. to S., and about the same from E. to W. The glen of the Kuntersweg, between Klausen and Bozen, cuts through these porphyries, and is indebted to them for much of the beauty of its scenery. Indications of volcanic outbreaks, presumably of the same age, are found in more than one locality further W., as on the shore of the lake of Lugano, where a dark porphyry, that has flowed over the denuded edges of crystalline schists, is overlain by a red porphyry, and on this (as may be seen by the lake-side at the foot of Monte Salvatore) rest Triassic strata. Smaller masses of porphyry also occur about the S. end of the Lago Maggiore, and of the lake of Orta, and for some distance further W. Similar rocks, probably of the same geological age, occur about Raibl, and at other places in Carinthia.

Trias (including Rhætic).—If we exclude from this group the 'schistes lustrées' of the Cottian Alps, and the 'Bündner Schiefer' of the Grisons and the immediate neighbourhood, we find that, over a considerable region of the Alps, Triassic rocks are either missing or very poorly developed. On the margin of the crystalline masses on the western side of the main watershed, from that of the Pelvoux to Mont Blanc, Jurassic deposits appear to rest directly upon the crystalline rocks, so that these regions, in all probability, were above water in Triassic times. Indeed, in all parts of the Pennine, the Lepontine, and the Central Alps on either side of the Reuss, Triassic strata, if represented, are commonly limited in thickness, and abnormal in character. Here the most usual type is rather a soft porous limestone or dolomite, of a yellowish colour, often called 'Rauchwacke' or 'Rauwacke,' with which beds of gypsum are sometimes associated; occasionally it passes into a breccia, containing fragments of the underlying crystalline rocks. In the heart of the Pennine and Lepontine Alps this deposit is found occasionally, appearing and disappearing in a curious 'patchy' manner. Here, as on the flank of the Hohthäligrat, a little strip is 'nipped in' among crystalline masses, far away from any rocks of Secondary age; there, as in the neighbourhood of the Nufenenstock, the Jurassic beds are, in one place, separated by a few feet of 'Rauchwacke' from the crystalline schists; in another, they rest directly upon them. In other localities, as in the Val Canaria, and on the S. slopes of the Lukmanier Pass, the 'Rauchwacke' attains to a considerable thickness. There can be little doubt that this peculiar friable rock has been deposited under exceptional physical conditions; probably much of it, like calcareous tufas, is not of organic but of chemical origin, a precipitate in the isolated recesses of a hilly district, which was subsiding somewhat irregularly, so that lagoons were formed, which communicated intermittently with the open sea, or salt lakes were produced in basins of inland drainage, as in Utah or Thibet.

Triassic and Rhætic deposits, however, assume a greater importance E. of the Rhine, and may be traced on the N. side of the central crystalline range through the great zone of limestone mountains almost up to the longitude of Vienna. South of the crystalline range, Triassic strata set in on the E. side of the S. part of Lago Maggiore, though a few outliers occur further W. ; they rapidly expand in thickness, and occupy a wider area, so that in the district from the Lake of Lugano to that of Garda, Jurassic and later rocks are confined to the S. border of the mountain district. Thus the sedimentary zone, south of the crystalline range which forms the watershed of the Tyrol, is practically composed of rocks belonging to the Triassic or Rhætic systems. Curving upwards from the N. part of the Lake of Garda, these continue to run south of the crystalline axis (one or two outliers occurring on the Brenner Pass) and extend to the E. end of the chain. The grand crags, towers, and battlements of the well known Dolomite Alps are all excavated from strata of Triassic or Rhætic age. In both these systems, from the valley of the Rhine eastwards, N. and S. of the central range, the dominant rock is light fawn-coloured limestone or dolomite ; this is sometimes interstratified with red or dark-coloured clays, and occasional sandy beds. The complete section from the base of the Trias to the top of the Rhætic, exhibited on both the N. and S. sides of the central range, indicates a great marine series, very different from the abnormal and imperfect Trias of Britain. Not only is the 'Muschelkalk' of the Vosges district represented, but also the sandstones and clays of the Bunter and Keuper are replaced by great masses of marine deposits. Of these the most noteworthy are the Dachstein dolomite ('Hauptdolomit') of both the N. and S. range (Rhætic), and the Schlern dolomite (Keuper). The last deposit is rather limited in extent, but of it the grand cliffs of the Schlern, Langkofel, and neighbouring mountains as far as the Marmolata are composed ; those of the Tofana, the Pelmo, the Antelao, and the mountains E. of the Ampezzo Pass are Dachstein dolomite, for the Schlern rock attenuates eastward. The last word has not yet been written on these stupendous masses of dolomite, but many geologists think that, directly or indirectly, they owe their origin to ancient coral reefs. Tuffs and lava-flows occur in the lower part of the Trias in the Schlern district ; these, however, are lithologically very different from the similar masses of Permian age, for the so called augite-porphyry of the Trias is in reality only a variety of basalt or dolerite. These are well displayed on the Seisser Alp. But a still more interesting group of igneous rocks, which is somewhat later in date, occurs in the vicinity of Predazzo. Here more than one species is found ; the earliest, according to Mojsisovics, is the so called syenite of Monzoni (now often called *Monzonite*), a coarse-grained rock, consisting mainly of two kinds of felspar, with augite or hornblende ; a Tourmaline-granite breaks through this ; later still are 'melaphyres' and 'augite-porphyries,' besides some others which occur in comparatively small masses or dykes. Volcanic rock of Triassic age does not occur further to the E.

Jurassic.—In the Eastern Alps the Triassic system is succeeded conformably by the Jurassic. South of the central crystalline range the representatives of the latter system are often reduced by subsequent denudation to isolated patches, but they become more continuous towards the S. margin of the sedimentary zone. They are well preserved on the W. side of the valley of the Adige, and about the head of the Lake of Garda, and may be followed to the neighbourhood of the Lago Maggiore. On the N. side, however, of the central range they are more widely developed, and may be traced, with occasional intervals, along the N. sedimentary range into Switzerland, occurring in force between the valleys of the Inn and the Rhine. W. of the latter river they form a considerable portion of the great sedimentary zone of the Glarus and Bernese Alps, and pass on, across the Rhône, through Savoy along the E. side of the crystalline axis which extends from the Mont Blanc group to that of the Belledonne, in Dauphiné. S. of the prolongation of the latter and of the Pelvoux group the whole Alpine region E. of the Rhône (much of which is drained by the Durance) consists of Jurassic rocks overlain by later Secondary, and in some places also by the earlier Tertiary deposits; these continue until the Maritime Alps slope steeply down to the Mediterranean. Strips of Jurassic sediments, generally narrow, are also enfolded among the crystalline rocks of the main watershed of the Alps, as, for instance, along the trough which is partly interrupted by the Oberalp and Furka Passes. Similar strips occur to a less extent on the S. side of the same great watershed, as in the upper part of the Val Bedretto. These last deposits belong to the Lias, and are generally dark slaty mudstones, occasionally interbanded with thin sandstones. On the Lukmanier Pass, as at the Vitgira Alp, and on the flanks of the Scopi, on the Furka and Nufenen Passes, and on the N. side of the Gries Pass, belemnites are found, much distorted by pressure, together with occasional fragments of other fossils. In these localities (except on the Furka) the dark calcareous mudstones also contain, often in the same blocks with the fossils, ovoid bodies ('knoten') and rather rounded prisms ('prismen'), which project from weathered surfaces, and have a curious 'spotted' appearance. The error, to which these have given rise, has been already mentioned. Belemnites thus crushed have also been found near the Plateau de Paris, above La Grave, in Dauphiné. About Bourg d'Oisans the cliffs of Lias often present very striking alternations of dark slaty and of lighter, more 'stony' layers, which recall some of the banded deposits in the Lower Lias of England, such as are worked for the manufacture of cement. The more slaty members, such as the rocks in the Val Ferret, or in places on the Furka Pass, were probably once a shale or clay, like some of the Upper Lias of Yorkshire or Rutland. But in the N. and S. ranges of the Eastern Alps, and in the more S. parts of the Western (French) Alps, especially where the Lias is some distance away from the crystalline massif, limestones become important constituents, and the beds often contain a rich and varied fauna, among which ammonites sometimes become abundant.

Except in the isolated localities already mentioned, the other members of the Jurassic system generally succeed the Lias, and representatives of the Lower, Middle, and Upper Oolites of this country have been identified. (The second is generally the most developed, the first and third are sometimes rather attenuated.) Still in some parts of the Alps the group as a whole is represented by a great thickness of rock. The necessarily restricted compass of this essay prevents any detailed discussion of the various subdivisions, and their numerous variations in different parts of the chain. It must suffice to say that the magnificent outer mountain zone which extends from the valley of the Reuss through the Bernese Oberland to the valley of the Rhône, above the Lake of Geneva, and then sweeps away to the S.W. into French territory, is largely formed from rocks of the Jurassic age. Limestones are frequent, and sometimes attain considerable thickness; in colour they vary from light to dark, but commonly change to a warm buff, or a dull grey tint, on weathered surfaces. The grand limestone cliffs which rise on the S. side of the Lake of Brienz, or above the valley of Lauterbrunnen, and the pastures on either side of Grindelwald, are also composed of rocks, which are the equivalents of the English Oolites (for in this district the Lias is but poorly represented). It may perhaps be said that wherever particularly fine cliff scenery occurs in the Central or Western Alps the rocks will probably be the equivalents of the English Oolites, though often very different in their lithological character, and that the upper (and major) portion of the Jurassic system plays in the scenery the part which in the Eastern Alps is taken by the Trias or Rhætic.

Neocomian and Cretaceous.—These systems, the Lower and Upper Cretaceous of many geologists, are also well developed in the Alps. On the N. range they come in succession to the Jurassic system, but in its most E. part, as, for instance, in the Salzkammergut, a rather marked break (which will be noticed presently) occurs between the Cretaceous and the Neocomian. This, however, disappears further W., and has not been observed in the Tyrol or in Switzerland. In the N.E. region also it is often difficult to separate the Cretaceous deposits from the Eocene, for they assume the character of a group of rocks, which are commonly called the *Flysch,* and will be more particularly noticed below. Passing over them for a time, the Neocomian and other Cretaceous rocks appear to occur only in strips and patches on the N. zone until they reach the W. side of the valley of the Ill. Then they form a continuous mass which extends through the N. Oberland across the head of the Lake of Geneva into Savoy, and so they run along the W. side of the chain by Chambéry and Grenoble, till they broaden out and occupy a large area between the Drac, the Durance, and the Rhône. Then they fringe the Jurassic zone which sweeps inland from the mouth of the Var to Toulon, reaching the sea near Nice and the Maritime Alps, and forming the subordinate ranges which lie E. of the lower course of the Rhône, and inland from the coast at Toulon. S. of the main watershed Neocomian and Cretaceous rocks begin in the neighbourhood of the Lago di Varese, and can be traced, with interruptions, to the Lake of Garda. To the E. of this they become more continuous, and extend over a larger area as far as the valley of the Tagliamento. Yet further E. they continue, after a short interruption, and are grandly developed about the Semmering Pass and in the ranges parallel with the Adriatic through Istria and Dalmatia. The pale cream-coloured limestones which are a characteristic feature in the mountains and islands of the E. coast of the Adriatic are of Cretaceous age.

The Neocomian system in the Alps consists partly of clayey, partly of calcareous rock, the light-coloured limestones called 'Schrattenkalk' belonging to the upper part of the system. It is the equivalent of the Urgonian group, and contains as characteristic fossils *Caprotina ammonia* and *Radiolites neocomensis*, over which comes a limestone containing very abundantly a foraminifer (*Orbitolites lenticularis*). The 'Schrattenkalk' is characterised by the curious rifts and fissures of its weathered surface, which gives to its scenery a singularly wild and sometimes rather desolate aspect. To this system also belongs the *Biancone* of the Venetian Alps, which also extends into Lombardy, where it takes the name *Majolica*. The Cretaceous system proper is variable in character, and in no part resembles the soft white chalk, which in England is its most important constituent. The horizon of the Gault and Upper Greensand, as well as different parts of the Chalk, have been identified by fossils. In the Salzkammergut region the system is represented by the Gosau beds, clays, and sandstones, which contain a rich fauna, and rest, with unconformity, on Neocomian beds. They are approximately contemporaneous with the upper part of the English Chalk. In Switzerland the 'Sewenkalk,' with beds representing the Gault and Upper Greensand of England, is well developed, and the whole system, together with those of the Neocomian and Jurassic, is implicated in the great folds on the N. margin of the Alps, as may be seen in the Bay of Uri by the side of the Axenstrasse. The Cretaceous system is well represented, generally by calcareous rocks, in the districts of the French Alps which have been mentioned above. Of its occurrence on the S. side of the Alps it may suffice to say that limestone is the dominant rock. This, in the Venetian Alps, where it is the equivalent of the Senonian or Upper Chalk, is an argillaceous limestone, stratified in thin layers, called 'Scaglia,' containing sometimes flint nodules, and varying in colour from white to dark red. In Lombardy this stage is represented by marly limestones and sandstones. Flint also occurs in the hard and nearly white limestones of Istria and Dalmatia, already mentioned, which are singularly compact, and furnish a splendid building stone. The mountains are rather barren, for much of the water disappears down swallow holes and fissures.

Eocene (including Oligocene).—The great break which in England separates the Secondary from the Tertiary series does not exist in the Alps, for the Cretaceous system is followed in regular succession by the Eocene, and in some places it is impossible to fix upon any well marked line of separation between them, owing to the rarity of fossils. The beds referred to the lower part of the Tertiary have commonly a rather peculiar character, and recent investigations have shown that the group, to which the name of *Flysch* has long been given, and of which the exact geological position has been a matter of dispute, belongs really in one part of the Alps to the Cretaceous and in another to the Eocene system. This indicates, of course, that the physical conditions of which the Flysch is a result began in one part of the Alps at an earlier date than they did in another. The Flysch in the E. part of the Alps is more arenaceous in character than it is in the W. part, and takes the name of Vienna sandstone. Here, in the extreme E., it seems, so far as can be inferred from the fossils (occasionally found), to begin even in the Neocomian period. But in the Salzkammergut district it appears to be truly Cretaceous, and W. of this to correspond with the higher members of the same system together with part of the Eocene, for it is overlain by beds containing nummulites. In the Algäu districts (Bregenzerwald) the Flysch follows upon the 'Sewenkalk,' where the latter represents the uppermost horizon of the Cretaceous, and has thus gradually mounted to the threshold of the Tertiary series, to which in Switzerland it is restricted. As in that region beds containing nummulites are included in the upper part of the Flysch, the latter must be the equivalent of the Eocene up to somewhere about the horizon of the Middle Bagshot beds in England. The Flysch, as distinguished by lithological characters, comes to an end about Chambéry, though Eocene beds are continued further southwards.

As the lithological peculiarities of the Flysch are more characteristic of the Eocene system in the N. than in the S. zone of the Alps, it may be convenient to describe them briefly before proceeding further. The Flysch consists of clayey or sandy limestones, sandstones, and conglomerates or breccias, with shaly or slaty beds (sometimes largely developed), which are frequently interbanded together, and form together a rather conspicuously stratified group several hundred yards thick. As a rule fossils are scarce, or consist only of obscure markings referred to plants, or of the tracks of worms and other organisms, though occasionally in certain localities a sufficiently abundant fauna has been discovered to indicate the geological position of the deposit. The noted fossil fishes of Glarus occur in strata corresponding with the uppermost Eocene or Oligocene, and the Brown coal of Haring in the valley|of the Inn occupies nearly the same horizon.

But the most interesting and most puzzling beds in the Flysch are the conglomerates or breccias. These, in many localities, include erratic blocks of great size, which long since attracted the notice of geologists. One of the best known localities is the Habkernthal, within a few miles of Interlaken. Another place, easily accessible, is on the road to Ormonts-Dessus, a short distance above Sepey, but these boulders occur in many other parts of the Alps. According to Dr. E. Fraas * 'they extend along the whole Flysch zone,' and near Vienna on the Waschberg and Holingsteinerberg, near Stockerau, contain huge erratic blocks, one of the largest of which, a red granite, has been used as an appropriate memorial to L. von Buch. Similarly, to the W., near Sonthofen, in the Algäu, and in Switzerland these foreign blocks are associated with a great line of overthrust. The erratics, large and small, consist of many kinds of rock, sedimentary and crystalline, but some of the latter call for special attention.' A diabase is conspicuous in the E. Alps ; but varieties of this rock have also been found in the Swiss breccias. Those, however, to which more attention has been paid are granites. Blocks of this rock about four yards long, and more than thirty cubic yards in volume, are not uncommon. In form they are generally somewhat

* *Scenerie der Alpen*, p. 257 (1892).

rounded, and resemble the blocks which have been lying for some time in an Alpine torrent, rather than on a moraine. The interesting collection from the Habkernthal in the Bern Museum contains about seven varieties of granite; most, if not all, of these are different from any known to the writer as occurring in the neighbouring crystalline zone, or, as a rule, in any other parts of the Alps. One of the most striking is a porphyritic granite not unlike a variety common in the Schwarzwald.* In the Habkernthal the Flysch, about the horizon of the boulders, is a brownish or blackish mudstone, rudely fissile, perhaps cleaved, containing hard calcareous lumps, seemingly segregatory. It is interrupted by streaks and lenticular patches of grit, conglomerate, or breccia. These, in some places, are frequent, and very curiously interspersed; this, however, may be due to the breaking up (by subsequent earth movements) of larger masses; still the sudden and sporadic occurrence of these patches of coarser material in the finer mudstone is very perplexing; this peculiarity and the aspect of the rocks themselves suggest that a load of grit and boulders has been suddenly thrown down (almost as if it had been tipped from a ballast waggon) in a deposit, which normally was more or less a mudstone. In the Sepey district the mudstones, sandstones, finer and coarser conglomerates are distinctly interbanded, but the biggish blocks, which sometimes are almost, if not quite, as large as those in the Habkernthal, occur sporadically. For instance, in one place a rather egg-shaped block of granite, about nine feet by six, lies in a bed of conglomerate (the materials of which are more or less rounded, but can hardly be called good 'pebbles'), about four yards thick, in which the other fragments range from about two feet in diameter downwards. In another place, a block, perhaps even larger, is apparently almost isolated in the ordinary mudstone. In the Ormonts valley, however, many of these boulders consist of a grey granite or gneiss, and more closely resemble Alpine types.

To account satisfactorily for the presence of these erratics is no easy task. Some geologists regard them as the relics of a vanished mountain range, which, at that epoch, existed to the N. of the region where these erratics now occur, or as indications of an ancient shore line. Still this solution of the problem presents serious difficulties. The beds, as a whole, do not resemble an ordinary shore deposit in the neighbourhood of low reefs or low cliffs, and, if the action of torrents be invoked to explain the presence of bands of conglomerates and of large boulders in a group of strata generally fine-grained, these could only have descended from a rather lofty mountain range, and it is very strange that all other traces of it should have so completely vanished since Eocene times. If, however, we suppose mountains to have existed on the site of the present Alps, then their crystalline rocks must often have differed from any which are now exposed. Indeed, neither supposition removes the main difficulty—namely, how these large blocks were transported. It seems impossible to suppose that the lower Habkernthal could have been the site of a great range of crystalline rocks in Eocene times. In that case Secondary rocks should be absent from the neighbourhood of the Lakes of Thun and

---

* Something like the lighter variety of the Shapfell granite in England.

Brienz. If then these blocks have travelled for some distance, how did they come? Either bergs or rafts of shore ice seem to be the only possible modes of conveyance. But to this supposition the palæontological evidence is directly opposed, for, according to it, the temperature throughout Eocene ages was always higher, and often very much higher, than it is at present; hence that the winters should be cold enough to form coast ice seems impossible, and that glaciers should reach the sea hardly more probable. Thus these erratics must remain for the present among the unsolved problems of geology.

On the S. side of the chain Eocene deposits are restricted to the E. part, where they present more than one feature of interest. In the Vicentin district the 'Scaglia' beds, which form the uppermost part of the Cretaceous system, are followed by a group of deposits, among which basaltic cliffs afford proofs of contemporaneous volcanic action. Over these, in the Middle Eocene, come the calcareous shales of Monte Bolca, which have been for long noted for their numerous fossil fishes and plants; in other districts further E., at about the same level, are beds with foraminifera (nummulites and alveolina). In the Vicentin, at a somewhat higher level, are beds of fresh-water origin, containing brown coal; with these is associated the most important lava-flow (basalt) in the district, which sometimes attains a thickness of about 100 yards. The remainder of the Eocene, and part of the Oligocene, is represented by the noted fossiliferous deposits of Castel Gomberto (among which are some tuffs); these are generally assigned to the Middle Oligocene, though in some places they also belong to the Upper. The top of this group is formed by fresh-water deposits. Further W. the Eocene is not well represented, and its upper parts assume the aspect of the Flysch.

Between the latest of the Eocene or Oligocene deposits in the Alpine region and the earliest of the Miocene a considerable time must have elapsed, and great physical changes occurred, for, during that interval, the Alps came into existence as a mountain chain. Doubtless their growth was slow. In the N.E. district it began, as we have seen, as early as the beginning of the Cretaceous era, but further to the W. no evidence is found of any marked disturbances at this date. Probably, however, a larger area was affected during the Eocene age, and the movements became more marked, as the disturbing forces acted with greater intensity, during the Oligocene era.*

In the Central and Western Alps the latest beds implicated in this series of movements are referred to the Lower Oligocene. Beds of this, or of late Eocene age, are now found at great elevations, as on the Diablerets (10,650 ft.) and the Pointe de Salles (8,183 ft.), while in the Aiguilles d'Arves they reach 11,520 ft. The earliest deposits which apparently formed outside the zone of upheaval are referred to the middle of the Oligocene; these, however, are limited in extent while the representatives of the remainder of that system and of the Miocene are spread over a much wider area. The beds consist largely of sandstones and conglomerates. These, for the most part, are of fresh-water

---

* The Upper Eocene and Lower Miocene of many geologists.

origin, but the occasional intercalation of marine deposits shows that the sea was still near at hand.

On the N. border of the chain these conglomerates, called nagelfluh, sometimes, as in the Rigi and the Speer, attain a great thickness. They present many resemblances to the stratified gravels on the lowlands N. and S. of the present chain, and were obviously deposited by strong and rapid rivers. Although a few pebbles of crystalline rock have not yet been identified *in situ* in the Alps, it can hardly be doubted that the nagelfluh represents the deltas of rivers, which flowed from the Alps as they then existed. These conglomerates are now referred to the upper part of the Miocene.* The molasse (mostly sandstone), in many places, has yielded abundant plant remains; the fauna is sometimes marine, or brackish-water, but is more frequently terrestrial or fresh-water, as at Oeningen. From this locality came, with many other vertebrates, the skeleton of a large salamander, which was described by J. J. Scheuchzer as *homo diluvii testis*.

Deposits of a character generally similar to the Swiss molasse (sandstones with occasional conglomerates or shales) may be traced along the border of the Alps on both sides of the chain; these indicate that the Miocene era was one of extensive and active denudation. With its representatives the geological record in the Alpine regions practically closed, for beds of Pliocene age are few, local, and unimportant. That era was probably marked, especially in the Central Alps, by another epoch of great earth movements, by which the deposits just named were sometimes elevated, as in the Rigi and the Speer, about 6,000 ft. above the sea. That period also, and all the subsequent time down to the present day, has been characterised in the Alps by denudation rather than by deposition. True, the Alpine rivers have spread deposits of sand and gravel, in some cases far from thin, over the lowland valleys; the Alpine glaciers, during their epoch of greatest extension, built up their moraines even beyond the mountains; the same glaciers, as they retreated, have scattered erratics over the district, and in several places have covered it with a mantle of boulder clay. According to some geologists these ice streams have left a record of their passage in the excavation of the basins of the great Alpine lakes. But this is a moot question, which will be more fully discussed below. It is, however, certain that since the end of Miocene times the N. margin of the Alps has never been washed by the waves of the sea. The S. side of the chain has also been above water, but probably the valley of the Po, during Miocene ages, at least, formed a shallow gulf, which gradually became filled up. There may have been some slight general elevation of the district, but probably the accumulation of materials, brought down by the rivers, would suffice to bring the surface to its present level.

Pleistocene.†—The deposits formed during this period are in most districts so insignificant in extent that they might be passed over without notice, were it not for the special interest that attaches to the history of the operations which were in progress in the Alps during the time thus

---

* By some geologists they are placed on a rather lower horizon.
† This section, with some omissions, is retained from the first edition.

covered. These operations, whatever they may have been, have resulted in the transport of enormous quantities of solid matter from the inner and higher parts of the chain to the wide channels of the main valleys, and to the low country surrounding the base of the Alps. This transported matter is of three kinds, each of which deserves a brief notice.

1. *The Ancient Alluvium.*—This is present to a greater or less extent on all sides of the Alps, and in the bottoms of most of the great valleys, but is mainly developed on the S. side of the chain, and may there be studied to the best advantage. To this is referred the masses of rolled stones, composed of crystalline or harder sedimentary rocks, that at a slight depth beneath the surface are seen to spread along the valley of the Po, extending to a variable distance from the foot of the mountains, and along the course of the wider and deeper valleys. A deposit of similar character, covered only by a thin skin of vegetable soil, covers the plain of Friuli, from the Piave to the Isonzo, and, in some places at least forms beds of considerable depth.

2. *Moraine Deposits.*—In a subsequent page the reader will find a brief notice of the geological action of glaciers, where the nature of those masses of mineral matter which are borne down from the upper regions of the Alps to the lower valleys, and are known by the name of *moraines*, is more fully described. At many points in valleys, to which, as we know from other evidence, glaciers formerly extended, mounds of transported matter, including large angular blocks irregularly dispersed through gravel and fine sand, still exist, and at the opening of the great valleys on the S. side of the Alps similar mounds appear on a great scale, sometimes forming hills of considerable height. Those which surround the S. side of the Lake of Garda are fully 35 miles in length, and some of them, as that of Solferino, are nearly 500 ft. in height. The ancient moraines opposite the opening of the valley of the Dora Baltea are on a still grander scale.

3. *Glacial Silt.*—The action of glaciers in pulverising the underlying rocks, and transporting the materials to a distance in the form of extremely fine mud, is referred to in Art. XIV. (on Glaciers.) Accurate measures are wanting to show the amount of solid matter thus annually transported from the Alps to the lower valleys, to the bottom of lakes, and to the sea. Whatever that amount may be, it must have been much greater during the period when all the valleys of the Alps were traversed by glaciers, and an extent of surface was exposed to the grinding action of those glaciers 20 or 30 times as great as the beds of existing ice-streams. A large share of this deposit must have been carried into the valley of the Po, and when beyond the reach of the ancient alluvium this must be the chief constituent of the subsoil.

4. *The Growth and Sculpture of the Alps.*

Though the subject has already been mentioned indirectly, the questions involved are so difficult that something may be gained by regarding it for a moment from a different point of view.

The Alps, as has been already said, commence their history as a mountain chain about the middle of the Tertiary era. This is generally admitted, but difficulties begin when we attempt to pass beyond that general statement. In any speculations as to the earliest chapters in the chronicle much, of course, must depend on the views held as to the age of the crystalline schists. Many geologists have maintained that not a few of these are metamorphosed rocks of Palæozoic or even later ages. For this opinion the writer, as already said, not only can find no warrant, but also can produce much evidence to prove the great antiquity of those crystalline rocks of which the higher peaks and ranges are wholly, or almost wholly, composed. The Silurian and Devonian strata of the N.E. Alps, if he may judge from the results of a limited investigation, have derived their materials from older crystalline rocks, which, however, may not have occupied the site of the existing Alps. But in Carboniferous ages the grits and conglomerates, full of fragments from the adjoining region, indicate that even then the Alpine region was one of hills, if not of mountains. Moreover these fragments often exhibit structures that prove that the parent rocks, prior to this era, had been affected by potent earth movements. It is, however, hopeless to attempt any restoration of the physical geography of the Alpine region during the Carboniferous period. No more can be said than that from the W. of the Gailthal to the S. of Dauphiné bold and fairly lofty hills must have alternated with marshy lowlands: the one giving birth to strong streams; the other supporting, not infrequently, a luxuriant vegetation. The Carboniferous period was followed by another epoch of mountain-making, certainly not less pronounced, which appears to have affected more especially Switzerland and the Western Alps. There the Carboniferous deposits were folded, often sharply, like a pamphlet shut up in a book, between the underlying crystalline masses, and these disturbances were followed by denudation, probably considerable and long continued. In many places, as near Le Fréney, in Dauphiné, and in the Bifertengrat, on the E. side of the Tödi, secondary strata may be seen resting both on the crystalline schists and the denuded edges of the infolded Carboniferous deposits, thus indicating that in parts of the Alps there is a great break between the last members of the Primary, or Palæozoic, series and the first of the Secondary, which corresponds with an epoch of disturbance comparable with that which gave birth to the present mountain chain. Of the outlines and contours of these pre-Secondary mountains nothing positive can be said. But, as will be explained, there is some reason to think that the folds, at any rate over a considerable area, trended not far away from N.N.E. to S.S.W. The area, however, occupied by these mountains did not wholly correspond with the present Alpine region. The sea, for instance, must have covered the latter to some distance W. of the Lake of Garda, at any rate from early Permian times,* for here, as already mentioned, the great outbursts of volcanic material are associated with, and followed by, a mass of marine deposits, which continue through the Trias and Rhætic into the Jurassic period. Seeing that the united thickness of the deposits, from the base of the Permian to the top of the Rhætic, can be hardly less in some parts of the Dolomite district than 9,000 feet, and that, in many parts of the Alps, the

---

* In the Gailthal Permian deposits appear to rest conformably on Carboniferous, both being marine. See Dr. E. Fraas, *Scenerie der Alpen*, p. 86.

Permian and Trias, as already stated, are either absent or very feebly and irregularly represented, and that the succeeding Jurassic beds usually are extremely well developed, we can hardly doubt that the first-named period saw the beginning of a long age of subsidence (perhaps initiated by the volcanic outbursts).

By the end of the Triassic period the greater part of these pre-Secondary Alps must have disappeared under water. The mountain ranges must have been replaced by lines of rocky islands, till at last the highest peaks alone rose above the sea as monuments of a drowned land, like the Lofoten islands, at the present day, on the W. coast of Norway. There is no reason to doubt that this downward movement continued practically throughout the Secondary era, but a minor question of some interest may be asked, to which opposite answers have been given. Did these islands remain above water until the Alps began once more to rise, and are they now represented by certain areas of the existing ranges, or did 'this silence of the central sea' prevail for a time where the mountain peaks once rose, and now have risen again? Many geologists, among whom E. Fraas may be quoted, are of opinion that the sea was always interrupted by long narrow islands which corresponded in direction with the present mountain ranges. Something may be said in favour of this view, but the writer thinks that, if any islands escaped submergence, they must have been very small. For instance, in several parts of the Pennine Alps little patches of 'Rauchwacke' still remain in the heart of the crystalline districts S. of the Rhône valley, which are identical with the deposit underlying the Jurassic in the same valley. As the latter system attains to a considerable thickness, and as the present differences in level, at which it now occurs, can be shown to be due to post-Secondary disturbances, it is highly probable that the 'Rauchwacke' was succeeded by other Secondary deposits, or, in other words, that the whole region was gradually submerged. Another point also must not be forgotten. In these Secondary deposits conglomerates are rare, and even beds of sandstone not very abundant. Their materials are fairly uniform in character. The Alpine Lias, like that of England, seems to point to the action of large rivers, with *embouchures* not very remote, and the existence of continental land, yet not quite close at hand. It might, indeed, be urged that a mountainous region, in subsiding, broke up into islands, and that its valleys were converted into fiords. If so, no doubt it would supply but little coarse material ; still it could hardly fail to interfere with the continuity of the deposits, and the general aspect of the Lower Secondary rocks in the Alps leads the writer to infer that their materials were laid down over an area comparatively uninterrupted, and were derived from a region at some little distance.

So for long ages deposition went on over the Alpine area ; if there was any interruption to, or discontinuity in, the subsidence, it was only local. The first sign of an upward movement occurs, as already stated, between the Neocomian and the Cretaceous period, and this only in the E. Alps. From the lithological character of the Vienna sandstone, or Flysch, of the E. Alps, it seems probable that by the close of the Neocomian period denudation had begun in that region, though there is no proof, so far as the writer is aware, that a mountain range, in the ordinary sense of the words, had been as yet produced. But the Alps had begun to grow; and the movements gradually extended westward, though, as far as can be ascertained, nothing like a mountain system existed in the latter region until after the nummulitic group had been deposited. Then, in late Eocene or in early Oligocene times, if the more modern grouping be preferred, the Alps apparently rather rapidly became a great mountain chain. But it must be remembered that though the uprising of the Alps is assigned, as a matter of convenience, to a particular geological epoch, no more is meant than that deposits prior to this epoch afford no indications of the existence of mountains, while those posterior supply ample evidence. But the chain may have continued to develope itself steadily for long ages after the epoch thus selected as a date. Accordingly the inner zones of the Alps very probably continued to rise, while the nagelfluh and molasse were deposited on the lowlands outside the chain, where very likely there was a corresponding subsidence.

But to this process also an end came towards the close of Miocene times. New disturbances began, produced apparently by thrusts from the S., or rather outwards from the plain of the Po and the head of the Adriatic, which, while they gave a general uplift to the bordering lowlands of France, Switzerland, and Austria, most intensely affected the middle part of the chain—that is, roughly speaking, the districts of the Oberland and Glarus Alps. The N. margin of this zone affords remarkable examples of folding and overthrust-faulting. The uplifted nagelfluh forms hills, which rise considerably more than 4,000 feet above the general level of the lowlands; in some places, as near the Rigi Scheidegg, the Eocene beds were thrust over the Miocene. Then also, in all probability, the remarkable double fold* of the Glarus region (described by Heim), and the complicated over-folding and faulting in the N. buttresses of the Jungfrau, unravelled by Baltzer, were, if not originated, at any rate brought to their present condition.

As the result of these movements, which doubtless were long continued, and perhaps may hardly yet have entirely ceased, the present mountain system of the Alps has been upraised. They have been carved by the destructive processes of Nature (to be presently indicated) into their present form; these have acted simultaneously with the upraising, and are certainly not yet at rest.

There is a question, however, which is still unanswered: Were the Alps formed by the inosculation of two chains produced by separate movements at different times, or are they a single chain, of which the E. end began to be developed at an earlier epoch than the W. one? Not a few authorities of the first rank approve the former view, the leading features of which may be briefly sketched as follows.†

The Alps are formed by the combination of two curved chains, the convexities of both being turned towards the N.W.; the outline of each of these two chains can be roughly compared with that of a pocket pistol, and they are so placed that their 'barrels' are nearly parallel, the muzzle of one touching the convex part of the handle of the other.

---

* Probably the folding is associated with thrust faults.
† Much of the following account is taken from a summary by Mr. J. Eccles (*Alpine Journal*, xv. p. 561 *sqq.*) of Dr. C. Diener's work entitled *Der Gebirgsbau der West-Alpen* (1891).

The West chain commences at the Maritime Alps, and consists of two principal crystalline zones—indicating regions of maximum disturbance —named respectively after Monte Rosa and Mont Blanc, between which is a zone (part of the Briançonnais) mainly consisting of sedimentary deposits, and forming an infolded trough. There is also an outer sedimentary zone, beyond which are others, less well defined, and more limited in extent, including the zone of the molasse and the chain of the Jura. *The Monte Rosa zone* extends from near Cuneo, in Piedmont, to the Adula group; it includes the central nuclei of the Cottian and Graian Alps, the group of Monte Rosa, with the neighbouring peaks, and the Alps of Ticino. In this zone the arrangement of the beds, broadly speaking, is comparatively uniform throughout, consisting, in the W. part, mainly of a regular series of anticlinals of moderate elevation, affected only by local disturbances, while further E., in the more central portion of the zone, steep dips and generally more complicated conditions prevail. This zone comes to an end about the Blegno and Leventina valleys, on the E. side of which the dip of its beds makes a high angle with that of the beds in a chain running S. from the Adula group. *The Mont Blanc zone* has been subjected to much greater disturbance, and is a region of intense lateral pressure. This zone begins in the Maritime Alps, and can be traced over a region often occupied by Secondary or Tertiary rocks, by occasionally outcropping crystalline masses, such as the Pelvoux, Grandes Rousses, and Belledonne groups. It follows, therefore, that over this region (and the same holds further N.) the zone exhibits a rather complicated structure, and consists of more than a single fold. It passes on through the Mont Blanc group and the parallel range of the Brévent, crosses the Rhône valley near Vernayaz, and runs through the Bernese Oberland to beyond the Reuss. In places, as in Mont Blanc itself, the fan structure is strongly developed. The Adula group, as it strikes approximately at right angles to the trend of the Monte Rosa group, cannot, according to Dr. Diener, be part of the system of the Western Alps. In the *East chain*, which it begins, the beds turn gradually eastwards, until at last they trend continuously nearly in that direction. The essential structure of the Eastern system is a central crystalline zone flanked by calcareous and other sedimentary rocks; it is thus more simple than that of the W. half of the Alps.

By Dr. Diener's theory of the separate origin of the two parts of the Alpine chain several difficulties in its structure are explained: notably the way in which the Alpine chain appears to broaden out in approaching the Lake of Garda, the marked N.N.E. and S.S.W. trend of the sedimentary deposits in this and the adjoining regions, and the apparently more complicated structure of the W. half of the Alps. But it creates other difficulties. For instance, the sedimentary deposits on the margin of the Alps appear to extend from E. to W. without any break such as the junction of two chains might be expected to present, and the structure of the outer zone seems to accord better with the hypothesis that the Alps were the result of sets of simultaneous movements, but that the later disturbances acted more powerfully in the central than in the E. region. Moreover, while the existence of a cross trend in the strata (*i.e.* from N.N.E. to S.S.W.) is most perceptible about the Lake of

Garda, it is by no means restricted to that region.* 'The Ortler *massif* and the district to its N. seem indicative of another and less clearly marked parallel trough; the rather abrupt cessation of the region of Secondary rock, on the S. side, near that end of the Lago Maggiore, and the remarkable bend of the watershed of the Pennine chain, on the E. side of the Vispthal, also suggest the effect of an anticlinal running in the same direction; while, yet further W., to beyond Mont Blanc, the general trend, both of the ridges of crystalline rock and of the troughs of Secondary, suggests similar disturbances. Obviously the whole course of the chain for a long distance S. of Mont Blanc corresponds with the same line of folding, but this might be an accidental coincidence. It can, however, hardly be a mere chance that the central *massif* of Dauphiné, with the parallel crystalline ranges of the Grandes Rousses and Belledonne, project so markedly in a S.S.W. direction, though the watershed of the Alpine chain is already beginning to curve towards the eastward side of a circle of longitude.'† These considerations have led the writer to suggest that this structure is a record of older disturbances. 'These folds may be due to earth movements which are pre-Triassic, but not improbably post-Carboniferous, in age. Certainly the deep sea, which, as already pointed out, covered the greater part of the E. Alps in Triassic times, appears to have shallowed rapidly westwards, and its coast in that direction to have had a general trend much nearer N. and S. than E. and W. The direction of the ridges of older rock in the Schwarzwald and Vosges agrees with this, as does the position and direction of the most important watershed in the Cévennes—namely, that from which the Allier and the main stream of the Loire descend—which also appears to be in intimate relation with the whole series of earth movements which have affected Dauphiné.' ‡ But further study of the Alps is necessary before the difficulties of this problem can be completely overcome.

The *sculpturing of a mountain region* is a subject which presents fewer difficulties than it formerly did. The peaks and valleys have alike been hewn out by Nature's carving tools, by the heat and the frost, the rain, the stream, and the glacier. This action, doubtless, has been modified and directed by the earth movements. Obviously before wave can batter, or river furrow, rocks must be upheaved from the quiet depths of ocean, and exposed to the action of the elements. The effects also of these cannot fail to be modified by the strike and dip of the rock masses, by the existence of folds and faults, by the alternation of hard and soft material. But while valleys may be connected with synclinal folds or anticlinal fissures, while their direction may have been affected by the slope of the rising ground or the outcrops of particular rocks, while they may have been guided or even initiated by faults, there is no ground for supposing that any one valley—not even such a gorge as that of the

---

* This synclinal trough, though less conspicuous N. of the line joining Meran and Bozen, seems traceable as far as Innsbruck, and is indicated by the outliers of Secondary rock on either side of the Brenner railway N. of Sterzing.
† See the writer's 'Tyndall Lectures' for 1888 on the 'Growth and Structure of the Alps,' in the *Alpine Journal*, vol. xiv. p. 106.
‡ *Ibid.* p. 107.

Tamina, or of the Trient—is in any proper sense a fissure. Whatever cracks may have been produced in the terrestrial crust by the strains of earth movements, the forces of Nature have worked so long and so vigorously on the lines sketched out that they have obliterated them as completely as the tools of the carver destroy the design pencilled on a piece of wood.

At the present day the subject of mountain sculpture generally receives full notice in text-books of Geology, and some details in that of the Alps have been discussed by the writer in three lectures published in the 'Alpine Journal,'* so that a brief outline may suffice. The valleys in a hill district, as a rule, may be divided into *valleys of dip*, or those which correspond in direction with the dip of the strata, and *valleys of strike*, or those which follow the trend of the beds. The former, as produced by the more rapid streams, are commonly narrower and steeper and more gorge-like; the latter, as excavated by rivers which have only a slow fall, are broader, more level, and enclosed by less abrupt slopes. The form, however, obviously depends much on the nature and structure of the rocks, and a traveller, with but a slight knowledge of geology, soon finds little difficulty in understanding the relation of the course of a river to the rocks which it traverses. Thus the valley of the Rhine, above Chur, and that of the Rhône, above Martigny, are, broadly speaking, valleys of strike. Their general direction is parallel with the outcropping edges or trough-like infolds of the softer sedimentary rocks, and these are modified, more especially in the second case, by irregularities in the outline of the underlying crystalline masses. The rivers which traverse the sedimentary zone, between the Lake of Geneva and the course of the Isère below Grenoble, as they make their way from their sources in the mountains to the bordering lowlands, often exhibit very conspicuously valleys of strike alternating with valleys of dip.

When the Alps first began to rise definitely above the sea their watershed must have been determined by the highest ground, and with this the present one may be roughly compared. Hence in the Tyrol the central range may have always been the watershed of the chain, and may thus indicate the zone in which the uplift has been the greatest. But, as a consequence either of the combination of two separate chains or of a complication due to the existence of an earlier structure, as suggested above, the line of watershed seems to run irregularly from the Oetzthal group along the Ortler group, and to betake itself to follow a range which apparently corresponds with the S. one in the E. Alps. But this change of direction, as the writer has pointed out in the lectures already mentioned, may be more apparent than real, due partly to removal by denudation of the westward extension of the Dolomite group, and to complications introduced, especially in the region of the Central Alps, by the second series of mountain-making movements. The inference, at any rate, seems legitimate that when the river valleys of the Central Alps were first defined the Oberland range can have offered but little obstruction to the northward flow of water, so that this part of Switzerland must then have more closely resembled in its structure the Central Tyrol. When the former range began to assume a more grandiose aspect, owing to the later series of disturbances, it must have been uplifted slowly enough to allow the Rhine, the Reuss, and the Rhône to keep open their channel of exit, by sawing down into the rising mass.

Two remarkable features in the Alpine valleys may be briefly noticed before quitting this subject. One is that occasionally the watershed between the valleys of strike, belonging to two distinct river systems, is very ill marked. Notable examples are to be found on the Reschen Scheideck between the drainage of the Inn and the Etsch, and on the Toblacher plateau, between the Rienz and the Drave. These may be explained by supposing that denudation has been more active at the head of one of the valleys, so that part of the territory of one of the river systems has been, so to say, annexed by the other as it has cut away the rising ground by which the two basins were once divided. A similar explanation may be offered for the second feature, viz. that the watershed between two river systems not unfrequently lies very near one end of an almost level trough, which overlooks a steep descent. The most conspicuous instance of this structure is presented by the Maloja Pass. The summit is a long and nearly level valley; the watershed, close to the Kulm, is so faintly marked that a cutting, a very few yards deep, would divert the waters of the nearest lake down the precipitous descent into the Val Bregaglia. This and similar structures may be attributed to the more rapid erosive action of the streams draining towards Italy. The original 'divide' between the waters of the Inn and of the Maira may have been situated as far S. as Vicosoprano, so that the streams from the valleys now occupied by the Forno and Albigna glaciers may once have been received by the Inn. On most of the great mountain high roads a comparatively level 'trough,' exists at the top of the pass, though the structure generally is not so marked as in the case of the Maloja.

The interesting question of the origin of the *Alpine lakes* is briefly noticed in the next section, so that it may suffice to say that, in the writer's opinion, some of the smaller tarns may be exceptional results of the erosive action of glaciers; some are formed by moraines, and some, like the Lago d' Alleghe, by dams produced by bergfalls. In many lakes, both large and small, the level of the water is raised by débris, which has been thrown down either by one of these two causes or by tributary streams. But it seems impossible to attribute the greater Alpine lakes to glacial erosion, for not only is there no evidence that glaciers under ordinary circumstances ever excavate basins, but also it is clear that in the Alps their effects have been comparatively superficial, and of secondary importance on the rocks over which they have passed. These larger basins, in the writer's opinion, have been produced by unequal movements in the floor of valleys, already excavated by the ordinary processes of denudation, and are thus comparatively modern features in the physical structure of the Alps. The deltas at their heads and the division between the Lake of Thun and of Brienz, are of course yet later in date, and are continually increasing in size.

5. *The Glacial Period.*[*]

As we have already seen, the relative level of the different portions of the Alpine chain has undergone no considerable change since the close of the Tertiary Period. This latest portion, however, of the history of the Alps is not less interesting, for it is marked by the extraordinary extension of the glaciers.

It is impossible here to enter into any detail of the evidence upon which the present conclusions of geologists have been based, and still less to refer to the prolonged discussions to which at every step they were subjected—discussions which ultimately served to establish the new theory upon more decisive proof, than if it had been more easily accepted.

In the brief description which is given (Art. XIV.) of the phenomena of existing glaciers, it has been shown that amongst other operations they transport large quantities of mineral matter from the upper ridges of the Alps to the lower valleys; that this transported matter consists partly of large blocks, partly of smaller stones and gravel. It is seen that a portion of these blocks are stranded upon the bank of the glacier, while others are carried down to its lower end, where, if the shape of the ground be favourable, and the glacier remain long enough stationary, they, along with the rest of the transported materials, enter into the formation of a terminal moraine. Again, it is seen that by the passage of a glacier, the bottom and sides of the valley are subjected to a peculiar process of smoothing and polishing, which leaves its tokens permanently impressed on the general form of the rocks, and on the condition of their surface. Finally, it appears that the pressure of the glacier against the bottom and sides of the valley reduces the rocks and gravel that find their way to the bottom partly to fine mud, and partly to flattened pebbles, scored by the friction they have encountered in the rocky bed of the glacier.

It has long been known that blocks, sometimes of great dimensions, and composed of rock utterly different from that of the district in which they are found, are scattered through the lower parts of the main valleys of the Alps, and over the low country at their base. Such blocks, with their edges still fresh, and without trace of violent transport, are seen resting on steep slopes. Further enquiry showed that in the places where these blocks were deposited, the rock *in situ* is often rounded and grooved—nay, even, that when hard enough, it has preserved the finer striæ and polish which we see under the beds of existing glaciers. One after another the moraines, the glacial mud, and the scored pebbles were discovered at long distances from the present limits of the glaciers, but associated with the distribution of the erratic blocks; and these appearances were shown not to be confined to the Alps, but to be equally distinct in other mountain districts, as, for instance, in the British islands, during the same recent geological period.

Though it was sustained by able advocates, foremost amongst whom must be reckoned the late M. Charpentier, the theory which accounted for the dispersion of the erratic blocks by the agency of extinct glaciers

---

[*] This section is retained with little change from the first edition.

encountered much opposition. It has perhaps suffered more from the exaggerations of some of its supporters than from the criticism of its opponents. At present the original controversy is nearly set at rest. The absolute identity of the operations of existing glaciers with the facts traceable throughout the Alps, and other mountain countries, has overcome the reluctance of many eminent geologists to admit the new theory, and the former extension of glaciers over a wide area in the Alps, and elsewhere, is now one of the admitted data of geological science.

The evidence is in some respects more complete and convincing on the southern than on the northern side of the Alps; and it is probable that if the phenomena had been sooner studied in that region, the period of resistance to the new theory would have been abridged. It has been fully proved that nearly all the secondary valleys that open into the valley of the Po were traversed by great glaciers which extended down as far as the opening of the valley, and in some instances, as already mentioned, were protruded into the plain.

On the north side of the Alps the area occupied by the ancient glaciers was even more extensive. The glacier of the Rhône, with a vast number of affluents poured into it from the tributary valleys of the Pennine and Bernese Alps, not only filled the basin of the Lake of Geneva, but also covered a great portion of the plain of Switzerland, and reached to a considerable height on the flanks of the Jura.

A map showing the distribution of the erratic blocks in Switzerland has been published by M. Escher von der Linth; a similar map, including the Alps of Lombardy and a part of Piedmont, accompanies a memoir by M. Omboni in the 2nd volume of 'Atti della Società Italiana di Scienze Naturali.'

In the 3rd volume of the 'Acts' of the same society, M. G. de Mortillet has published a more complete map of the ancient glaciers of the Italian side of the Alps, with an interesting memoir, in which he discusses at length various questions to which in this brief essay it is impossible to do justice. The latest speculations upon the part played by glaciers in the past history of the Alps lead to conclusions that have not as yet gained the general agreement of geologists. M. de Mortillet, M. Gastaldi, and other distinguished Italian geologists hold that during the period preceding the utmost extension of the glaciers, the Italian lakes were filled with the waterworn materials that constitute the so called ancient alluvium, and that the cavities so filled were scooped out by the action of the glaciers when they descended into the lake basins. Other theorists, and among them the eminent English geologist, Sir A. Ramsay, have gone further still, and have sought to prove that the ancient glaciers were competent not only to clear out the bed of a lake, supposing it filled with alluvium, but to excavate the rock-basin itself. When we recollect the depth of the Italian lakes, which vary from 900 feet in the Lake of Lugano to over 2,600 feet in the Lago Maggiore, we feel that more cogent evidence than any yet produced is required before we can admit the probability of even the more moderate of these hypotheses. The subject is interesting from its novelty as well as its geological importance; but, pending its further discussion, we concur in the objections to the new theories urged by Mr. Ball in the 'Philosophical Magazine' for

February and December 1863.* On somewhat similar grounds we can give no credence to the supposed operation of glaciers in the excavation of the valleys of the Alps, while we admit the probability that the action of ice has, along with other agents, had a large share in modifying the details, and shaping the minuter features, of the surface of the Alpine valleys.

Notwithstanding the labour that has been bestowed by geologists upon the study of the glacial period in the Alps, there remain many branches of enquiry which are far from being exhausted. One of these relates to the probable oscillations in the extent of the glaciers. The great moraines which are so remarkable on the S. side of the Alps prove that the glaciers must have remained for a long period at or about the limit which they indicate, and that this limit has not since been surpassed; but this does not imply that at an earlier date the great ice streams may not have flowed further into the plain, without remaining long enough to leave such moraines as would survive to the present period. One of the difficulties found in studying the glacial phenomena in that region arises from the fact that during the period of the retirement of the glaciers, and since that time, the materials of the ancient moraines have been constantly attacked by torrents, sometimes transported to a distance, and partially stratified. The region of ancient moraines along the southern base of the Lombard Alps is extremely interesting from its diversified scenery, and the small lakes formed by the mounds of moraine matter add much to its beauty; but laborious and patient study is necessary for those who would unravel the phenomena.

The glacial deposits in some valleys show that the onward movement of the great ice-stream was by no means uniform. One of the most notable, and in some ways most perplexing, of these indications is afforded in the valley of the Limmat. A morainic deposit occurs on the upper part of the Uetliberg overlain by a coarse gravel, called the 'löcherige Nagelfluh,' to distinguish it from the well known conglomerate of earlier Tertiary age. But that pebble-bed descends to near the level of the Limmat at Baden, fifteen miles below Zürich. In the intervening district another extensive morainic deposit, newer than it, occurs, about and at some height above the Lake of Zürich, and this is followed by the stratified river gravels forming the bed of the valley to the west of the town. But the ice must have advanced over this also; for, near Kilwangen, about four miles above Baden, moraine is seen resting upon it. Of these three records of the actual presence of ice the second is supposed to mark the epoch when the Alpine glaciers reached the Jura and attained their greatest extension.

Another branch of enquiry connected with the same subject regards the effects of the glacial period in the Alps upon animal and vegetable life. It is probable that the period of the utmost extension of the glaciers was unfavourable to most forms of life, and that the present fauna and flora began to appear on the flanks of the chain only as the glaciers retired to the upper valleys. Among the mammalia whose remains belong to that period are a few now extinct species. There is nothing to

* See a further paper by Mr. Ball, *Geol. Mag.* 1871, p. 359; also papers by Prof. Bonney, *Quart. Journ. Geol. Soc.* 1871, p. 312, 1873, p. 382, 1874, p. 479.

show that the new inhabitants appeared simultaneously, but some reason to hold the contrary opinion. The fish, insects, and mollusca that inhabit the Alpine lakes could have made their appearance only after these were clear of ice, a period which must be separated by a long interval from the commencement of the retirement of the glaciers.

On the questions concerning the antiquity of man, which now so much interest geologists, the glacial deposits of the Alps have hitherto been silent, and we cannot determine whether the earliest human inhabitants witnessed the presence of great glaciers in the lower valleys of this mountain chain.*

6. *Geological Literature and Maps.*

The Alps have in recent years loomed large in geological literature. It would be a laborious task to draw up anything like a complete list even of the books and papers which are restricted to questions of Alpine Geology, and, if accomplished, it would be too long for publication in these pages. Hence it must suffice to enumerate a few of the larger books which deal with the geology of the Alps, or of some important district, and to mention the official publications or periodicals in which valuable information is likely to be found. The list is restricted, with a few exceptions, to books published within about the past thirty years, because although the older books often contain valuable material they have been in part superseded by the rapid advance made during that time by some departments of natural science.

1. *Books.*

Baretti (*M.*). Geologia della provincia di Torino. With Atlas. Turin, 1893.
Diener (*C.*). Der Gebirgsbau der West-Alpen. Prague, Vienna, and Leipzig, 1891.
Favre (*A.*). Recherches Géologiques dans les Parties de la Savoie, du Piémont et de la Suisse Voisines du Mont-Blanc. 3 vols. With Atlas. Paris, 1867.
Fraas (*E.*). Scenerie der Alpen. Leipzig, 1892.
Frech (*F.*). Die Karnischen Alpen. Halle, 1892.
Gümbel (*C. W.*). Geognostische Beschreibung des bayerischen Alpengebirges. Gotha, 1861.
Heer (*O.*). Die Urwelt der Schweiz. Zürich, 1st edition, 1865; 2nd enlarged edition, 1879. The English translation, 2 vols. 1876, is entitled 'The Primæval World of Switzerland,' edited by James Heywood.
Heim (*A.*). Untersuchungen über den Mechanismus der Gebirgsbildung. 2 vols. and Atlas. Basel, 1878.
  ,,   Handbuch der Gletscherkunde. Stuttgart, 1885.
Lory (*C.*). Description Géologique du Dauphiné. Paris and Grenoble, 1860-64.

* Here followed, in previous editions, an account of the geological divisions of the entire chain of the Alps. This section would have required searching revision, if not recasting, and the subject is one which cannot be satisfactorily treated in the present state of our knowledge of Alpine Geology. Accordingly it has been thought best to omit it altogether, except so far as the matter has been dealt with in earlier parts of this Article. I may, however, refer to the suggestive papers on Alpine geology by Professor Rothpletz. His writings and those of Mrs. Gordon (Miss Ogilvie) show that the structure of the Dolomite region is much less simple than geologists in general have supposed, and that in it also folding and faulting, especially by overthrusting, have produced very marked effects.—T. G. B.

Mojsisovics (E. von). Die Dolomit-Riffe von Südtirol und Venetiens. Vienna, 1879.
Richthofen (F. von). Geognostische Beschreibung der Umgegend von Predazzo, &c. Gotha, 1860.
Studer (B.). Geologie der Schweiz. 2 vols. Bern and Zürich, 1851–53.
Suess (E.). Die Entstehung der Alpen. Vienna, 1875. (See also references in 'Das Antlitz der Erde.')
Zaccagna (D.). Sulla Geologia delle Alpi Occidentali (article in the 'Bollettino del Reale Comitato d' Italia,' 1887).

A useful book in its way is the 'Livret-Guide Géologique dans le Jura et les Alpes de la Suisse' (Lausanne, 1894), published to help the members of the 6th International Geological Congress in their scientific excursions in the Jura and Swiss Alps. It has maps and plates, so that it is a very handy geological guide for Swiss travellers.

2. *Official Publications.*

Austria.—K.K. Geologische Reichsanstalt.
    Abhandlungen. Vienna. From 1852 onwards.
    Jahrbuch.   ,,   ,,   1850 ,,
France.—Bulletin des Services de la Carte Géologique de la France. From 1889.
Italy.—Reale Comitato Geologico d' Italia ('Bollettino'). From 1870.
Switzerland.—Beiträge zur geologischen Karte der Schweiz. From 1864 onwards.

3. *Publications of Scientific Societies in which Papers of Importance have appeared.*

Académie des Sciences de l'Institut de France ('Comptes Rendus').
Accademia Reale dei Lincei ('Atti').
Annales des Mines. Paris.
Deutsche Geologische Gesellschaft ('Zeitschrift').
Geological Society of London ('Quarterly Journal').
Kaiserliche Akademie der Wissenschaften (Vienna) ('Sitzungsberichte').
Königliche Bayerische Akademie der Wissenschaften ('Sitzungsberichte').
Società Geologica Italiana ('Bollettino').
Société Géologique de France ('Bulletin').

A summary of the papers dealing with Alpine Geology by MM. Favre and Schardt is now printed in 'Eclogæ Geologicæ Helveticæ' (the periodical of the Swiss Geological Society).

Geological papers occasionally appear in the publications of the French, German and Austrian, Italian, Swiss, and other foreign Alpine Clubs and Societies, but there are few in that of the English Alpine Club.

4. *Maps.*

The best and most recent geological map of the whole chain of the Alps is that by F. Noë, entitled 'Geologische Uebersichtskarte der Alpen.' $\frac{1}{1000000}$. Vienna, 1890.

The following are geological maps of more limited regions:—

Austria.—Franz Ritter von Hauer. Geologische Uebersichtskarte der Oesterreichisch-Ungarischen Monarchie. $\frac{1}{576000}$. Vienna, 1867–1871. Two sheets, which include the greater part of the Eastern Alps. This is the map of the Austro-Hungarian Geological Survey.

E. Mojsisovics v. Mojsvar.—Geologische Uebersichtskarte der Tirolisch-Venetianischen Hochländer zwischen Etsch und Piave. $\frac{1}{75000}$, 6 sheets. Vienna, 1878.

France.—Carte Géologique détaillée de la France. $\frac{1}{80000}$ (in process of publication, but only a few of the Alpine sheets have as yet been issued).

Carte Géologique de la France. $\frac{1}{1000000}$. This includes the French part of the chain and somewhat more.

G. Vasseur and L. Carez. Carte Géologique Générale de la France. $\frac{1}{500000}$. This map was completed about three years ago, and includes the French part of the chain with the adjacent territory.

Italy.—Carta Geologica d'Italia. $\frac{1}{1000000}$. Rome, 1889. This map includes considerably more than the Alps of Italy, as well as a bit of the east side of the Adriatic.

A geological map of the Italian kingdom, on a scale of $\frac{1}{100000}$, is in course of publication, but the Alpine sheets have not yet appeared.

Switzerland.—Geologische Karte der Schweiz. $\frac{1}{100000}$, 25 sheets. 1862–1888.

To these may be added, as dealing with a single point in geology—

A. Favre—Carte du Phénomène Erratique et des Anciens Glaciers du Versant Nord des Alpes Suisses, et de la Chaîne du Mont-Blanc. $\frac{1}{250000}$ (published by the Swiss Geological Survey). 4 sheets. 1884.

Art. XII.—Alpine Zoology.[*]

The zoology of the Alps is replete with many points of interest. Although some of the more remarkable animals have passed away; although the gigantic urus (*Bos primigenius*), which flourished in the forests of Mid-Switzerland during the prehistoric human period, and perhaps gave its name to the Canton of Uri, is now extinct; although the marsh hog (*Sus scrofa palustris*), which survived in the Lake habitations, exists no longer, having given place to the modified wild boar and domestic hog, that afford sport and food to the present population, yet the mountains at a higher elevation, and far above the snow line, afford examples of the Alpine fauna, which, as might *a priori* have been expected, represents in many important points the faunas of other and still less accessible regions. We purpose briefly to recapitulate the more striking forms, and to comment on their vertical distribution.

1. *Alpine Mammals.*—The order *Carnivora* is well represented in Switzerland. The lynx (*Felis lynx*) and the wild cat (*F. catus*) are to be found at high elevations in the Alps. The former, in the Pyrenees, is said to reach the vertical height of 11,300 feet; its 'bathymetrical' distribution in the Alps is unrecorded. Up to a thousand feet are found the marten (*Mustela foina*), the weasel (*Putorius vulgaris*), and the

[*] This article was originally written by Mr. C. Carter Blake. It has been carefully revised by Dr. P. L. Sclater, F.R.S., Secretary of the Zoological Society, with the assistance of Mr. Boulenger and of Prof. Bell. Mr. W. Warde Fowler has contributed the Section on 'Alpine Birds.'

polecat (*P. fœtidus*). The stoat or ermine (*P. erminea*) reaches a higher elevation than any other Alpine carnivore; it is found at the height of 10,000 feet. Next beneath it, at 9,000 feet, lives the brown bear (*Ursus arctos*), which, however, is now getting very scarce, except in one or two remote districts of the Alps. The fox (*Canis vulpes*) and the badger (*Meles taxus*) occur on the lower slopes.

The order of *Ungulates* exhibits many interesting examples. In the whole world, the Alps, the Pyrenees, the Carpathians, the Albanian mountains, and the Caucasus are the sole spots where the chamois, or 'Gemse' (*Rupricapra tragus*), still survives, the solitary representative of the group of mountain-antelopes in Europe. The chamois ranges to an elevation of 12,000 feet. It has so long been selected as the representative of the Alpine fauna that any comment on the most striking and picturesque animal in the Alps is superfluous, and a general reference to the monograph * on it written by F. C. Keller ('Die Gemse,' Klagenfurt, 1887) is all that is necessary. It is rarely seen in the more frequented parts of the Swiss mountains, and can be best studied in the Eastern Graians and the Maritime Alps, in both of which districts it is carefully preserved for hunting purposes by order of the late and present Kings of Italy. In Switzerland chamois are most common in the less known parts of the Grisons. The goats are represented by the ibex, bouquetin, or steinbock (*Capra ibex*). The horns of the male bouquetin are strong, thick, and subquadrangular, frequently extending to a length of several feet; those of the female are much smaller. In Switzerland the steinbock was rapidly disappearing as early as the sixteenth century, and the last authenticated cases of its occurrence in the Swiss Alps were in the neighbourhood of Arolla about 1830-1840. They exist in numbers only in the Eastern Graians (Cogne), where they are preserved by the King of Italy, whose father purchased all the hunting rights in these districts from 1856 onwards. The herd now numbers about 300. Attempts to reintroduce the steinbock into the Grisons and Eastern Alps, by means of the importation of specimens from the E. Graians, have not been attended by success. Yet the steinbock was once far more common. Its remains are found in the Swiss Lake dwellings; the arms of the Grey League of Rætia (from 1650 at least, and probably from a far earlier date), and of the city of Chur (from 1466), the names of the Col and Dents des Bouquetins, near Arolla, and those of the well known Hôtels Steinbock at Chur and at Lauterbrunnen all serve to show that the steinbock was once no rare phenomenon in the Swiss Alps.† An allied wild goat is found in the Pyrenees, and in other mountains of Spain, the Pyrenean tur (*Capra pyrenaica* ‡); other wild goats are found in Crete, and in the Caucasus.

The deer of Switzerland belong to the South German forms—the red deer (*Cervus elaphus*) and the roebuck (*Capreolus capræa*). Neither of these ranges to so great an elevation in the Alps as the chamois or the

---
* See a notice of this book in the *Alpine Journal*, vol. xiii. pp. 344-7.
† See Dr. Girtanner's monograph, *Der Alpensteinbock* (Trèves, 1878), of which an Italian translation appeared in the *Bollettino del Club Alpino Italiano*, 1879, pp. 412-461. A short article on bouquetins by Mr. Coolidge in the *Alpine Journal*, vol. xvii. pp. 193-6 (an addition on p. 276), is followed by a detailed list of allusions and articles relating to bouquetins.
‡ See Mr. Buxton's *Short Stalks*, First Series, chap. vii.

ibex, the firmer feet and coarser digestive apparatus of the two latter animals enabling them to ascend to higher vertical zones, and to subsist on a less nutritive diet than the cervine ruminants. The hog of Switzerland is of the same race as the wild boar of France and Germany.

2. The *Chiroptera*, or bats, of the Alps are confined chiefly to the mountains of inferior height, and do not ascend above the snow line. The ordinary Pipistrelle bat (*Vesperugo pipistrellus*), the noctule (*V. noctula*), the barbastelle (*Synotus barbastellus*), the small horseshoe bat (*Rhinolophus hipposideros*), the great horseshoe bat (*R. ferrum equinum*), Natterer's bat (*Vespertilio nattereri*), and the large-eared bat (*Plecotus auritus*) belong to the Alpine fauna. It is stated that other species have been found, but according to F. von Tschudi they are of less frequent occurrence than the species named above.

3. The Alpine *Insectivora* are all of a characteristically European type. The hedgehog (*Erinaceus europæus*), the Alpine shrew (*Sorex alpinus*), and the water shrew (*Crossopus fodiens*) are Alpine forms. The white-toothed shrew (*Cocidura leucodon*), a beautiful species, of which the back is reddish brown and the belly white, is also frequently met with. Besides these the mole (*Talpa europæa*) is common, and is even found in places, like the Urseren valley, surrounded on every side by rocky ground in which the animal cannot subsist.

4. The *Rodentia* of the Alps are not numerous. The marmot, 'Murmelthier' or (in patois) 'Munk' (*Arctomys marmotta*), is to be found in its small burrows up to the snow line; it is persecuted for the sake of its flesh (considered a great delicacy by the Alpine folk) by hunters, who sell its fat at a high price as a remedial agent. Several kinds of campagnol (*Arvicola*) occur in the Alps, amongst which is the snow mouse (*A. nivalis*), a peculiar species, first discovered on the Faulhorn by Martins and Bravais in 1841. The mountain hare (*Lepus variabilis*) is also found in the Alps; the same species extends from the 55th parallel in the eastern hemisphere northward to the Arctic circle.

5. *Alpine Birds.*—The distribution of birds in the Alps is peculiarly interesting owing to the great variety of elevation, and therefore also of food, temperature, and cover. The mountainous district may be roughly divided into three successive regions of elevation, each with its characteristic avifauna.

(1) The region of the *valleys and lakes*, with the slopes immediately above them up to 3,000 ft. Here the species are numerous, and in great part identical with those of southern England. Some striking differences, however, will be noticed at once. The black redstart is perhaps the most abundant bird, and plays for the Swiss peasant the part of our robin; our pied wagtail is replaced by the white wagtail (*Motacilla alba*); the willow warbler, so abundant with us, is rarely heard, while Bonelli's warbler is abundant on all wooded slopes. The rook is seldom to be found, while the crow is abundant and gregarious. Of species rarely or never met with in England may be mentioned the serin finch, the crag martin, the Alpine swift (which breeds in the tower of the Münster at Bern), the meadow bunting (*Emberiza cia*), and the marsh warbler (*Acrocephalus palustris*), which here seems to take the place of our common sedge warbler. Ducks, sandpipers, and other water-loving

birds are rarely met with in summer; but the dipper is common, and on the lakes the black-headed and common gulls may be seen, as well as the black and common terns. The white-tailed eagle, the osprey, and the black kite are often seen on or near the great lakes.

(2) On ascending to the *middle region* (3,000 to 6,000 ft.) we find on its pastures and in its forests a comparatively new avifauna, though in summer some species are common to this and the lower region. This is the home of the woodpeckers; besides our three English species we have here in the pine woods the great black woodpecker and the rarer three-toed woodpecker (*Picus tridactylus*), while among deciduous trees the grey woodpecker (*P. canus*) occurs. The pines are full of titmice, including the crested titmouse, which is hardly less common than the other species. Nutcrackers and jays are here found in summer up to 6,000 ft., but descend to a lower level in autumn. With these are crossbills, robins, nuthatches, and, in sunny spots, siskins and the interesting citril finch (*Chrysomitris citrinella*). Of the grouse kind the capercaillie, the black grouse, and the hazel grouse are met with; but these seem to be getting rarer in the Central Alps. Owls, including Tengmalm's owl and the great eagle owl, are not uncommon, but are seldom seen by travellers.

(3) The third region includes the *highest pastures*, which the cattle do not reach till mid-July, *and the desolate tract of rock and snow above them*. Here the species are fewer, but of great interest. On the pastures breed the Alpine accentor and Alpine pipit (*Anthus spinoletta*), the ring ouzel, and the mealy redpoll. Still higher may be found the beautiful snow finch, which builds where it can on human habitations, as at the Furka and the St. Gotthard, and 'packs' in late summer in large flocks. The partridge of this region is the so called Greek redleg (*Caccabis saxatilis*, or *Steinhuhn*); the grouse is the common ptarmigan (*Schneehuhn*), which in summer is found at great altitudes, and even on the summit of Monte Rosa. On rocks above glaciers (such as the Aletsch) the mountaineer may look out for the red-winged wall-creeper (*Tichodroma muraria*), which is also found at lower elevations. Perhaps the most characteristic bird of the mountains is the Alpine chough, which breeds in rocks at 8,000 ft. and higher; beautiful as it is in form and flight, it shares here, with its relative the raven, the reputation of being a bird of ill omen, and is apt to appear over the precipices when bad weather is at hand, and when the climber is involved in difficulties. The birds of prey are hardly so numerous here as might be expected; the great bearded vulture (*Lämmergeier*) is fast becoming extinct in Switzerland, and the golden eagle is rare.

The above account of the distribution refers to the summer only; but it should be added that the movements of Alpine birds in spring and autumn offer a very interesting study. For further information the reader is referred to papers in the 'Ibis' (1887 and 1891), by Mr. Howard Saunders and Mr. Scott Wilson, and to two chapters in 'A Year with the Birds,' by W. Warde Fowler. (W. W. F.)

6. *Alpine Reptiles and Batrachians.*—The common frog (*Rana temporaria*) and the common lizard (*Lacerta vivipara*) are found at the height of nearly 10,000 feet, the Alpine newt (*Molge alpestris*) and the

viper (*Vipera berus*), at nearly 9,000 feet, the common toad (*Bufo vulgaris*), and the slow-worm (*Anguis fragilis*) at 7,000 feet, and the common snake (*Tropidonotus natrix*) at 5,000 feet. All these species, however, are also met with, at least locally, in the plain. One species only can be considered as exclusively Alpine, the black salamander (*Salamandra atra*), which occurs at between 2,500 and 10,000 feet. On the southern aspect of the Alps a second species of viper (*Vipera aspis*) ascends to 6,500 feet.

7. *Alpine Fishes.*—Few fishes are found at great altitudes. These are the minnow (*Leuciscus phaxinus*) to 8,000 feet, miller's thumb (*Cottus gobio*) to 7,000 feet, the trout (*Salmo fario*) to 6,500 feet, the loach (*Cobitis barbatula*) to 5,500 feet, and the grayling (*Thymallus vexillifer*) to 4,500 feet. The occurrence of other fishes, such as the burbot (*Lota vulgaris*) at 5,500 feet, the rudd (*Leuciscus erythropthalmus*) at 6,000 feet, the perch (*Perca fluviatilis*), the carp (*Cyprinus carpio*), and the tench (*Tinca vulgaris*) at from 4,000 to 5,000 feet, is probably the result of importation from lower altitudes. The presence of trout in the Sgrischus lake in the Fex glen, above Sils, in the Upper Engadine, at a height of 8,600 feet, is also probably to be ascribed to human agency.

8. *Invertebrata.*—Many of the numerous groups of Invertebrates attain high altitudes in the Alps, but when application is made for definite information it is astonishing to find how small our knowledge of the Alpine invertebrate fauna is. It is, therefore, certain that travellers who collect specimens at accurately ascertained heights will aid the progress of natural science. What is known is of much interest. Mr. A. E. Craven, in 1888, took, near Zermatt, *Helix harpa*, a snail otherwise known only from South America, Lapland, and Amurland. *Vitrina diaphana*, another snail which is common enough all over France and Germany, ranges as high as 7,500 feet. Protective colouring is exhibited by the high-ranging grasshopper (*Ædipoda fasciata*), which is clearly seen when on the wing; but becomes almost, if not quite, invisible when it closes its wings, and settles on the rock.

As regards Alpine *Butterflies*, a good idea of the various kinds may be gained from a paper by the late W. A. Forbes in the 'Entomologist's Monthly Magazine' for 1879. Beetles are rarer at great heights than butterflies; bees are occasionally carried up by the wind or desire of exploration to heights of over 12,500 feet, and of the other orders of insects it can only be said that the Alpine species are very poorly represented in public collections in this country.

A scorpion (*Euscorpius germanicus*) is found at heights between 5,000 and 7,000 feet, and two species of earthworms (*Allobophora profuga* and *Lumbricus castaneus*) were collected at 5,500 feet by Mr. Whymper.

With regard to the deep-water fauna of the Alpine lakes Professor Forel, of Morges, and other naturalists have worked assiduously on this subject.

BOOKS TO CONSULT.

The chief authority on Alpine Zoology is F. von Tschudi's 'Das Thierleben der Alpen,' first published in 1853, which has passed through ten editions in

German, and was translated into English in 1858; see also V. Fatio's 'Faune des Vertébrés de la Suisse' (5 vols. 1869-1894). A recent pamphlet, 'Alpenthiere im Wechsel der Zeit,' by Conrad Zeller (Leipzig, 1892), gives a sketch of the history of the subject. See too the zoological section (by K. W. v. Dalla Torre) of the 'Anleitung zu wissenschaftlichen Beobachtungen auf Alpenreisen,' published at Vienna between 1878 and 1882, by the German and Austrian Alpine Club.

Art. XIII.—Climate and Vegetation of the Alps.*

CONTENTS.

		PAGE
1. Climate and Vegetation of the Alps		ciii
2. Additional Notes :—		
(a) *Climate of the Alps.*		
i. Diminution of the Pressure of the Air		cviii
ii. Increase of the Intensity of Solar Radiation		cviii
iii. Fall of the Temperature with Increased Altitude		cix
iv. Aqueous Vapour in the Alpine Air		cix
v. Winds in the Alps		cx
(b) *Vegetation of the Alps.*		
i. General Conditions affecting Plant Life		cxi
ii. The Direct Effect of the Alpine Climate upon the Forms of Alpine Plants		cxiv
iii. The Flowers of Alpine Plants		cxv
iv. Origin of the Alpine Flora		cxix

The narrow limits of this Introduction admit but of a brief reference to a subject which it is difficult to treat without entering into some detail. The climate of the Alps determines the character of the vegetation, and upon this depend the occupations and manner of life of the inhabitants. Writers upon this subject have attached too much importance to the absolute height above the sea-level, as though this had a predominant influence upon the climate; whereas the position of each locality in respect to the great mountain masses, and the local conditions of exposure to the sun and protection from all cold winds, or the reverse, are of primary importance in deciding the climate and the vegetation.

Olive Region.—Along the southern base of the Alps we find a first illustration of the remark above made. The climate of the lower declivities and the mouths of the valleys is markedly warmer than that of the plains of Piedmont and Lombardy. While the winter climate of Milan is colder than that of Edinburgh, the olive ripens its fruit along the skirts of the mountain region, and penetrates to a certain distance towards the interior of the chain along the lakes and the wider valleys of the Southern Alps. The olive has even become wild on the shores of the Lake of Garda, where the evergreen oak is indigenous, and lemons are grown on a large scale, with partial protection during the winter. The climate of the Borromean islands and some points on the shores of the Lago Maggiore is known to permit the growth of many plants of the warmer temperate zone, while at a distance of a few miles, and close to

---

* This article has been carefully revised throughout by Mr. Percy Groom, M.A., F.L.S., who is solely responsible for the valuable 'Additional Notes' which follow the revised text.

the shores of the same lake, but in positions exposed to the cold winds from the Alps, plants of the Alpine region grow freely, and no delicate perennials can survive the winter. As regards the conditions under which the olive flourishes, it requires a *dry* soil, and is at home in regions of Italy where the summer is dry. According to Grisebach at Nice the olive unfolds its buds in the month of January, when the temperature is 8·2° cent., but the fruits do not ripen till the following November. At Lugano, for instance, the mean temperature in January is ·9° cent., in February 4·2°, and it is not till March and April that the mean temperature, 8·2° cent., is passed. Thus it appears that the tardy awakening of the olive at Lugano would not permit it to ripen its fruit, though it might allow its existence. In the canton of Tessin, of which Lugano is one of the chief towns, the annual mean minimum in winter (for twelve years) was −6·8°, at which temperature the olive is not killed. At Montpellier, where the tree flourishes, the mean minimum is −9·23°. Martins says that the olive is not seriously menaced at −15·9⅜°. Its successful cultivation may be held to indicate a winter in which frosts are neither long nor severe, where the mean temperature of winter does not fall below 42° Fahr., and a heat of at least 75° Fahr. during the day is continued through four or five months of the summer and autumn.

Vine Region.—The vine is far more tolerant of cold than the olive, and will produce fruit with a much lower summer temperature; but to give tolerable wine it demands, at the season of the ripening of the grape, a degree of heat not much below that needed by the olive. These conditions are satisfied throughout a great part of the Alpine chain in the deeper valleys, and in favourable situations up to a considerable height on their northern slopes. While the olive region is but exceptionally represented on the S. side, the vine not only extends to form a girdle round the base of the chain, but reaches near to the very foot of the greater peaks. The fitness of a particular spot for the production of wine depends far more on the direction of the valley, and of the prevailing winds, than on its height. Hence it happens that in the Canton of the Vallais, the valley of the Arc in Savoy, and some others on the N. side of the dividing range, tolerable wine is made at a higher level than in the valleys of Lombardy, whose direction allows the free passage of the keen northern blasts. It is not uncommon to see vineyards rising in terraces on the N. slope, exposed to the full force of the sun, while on the opposite declivity the pine descends to the level of the valley. The vine in the Alps often resists a winter temperature which would kill it down to the roots in the low country, possibly because of the protection afforded by the deep winter snow. An early thaw followed by spring frosts often injures the crop. A mean summer temperature of 68° Fahr. is considered necessary to produce tolerable wine, but in most of the places where the vine is grown in the Alps the heat rises, at least occasionally, much beyond the required limit. In fine weather the thermometer often stands at and above 80° Fahr. in the shade in the valleys. Along with the vine many species of wild plants, especially annuals, characteristic of the flora of the S. of Europe, show themselves in the valleys of the Alps.

The Mountain Region, or Region of Deciduous Trees.—Many writers take the growth of corn as the characteristic of the colder temperate zone, corresponding to what has been called the mountain region of the Alps. But so many varieties of all the common species, with widely different requirements, are in cultivation, that it is impossible to identify the growth of cereals in general with any natural division of the surface. A more natural limit is marked by the presence of the principal deciduous trees. Although the oak, beech, and ash do not reach exactly the same height, and are not often present together in the Alps, their upper limit corresponds accurately enough to that transition from a temperate to a colder climate that is shown by a general change in the wild herbaceous vegetation. The lower limit of this district is, as we have seen, too irregular to admit of definition; its upper boundary, marked by the gradual disappearance of the above-mentioned trees, is at about 4,000 ft. on the N. side of the Alps, and often rises to 5,500 ft. on the southern slopes. It would be a mistake to suppose that the aspect of this region is mainly characterised by its tree vegetation. The climate appears to be favourable to one or other of the trees which have been named as marking its limits, but the interference of man has done much to eradicate them. It is probable that at a very early date they were extensively destroyed for use in building, and to clear space for meadow and pasture land; so that, if we except the beech forests of the Austrian Alps, there is scarcely a considerable wood of deciduous trees to be seen anywhere in the chain. In many districts, where population is not too dense, the Scotch pine (*P. sylvestris*) and spruce (*Picea excelsa*) have taken the place of the oak and beech, mainly because the young plants are not so eagerly attacked by goats, the great destroyers of tree vegetation. On the S. side of the Alps the chestnut, although naturally an inhabitant of a warmer region, has in many districts replaced the other deciduous trees, rising to within 1,000 ft. of the same height, being met by the spruce, which descends through the intermediate space. To this region belong many of the lower ranges on the outskirts of the Alpine chain, and some highland pastoral districts, such as those of the Bauges, in Savoy, of the Swiss Canton of Appenzell, and the plateaux of the Venetian Alps between the Adige and the Piave. We find here one form of the peculiar condition of society charactertstic of the Alpine highlands, but this is more conveniently described in connection with the next region. The annual mean temperature of this region is not very different from that of the British Islands, but the climatal conditions are as different as possible. Here snow lies for several months together, till it disappears rapidly in a few weeks of warm spring weather, and gives place to a summer considerably warmer than the average of our seasons.

The Subalpine Region, or Region of Coniferous Trees.—This is the region which mainly determines the manner of life of the population of the Alps. On a rough estimate of the region lying between the summits of the Alps and the plain country that encircles them, we may reckon the whole amount of land in cultivation at about one-quarter of the surface, and of which but little more than a half is under vineyards or corn-fields, and the remainder produces forage and artificial meadow. Nearly another quarter may be set down as utterly barren, consisting of snow-fields, glaciers, bare rock, lakes, and the beds of streams, leaving about one-half of the entire surface which is divided between forest and grass land, either natural meadow or pasture. These proportions show clearly that if any considerable population is to derive a subsistence from the soil, it must be from feeding animals, and not from the direct production of human food. It is principally from the subalpine region that these animals draw their support. Grass-land is, indeed, abundant in some parts of the mountain region, but it is chiefly reserved for hay, while the upper pastures of the subalpine and Alpine regions support the herds and flocks during the fine season. Botanically this region is best distinguished by the prevalence of coniferous trees, forming vast forests that, if not kept down by man, and by the tooth of the goat, would cover the slopes of the Alps. The prevalent species are the spruce (*Picea excelsa*) and the silver fir (*Abies pectinata*). In granitic districts the larch (*Larix Europœa*) flourishes, and reaches a greater size than any other tree. Less common are the Scotch pine (*Pinus sylvestris*) and the arolla (*Pinus cembra*) or Siberian fir. In the Eastern Alps the mughus, dwarf-pine, or *Krummholz* (*Pinus pumilio*) of the Germans, becomes conspicuous, forming a distinct zone on the higher mountains, above the level of its cogeners. The pine forests play a most important part in the natural economy of the Alps, and their preservation is a matter of vital consequence to the future inhabitants. Through ignorance or recklessness, the destruction of the forests has in some districts been carried much too far; for the present gain derived from the sale of timber, and the additional space gained for pasture, may be dearly purchased by future sterility. In the Northern Alps the coniferous trees scarcely attain to a height of 6,000 ft., while on the S. side they often reach 7,000 ft. The larch, the arolla, and the mughus are the species that ascend highest, not uncommonly surpassing the above limits.

The Alpine Region.—In defiance of etymology, which would make the term Alpine coextensive with the entire tract available for pasturing cattle, this epithet has been attached by writers of authority to the zone of vegetation extending between the upper limit of trees and the first appearance of permanent masses of snow. Shrubs are not wanting throughout this region. The common rhododendron, several small species of Alpine willow, and the common juniper extend up to, the latter even beyond, the level of perpetual snow. It is in this region that the botanist finds fully developed the peculiar vegetation characteristic of the Alps. Many alpine species may, indeed, be found here and there at lower levels, either accidentally transported from their natural home, or finding a permanent refuge in some cool spot sheltered from the sun, and moistened by streamlets descending from the snow region; but it is here that the varied species of saxifrage, primrose, pedicularis, anemone, gentian, and other genera that give to the Alpine flora its utmost brilliancy of hue, have their peculiar home. In valleys where pasturage is scarce, the inhabitants are forced to send their cattle up to the very limit of vegetation in order to support them during the summer, while the grass of the subalpine region is in great part turned into hay for winter use. In such cases one or two men remain for several weeks on some isolated slope of Alpine pasture, many hours' walk from the nearest village, until the day arrives when the cattle are led back, perhaps across a glacier, or by some very difficult track, to the lower chalet which serves as an intermediate station between their summer and winter quarters. In other parts of the Alps, where sheep and goats are more common, the pastures of the higher region are left exclusively to them. The limits of this region in the Northern Alps may be fixed between 6,000 to 8,000 ft. above the sea, and at least 1,000 ft. higher on the S. slopes of the Alps and in some parts of the main chain. In Piedmont it is not uncommon to find chalets at 8,500 ft. above the sea-level, and vegetation often extends freely up to 9,500 ft.

The Glacial Region.—This comprehends all that portion of the Alps that rises above the limit of perpetual snow. We continue to use that term, which is convenient and cannot well be replaced, but without explanation it is apt to mislead.

Since the mean temperature becomes constantly lower as we ascend above the sea-level, there must be some point at which more snow falls in each year than is melted, or carried off by the wind, or otherwise removed. It is found that, one year with another, this occurs at pretty nearly the same point, and that the same patches or fields of snow are found to cover the same slopes of the mountain. But we never find, unless after fresh snow, that the entire surface of a mountain above a certain height is covered with a continuous sheet of snow. The form of the surface causes more snow to rest on some parts than upon others; the prevalent winds blow away the freshly fallen snow from the exposed ridges, and cause it to drift in the hollows; and the sun acts with great force, even on the highest peaks, upon the slopes fully exposed to his rays. The consequence is, that portions of the surface remain bare at heights greatly exceeding the so called limit of perpetual snow; and that limit is far from retaining a constant elevation throughout the Alps, or even on opposite sides of the same mountain. The term, nevertheless, has a definite meaning when rightly understood. Leaving out of account masses of snow that casually accumulate in hollows shaded from the sun, the formation of permanent snow-fields takes place at about the same height when the conditions are similar. Hence it happens that, on viewing an Alpine range from a distance, the larger patches and fields of snow on adjoining mountains, with the same aspect, are seen to maintain a pretty constant level. Vegetation becomes scarce in this region; all the more level parts are covered with ice or snow, and the higher we ascend, the less of the surface remains bare, with the exception of projecting masses of rock, which usually undergo rapid disintegration from the freezing of whatever water finds its way into the superficial fissures. Many species of flowering plants have nevertheless been found at a height of 11,000 ft., and even above 12,000 ft. As only a thin covering of snow can rest upon rocks that lie at an angle exceeding 60°, and this is soon removed by the wind or melted by the sun, some portions of rock remain bare even at the greatest height attained by the peaks of the Alps. There is, indeed, reason to believe that the quantity of snow falling on the higher summits is very much less than falls a few thousand feet lower down.

2. ADDITIONAL NOTES.

(a) *Climate of the Alps.*

i. *Diminution of the Pressure of the Air.*—As we ascend a mountain the air constantly becomes more and more rarefied. The actual rate at which the atmospheric pressure, registered by the barometer, falls with increasing altitude depends, however, on the temperature, the rate of decrease in the pressure of the air being slower at high temperatures than at low ones. These facts are illustrated by observations made at the Hospice on the Great St. Bernard Pass and on the St. Théodule Pass.

—	Height	Mean Annual Atmospheric Pressure in Millimètres of Mercury	Deviations from the Annual Mean Atmospheric Pressure	
			Cold Month (March)	Warm Month (July)
Great St. Bernard	2,472 m. (8,111 ft.)	563·9	−4·2	+4·6
St. Théodule	3,322 m. (10,899 ft.)	506·2	−4·6	+5·8

ii. *Increase of the Intensity of Solar Radiation.*—The higher a spot is situated above the sea-level the thinner will be the stratum of air interposed between the sun and that spot; hence the less will be the amount of sunlight which is intercepted and absorbed by the air before reaching the earth. The sun's rays will thus strike the earth at the top of a mountain with greater intensity than at the foot of it. This increased intensity of insolation with rise above the sea-level is not due solely to the decreased thickness of the layer of air intervening between sun and earth. It is further occasioned by the simultaneous diminution in the absolute amount of aqueous vapour in the atmosphere. Consequently intensity of insolation increases more rapidly than the atmospheric pressure lessens, with rise in altitude. M. Violle's and M. Margottet's simultaneous measurements on the summit of Mont Blanc and at the foot of the Bossons glacier illustrate this. They were made on August 16 and 17, 1875, both fine days.

—	Altitude	Atmospheric Pressure in Mm.	Pressure of Aqueous Vapour	Relative Intensity of the Sun's Rays
Mont Blanc	4,810 m. (15,782 ft.)	430	1	·94
Bossons glacier	1,200 m. (3,937 ft.)	661	5·3	·79

This intense insolation at increased altitudes causes by day a greater difference between the temperature in the shade and in sunlight, and also between the temperature of the air and that of the soil. M. Charles Martins's observations made in the Pyrenees illustrate this last statement. His measurements were made on three fine days in September, the two points being less than fifteen miles apart.

	Altitude	Mean Temperature of	
		Soil	Air
Bagnères	551 m. (1,808 ft.)	36·1° (cent.)	22·3° (cent.)
Pic du Midi	2,877 m. (9,439 ft.)	33·8° ,,	10·1° ,,

The same circumstances which lead to magnified insolation by day cause a constantly increasing radiation of heat from the earth's surface by night as the altitude is greater. Comparing, for instance, Chamonix with the Grand Plateau on Mont Blanc, situated 2,882 m. higher, radiation at night was nearly twice as great at the higher spot. The temperature of the snow sank, on the nights of August 28-31, to −19·2° (cent.), whilst the temperature of the air was −6·5° (cent.) Thus it comes to pass that on mountains more intense insolation by day, together with increased radiation by night, causes the soil to undergo greater changes of temperature than in the plains below.

iii. *Fall of the Temperature with Increased Altitude.*—As we ascend a mountain the temperature of the air falls about half a degree (cent.) for each 100 yards of vertical ascent. The exact rate of the fall of the temperature varies slightly according to the aspect, the mean temperature, and the configuration of the mountain. Both the diurnal and the annual variations of temperature of the air decrease as the altitude increases. On the St. Théodule Pass (3,322 mètres, 10,899 ft.) the mean monthly temperature of the air is below freezing point in all months excepting June (0° cent.), July (1° cent.), August (1·1° cent.), and September (1·1° cent.) Observations there in 1865-6 showed that the temperature of the air rose above 0° cent. four times in May, though but twice in October, and then only at midday, while in the four months from June to September the temperature of the air rose at about midday (1 o'clock actually) 110 out of 122 days. At night it exceeded 0° cent. on no occasion in June, but in the three following months it did so eleven times. Thus in the higher region of the Alps the temperature of the air falls below freezing point on most summer nights.

iv. *Aqueous Vapour in the Alpine Air.*—The *absolute amount* of water vapour in the air diminishes with increasing altitude more rapidly than does the atmospheric pressure. But the *relative humidity, i.e.* the degree to which the air is saturated with aqueous vapour, shows no *regular* changes as the altitude varies. That is to say, though the air at the top of a mountain contains less aqueous vapour than that at the foot, it is not necessarily drier. In the Alps it appears that, on the average, above the altitude of 1,000 mètres, the air is drier in winter and moister in summer than below that limit. The important and prominent feature of the hygrometric condition of the air at great heights in the Alps is the rapid changes in the relative humidity of the air in fine weather: wet fogs and mist alternate with spells of fine weather, during which the air may be extremely dry.

The *rate of evaporation* is greatly accelerated on mountains, in consequence of the diminished pressure of the air. In addition the extreme dryness of the air on fine days aids the process. Consequently objects dry rapidly on the mountains; perspiration evaporates quickly from the human body, the skin tends to become parched, and the feeling of thirst is increased.

Cloudiness.—As might be anticipated from some previous remarks the cloudiest weather in the Alps is in the spring and summer, but in the low-lying parts of Switzerland it is in winter.

Rainfall.—On many mountains the fall of rain (including snow) increases with the rise above the sea-level, but only to a certain altitude, above which it again diminishes. It is, therefore, possible that the maximum snowfall is not on the actual summits of the Alps.

Duration of the Snow.—The snow line descends to its lowest limit at the end of January, after which it gradually ascends till it attains its highest point (*circa* 2,700 mètres, or 8,859 ft.) about August. In the middle of March the snow clothes the mountains to approximately the same extent as in the middle of December; even at the end of October the snow line (*circa* 1,510 mètres, or 4,954 ft.) is higher than at the end of May (*circa* 1,470 mètres, or 4,823 ft.)

v. *Winds in the Alps.*—In the Alps, as on other mountains, the general rule holds good that during the day-time there is a wind ascending from the valleys to the mountain tops, whereas at night-time the exact contrary takes place. These alternating day and night winds are familiar to the inhabitants of the different regions of the Alpine chain, and are known by various local names.

The diurnal formation of clouds and rain is greatly influenced by these winds. The wind ascending the slopes by day takes with it the moisture from the valleys, and dries the air of the latter. As the air ascends it cools, and the moisture condenses in the form of clouds hovering on or over the mountain tops, or even forms rain. The descending night wind dissipates the clouds, and carries moisture down to the valleys.

The *Föhn wind* is a warm, dry, irregular wind, blowing from southern points (S., S.E., or, rarely, S.W.) It blows about thirty to forty days in the year, most frequently in autumn and winter, least often in summer. On a winter's day it causes the temperature of the air to be as high as in summer, and the atmosphere to become extraordinarily dry. It is greeted with joy in spring-time, because in one day it melts enormous masses of snow and ice, doing, according to Hann, as much work in this direction as the sun unaided would normally accomplish in fourteen days.

(b) *Vegetation of the Alps.*

In discussing the causes of the presence of a plant in a certain region it is necessary to answer two questions: 'How did the plant originally come there?' and 'What characters enable it still to exist there?' Similarly, in dealing with the form and behaviour of the plant, two problems present themselves: 'To what extent are the characters of the plant due to those of its ancestors?' and 'How far are they to be attributed to the direct action on a plant of its surroundings?'

i. *General Conditions affecting Plant Life.*—A plant derives its food from the soil and the air. The green parts, particularly the leaves, under the influence of light, absorb carbonic acid from the atmosphere. In order to build up new plant material the carbon thus absorbed by the leaves requires to be supplemented by water and substances contained in solution in the soil. The latter are absorbed by the roots, and conveyed up the stems to the leaves, where they combine with the carbon to form complex food substances (process of *assimilation*). From the leaves the excess of water is excreted, mainly in the form of vapour (process of *transpiration*). For its existence and growth an ordinary plant requires carbonic acid and oxygen (both occurring in the air), water, and substances in solution (found in the soil); and further needs an adequate supply of light and an appropriate temperature.

Effect of Temperature.—As a rule flowering plants exhibit no vital activity at a temperature below the freezing point of water. Usually a temperature several degrees above this point is essential to arouse the growth of a plant. No experiments have been made with regard to this question upon plants growing at high Alpine altitudes. It is, however, known that certain of them can push out their flowers just at the snow line in the melting or unmelted snow (*Crocus vernus, Soldanella alpina* and *S. pusilla, Ranunculus alpestris, Anemone vernalis,* &c.) It is safe to assume that when they are at a temperature below $0°$ cent. the vast majority of Alpine plants are incapable of any appreciable vegetative activity. They must, therefore, rest during the long season at which the temperature is very low and the ground is covered with snow. It is impossible to foretell by means of observations on the temperature of the air at different altitudes when the plants at those altitudes will first commence active vegetation in the summer, or first enter upon a rest at the approach of the winter. One reason of this is that the distribution of snow over the surface is not equable, and the intense insolation may cause the temperature of patches of ground uncovered with snow to rise considerably above that of the surrounding air. The active vegetative season at the different altitudes, however, has been found to run parallel with the mean monthly temperature and the rate at which the snow line ascends. For instance, the mean monthly temperature of the air on the St. Théodule Pass (3,322 mètres) does not reach as high as $0°$ cent. till June, but remains above this point during the three following months, and sinks again below it in October. Again, the snow line in the Alps at the end of May is lower than it is at the end of October; it lies at about the same altitude at the end of September as it does towards the end of June. Both these sets of facts correspond to the late commencement of spring, and the lingering second summer in autumn time, also to the short vegetative season and the long period of rest.

Owing to this shortness of the active season plants at high altitudes in the Alps require to produce flowers rapidly and to mature their seeds quickly. As an aid in this respect many Alpine plants have relatively well developed subterranean stems, or thick roots, in which they store food during winter, so that at the commencement of the active season the reserve stock of food may be at once available for the rapid production of new leaves and flowers. Later in the season, when the leaves are actively manufacturing food, the nutriment is being consumed not only in the production of seeds and in growth, but is also being stored up in the subterranean parts for use in the following spring.

In the lowlands of Switzerland, as elsewhere in Europe, there exists a considerable number of *annuals*, *i.e.* plants which in a single season germinate from seeds, produce flowers and seeds, and then die. They rest during the unfavourable season only in the form of seeds. Opposed to these are *perennial* plants, which can live year after year, and can rest during the unfavourable season. The shortness and severity of the Alpine summer would render the continued existence of *annuals* precarious, because one especially severe season, by preventing the ripening of fruits, would threaten an annual species with extermination. In addition the annuals labour under the disadvantage that a seed cannot store up such a large amount of food as a subterranean organ of a mature plant, nor can the root of a tiny seedling at once have at its command such supplies of water and substances in the soil as an already well developed plant. Hence at high altitudes very few annuals occur in the Alps; and the few which exist there are, for the most part, small plants living in a moist sand (e.g. *Gentiana tenella*). Kerner gives the following numbers, which illustrate the gradual disappearance of annuals in the Alps: on the Danube plains there are in every 100 plants 56 annuals and 44 perennials, whereas in the Alps out of every 100 plants 4 only are annuals and 96 perennials.

Even when the plants are in a state of activity variations of the temperature influence their behaviour. There is for each of the various functions a certain *minimum* temperature, below which the function is in abeyance. Above this each rise in temperature causes the process to become more active, till a certain *optimum* temperature is attained, above which again there may be a waning of activity, till at a certain maximum temperature the performance of the function ceases. This holds good for the processes of absorption by means of the roots and leaves and the process of growth. The process of transpiration has, however, no temperature maximum or minimum. The temperature of the Alpine plant depends more on the illumination than on the temperature of the air, and it is quite impossible to dissociate the influence of temperature, light, and moisture on active vegetative processes in Alpine plants.

Effect of Light.—Light is essential to green plants in order that they may obtain from the air the carbonic acid required for their continued existence. Light directly promotes assimilation and transpiration by the leaves, and indirectly accelerates absorption of liquids on the part of the root; and the activity of these processes is proportional to the intensity of the light. Light has the reverse effect on growth in the length of stems, as it retards the process with a strength proportional to its intensity.

Effect of the Relative Humidity of the Air.—Dryness in the air promotes transpiration; moisture in the air has the reverse effect. Indirectly the same effects are produced on the rate of absorption by the roots.

Effect of the Rarefaction of the Air.—The decreased pressure of the air promotes transpiration, but by diluting the carbonic acid in the atmosphere retards the assimilation of carbon.

Relation of the Behaviour of Alpine Plants to Climate.—These brief considerations with reference to the influence of temperature and light, as well as moisture and pressure in the air, suffice to show that Alpine plants are exposed to considerable risks. The most striking danger appears to be loss of too much water by excessive transpiration. Intense insolation, the frequent dryness of the air, and its low pressure all unite in inducing rapid transpiration. During the day-time, however, the intense insolation, inasmuch as it warms the soil to a temperature considerably above that of the air, at the same time promotes absorption by means of the roots. At night-time intense radiation cools the soil to such a degree as seriously to retard, or quite stop, absorption of water from the soil, and a plant itself is almost equally cooled, but the air is not. Hence at night-time the plant is doubly in danger of being dried up, owing to the fact that conditions causing the slowing of the absorption of water are not counterbalanced by external influences initiating an equivalent retardation of its exhalation of aqueous vapour. These considerations, together with the necessity of having a proper proportion between transpiration and the absorption of carbonic acid by the leaves, give the clue to the structure of many of the Alpine plants. In the first place an extensive development of the subterranean parts is very characteristic, and this, apart from the significance already attached to it, is of importance in that a large surface is thus provided for absorbing nutritive bodies and water from the soil. The Alpine plants are usually of low stature, often forming little mats of turf, or even hemispherical cushions, with close-set, small leaves. As examples of plants forming mats or cushions the following may be mentioned: *Petrocallis pyrenaica*, a number of species of *Draba*, *Silene pumilio* and *S. acaulis*, *Cherleria sedoides*, some species of *Androsace*, including *A. imbricata* and *A. helvetica* (both of which form small, hemispherical mounds), *Herniaria alpina*, and a number of species of *Saxifraga*. Even where no distinct tufts or mats are formed the leaves are frequently arranged in rosettes, pressed against the ground. In all these cases the leaves are set closely together, and only the flower stalks, when of any length, represent an elongated stem. This compressed arrangement of the leaves diminishes transpiration by exposing less of the leaf surface freely to the atmosphere, and by leading to the accumulation of moisture in the air between the leaves. In many cases the small size of the leaves works in the same direction. Transpiration is often further depressed by the copious development of hairs (*e.g.* in Edelweiss), by succulence in relatively decreasing the surface in comparison with the volume (e.g. *Sedum sempervivum*), or by the stiff or leathery nature of the leaves, which are then clothed with a thicker, more impermeable membrane. It will, therefore, be found that there are many Alpine plants which have small, stiff leaves, with a greater or less extent of succulence or hairiness. Occasionally the exposed surface of the leaf is diminished by the blade being rolled on itself (in some grasses and *Empetrum nigrum*). The low stature of the Alpine plants possibly confers a double advantage, first by diminishing the effect of wind (which increases transpiration) and secondly by placing the plant in a layer of atmosphere which soon tends to assume the temperature of the soil and the plant, particularly at night-time. In contrast to those Alpine plants, which are obviously constructed in harmony with their surroundings, there are others which appear to be devoid of any special structural characteristic enabling them to economise water. These may have relatively tall leafy stems, or comparatively large, thin, smooth leaves. At present no sufficient explanation has been offered which will account for the power undoubtedly possessed by these forms of resisting the trying Alpine conditions. Neither can we offer any adequate reasons for the power which Alpine plants possess of withstanding the almost regular frosts at night-time in summer; we can only assume that it is a character stamped into their 'constitution.' The relatively large amount of green colouring matter in Alpine plants, which is to be noted by their frequently dark green colour, enables them to absorb sufficient carbonic acid, in spite of the shortness of the vegetative season and the rarefaction of the air.

ii. *The Direct Effect of the Alpine Climate upon the Forms of Alpine Plants.*—If we succeed in cultivating in our gardens plants which grow in high Alpine situations, it is our experience that the garden individuals are frequently very different from individuals of the same species on the mountains. If naturally woolly their hairy covering often diminishes, their stems tend to become longer, and their leaves are separated by greater intervals along the stem. In addition the leaves tend to become thinner. This proves that in such Alpine forms the shape of the plant is largely induced by the Alpine conditions. In order to ascertain to what extent these conditions are directly responsible for the shapes of Alpine plants Bonnier cultivated plants in the lowlands, at high altitudes in the Alps and Pyrenees, and at intermediate stations. When the plants remained healthy he found that with increasing altitude they became more dwarfed, the stem being shorter, and the leaves pressed closer together; often, in place of being inserted at intervals up a distinct stem, the leaves formed a rosette at the base. For instance, the Jerusalem Artichoke (*Helianthus tuberosus*), which in the plains produces a tall, leafy stem, in the Alps assumes a dwarfed shape, with all its leaves arranged so as to form a flat radical rosette, like a dandelion. With increasing altitude the leaves became thicker, often smaller, and deeper green in colour. The subterranean parts of the plants at the higher stations were much more developed relatively to the parts above ground than in the lowlands. These facts prove that the forms of the Alpine plants are largely determined by the external conditions; and, as these structural modifications have been shown above to be of direct advantage to the plant, we are entitled to say that the Alpine plants are so constituted that they adapt themselves to their surroundings.

But it is not alone on the structural characteristics of the Alpine plants that the Alpine climate acts in a manner which aids them to resist the trying nature of surrounding conditions. Some plants that are annual in the plains become perennial in the Alps—for example, the annual meadow grass (*Poa annua*). Again, seeds ripened in intense sunlight, or in dry places, germinate more rapidly than those matured in the shade or in damp regions. This character is doubtless a great advantage to Alpine plants, which have only a short active season. It is known that if seeds of cereals, which have absorbed water and become swollen, be frozen a number of them will be killed, but those that survive will germinate much more rapidly than seeds not frozen; and it is further established that potatoes kept frozen for a time during winter will shoot up more rapidly than specimens kept in warmer places. Hence it seems probable that the very severity of the cold at high altitudes causes the Alpine plants to shoot up with greater rapidity when spring-time does set in. This hastened development in flowers growing at considerable altitudes is to be seen in the times of flowering of plants found also in the lowlands. Thus, for instance, *Gnaphalium dioicum*, *Gentiana germanica*, and *Dianthus superbus* are in full flower in the Alps in July, whereas in the valleys they scarcely open their flowers in August.

As to the precise factors in the Alpine climate which induce the structural changes above mentioned it is not easy to speak with any confidence. The intensity of the light, and the low temperature at night, both work in the same direction, retarding the growth of the stem, and thus rendering it dwarfed, with close-set leaves. The rarefaction of the air has no influence in this direction; in fact it appears to operate in an opposite manner, for stems grow more rapidly in rarefied air than in air at ordinary atmospheric pressures. The intensity of the light is, at any rate, partially responsible for the relatively increased thickness of the leaves. In confirmation of this view we find *Arabis anachortica*, a supposed species differing from *A. alpina* in having thin papery leaves, occurs only in the shady hollows of rocks. On removing it to Kew it changed into *A. alpina*, the papery consistence of the leaves being thus induced by the peculiar habitat, and the plant proving to be merely a variety of *A. alpina*. *Zahlbrücknera paradoxa* and *Saxifraga arachnoides* occupy similar shady cavities in rocks, and have thin, papery leaves, probably for the same reason. Alpine plants in exposed positions have, for the most part, leathery or hairy leaves, whereas among those growing in shaded ravines, torrent beds, &c., we find plants with more delicate leaves. Finally it has been shown by experiments on lowland plants that increased illumination tends to cause increased thickness of the leaf, and that dryness of the air has the same effect, tending to increase the hairiness of leaves.

iii. *The Flowers of Alpine Plants.*—The first impression one has on seeing Alpine flowers is that they are more beautiful and more brilliant than lowland plants. It is, however, a mistake to suppose that the flowers of Alpine plants are larger than those of their relations in low-lying lands; in fact, the reverse is sometimes the case. As a rule the flowers of Alpine species are about the same size as those of lowland species belonging to the same genus. It is the smaller size of the leaves of the Alpine species, the frequent crowding of the flowers, which thus form bright and isolated patches on the ground, and the increased depth of tone of the floral tints, that, taken together, give rise to the illusion that flowers growing high up on the Alps are larger than similar flowers growing in the plains. The brilliancy of colour is, to a certain extent, directly caused by the Alpine conditions. If we examine individuals of the same species growing at different heights we find that with increasing altitude there is generally a deepening of the tints of the flowers ; for instance, the light blue of the forget-me-not becomes deeper, the yellow of hawkweeds tends towards orange. It is a well known fact that the colours or shades of Alpine flowers change when the plants are cultivated in gardens. In any family of flowering plants in which flowers having different tints occur it is often found that the yellow flowers are the simplest and most lowly organised, and that the blue flowers are the most highly organised. Further, it is known that, speaking broadly, in a family the successive advance of the complication of the flowers corresponds more or less to the colours in the following order : yellow, white, pink, red, crimson, violet, blue. In Alpine flowers there is a larger percentage of the colours corresponding genetically to high organisation than there is in the lowland. For instance, the yellow of the lowland primrose and cowslip is supplemented by the violet tints of several species in the Alps. There is a pink-flowered Alpine saxifrage in addition to the ordinary yellow and white-flowered species. An orange-red Alpine hawkweed contrasts with the paler yellow lowland species. There are many flowers which are violet, or brilliant sapphire, or deep ultramarine (*Campanula*, *Phyteuma*, *Saussurea*); the gentians vary in their different species from yellow, whitish green, to deep yet vivid blue; the speedwells (*Veronica*) from pink to sapphire, with a central spot, white or yellow, fringed with orange or vermilion.

Frequently too the Alpine flowers have stronger scents, and pour out more honey than their lowland allies. The increased yield of honey of Alpine flowers is illustrated by observations of the average yield of hives in the Pyrenees, as shown in the following table (there were, at the time of observation, no less than 19,829 hives in the Eastern Pyrenees, scattered at altitudes varying from 0 to 1,500 mètres, or 4,921 ft.) :—

Altitude in Mètres	Mean Annual Yield of Hives in Kilogrammes of Honey
0–300	3·06
300–600	4·08
600–900	5·00
900–1,200	7·00
1,200–1,500	9·33

Bonnier has shown that, comparing individuals of the same species, but growing at different altitudes, the amount of honey poured out by the flower increases with the altitude, and that often there is a parallel increase in the strength of the scent of the flowers. Altogether the heightened brilliancy of Alpine flowers, the increased yield of honey, and often of the more potent scents are to be attributed, partly at any rate, to the direct action of the Alpine conditions on the plants themselves.

It is a matter of doubt whether these facts would afford a sufficient basis for the explanation of the colours of Alpine flowers, because it is still doubtful whether such changes as are merely wrought by the direct action of environment are ever hereditary. Still more problematical is it

CLIMATE AND VEGETATION OF THE ALPS.

whether, in consequence of such direct action of the surroundings operating for generations, a plant with, say, yellow flowers could give rise to descendants possessed of blue flowers. A second explanation has been offered—namely, that the rarity of insects in the Alps necessitates increased powers of attraction, in order that cross-fertilisation by their agency may be sufficiently secured. It must be noted, however, that both the flora and the insect fauna become poorer in species as the Alps are ascended, and additional attraction would only be necessary if the flower-visiting insects decreased in numbers at a greater rate than did the flowers fertilised by their agency, or if the opportunities of visiting flowers were lessened. As regards the absolute number of flowers and insects it is impossible to judge. It is possible only to glean an indication of their relative numbers by comparing the insect visitors of flowers in the Alps and in the plains. H. Müller found that Alpine flowers had at least as many sorts of visitors as flowers in the plains. In fact, he showed that some flowers in the Alps had visits from a larger number of varieties of insects than those in the plains; for instance, *Polygonum bistorta*, whilst visited by only 7 varieties of insects in the plains, had 38 sorts of visitors in the Alps. Selecting 12 of the most frequently visited plants in the plains, and comparing their visitors with the visitors in the Alps, the numbers were found to be 80 and 85 respectively. By this method he concluded that there is at least as great a probability of cross-fertilisation in the Alps as there is in the lowlands, and also as proportionately great a number of insect visitors. It must not be forgotten that the Alpine conditions render the flowers more attractive by increased supplies of honey and stronger scents.

From the point of view of their relations to insect visitors insect fertilised flowers may be ranged under five general heads :—

a. Po. A.—Flowers visited for their *pollen* alone, or for *honey* which is *freely exposed* (*e.g.* elder, *Umbelliferæ*). Such flowers are visited by all classes of flower-visiting insects.

b. A. B.—Flowers with *half concealed honey* (*e.g.* buttercups, saxifrages). Compared with the first class there is a decrease in the variety of visitors, and a relative increase in the number of insect visitors with long tongues.

c. B. and B.—Flowers (*e.g.* geraniums) and heads of flowers (*e.g.* daisy family) with *completely concealed honey*. This is an advance on the second class, but yet the flowers are not restricted to any particular class of insects.

d. H.—*Bee flowers* (*e.g.* pea family, gentians). In these the honey cannot be reached by insects with short tongues, and so these flowers are specially adapted for bees. Under this head there are three sub-groups specially adapted for (i) ordinary bees, (ii) humble bees, (iii) wasps.

e. F.—*Butterfly and moth flowers* (*e.g.* pinks, ordinary honeysuckles). These are especially adapted for Lepidoptera, and have their honey so deeply stored that it is not accessible to any insects save butterflies and moths.

It is obvious that the insect fauna of a region will be more or less reflected in the forms of the flowers. The following table, condensed from Müller's observations, summarised by Loew, illustrates the relative parts played by the different classes of insects on the groups of flowers mentioned above :—

			Percentage of Visits by		
Group of Flowers	Region	Butterflies and Moths	Bees with Long Tongues, including Humble Bees	Bees with Short Tongues and other Hymenoptera	Flies, Beetles, and other Insects
Po. A. and A. B.	Plains	1·7	6·1	34·7	56·5
	Alps	18·8	7·4	13·8	59·7
B. and B.	Plains	13·1	27·4	26·3	32·9
	Alps	47·2	12·6	10·7	29·2
H.	Plains	15·6	59·6	16·3	8·5
	Alps	45·7	47·5	2·0	4·6
F.	Plains	76·5	2·9	5·9	14·7
	Alps	79·6	8·7	2·7	9·0

This table illustrates the relative decrease in the number of the Hymenoptera, especially the short-tongued bees, but the increased number of humble bees in the Alps. It also shows clearly the vastly increased importance of butterflies and moths as fertilising agents. These facts stand out too in the composition of the flora. There is an increased number of flowers belonging to group F., especially adapted for Lepidoptera (butterflies and moths). To select an example, the genus *Primula* is represented in the plains by no flower adapted for Lepidotera, but has one species adapted for humble bees, viz. *P. farinosa*. There are, on the other hand, six Alpine species adapted for Lepidoptera, viz. a variety of *P. farinosa*, and the species *P. integrifolia*, *P. villosa*, *P. viscosa*, *P. longiflora*, and *P. Allionii*. The curious case of *P. farinosa*, in which there are two forms, Alpine and lowland, adapted for Lepidoptera and humble bees respectively, leads on to the interesting fact that in the Alps there are a number of flowers which are transitional between humble-bee flowers (H.) and Lepidoptera flowers (F.) Such, for instance, are the Alpine variety of the pansy (*Viola tricolor*) and some Alpine gentians (*Gentiana tenella*, *G. nana*, *G. campestris*, *G. obtusifolia*). These transitional flowers are, too, more or less closely genetically related to Alpine species, which are completely adapted for Lepidoptera: *Viola tricolor var. alpestris*, is allied to *V. calcarata* (a butterfly flower); the transitional gentians are allied to *G. verna* and *G. barbarica*, which are adapted for butterflies; *P. farinosa* has as close relations *P. integrifolia*, *P. villosa*, and *P. viscosa*. These facts suffice to suggest strongly that, in the Alps a number of flowers have been evolved under the influence of Lepidoptera. Thus the peculiar forms of Alpine flowers have been developed, at least partially, under the influence of the Alpine insects, and there is no reason for disbelieving that the insects have had a share too in the evolution of the colours and scents of the flowers. In particular Müller attributes to butterflies the evolution of a large number of flowers ranging from pink to crimson, such as Alpine primulas, pinks (*Dianthus*), *Silene acaulis*, *Erica carnea*, &c. Flowers of these tints are, in general, much visited by butterflies. Further, the clove-like smell is characteristic of many butterfly flowers (pinks, *Daphne striata*). The increased variety of tints in the bee flowers is associated by Müller with the relatively greater number of humble bees in the Alps, and he regards flies as responsible for the abundance of white-flowered *Alsineæ*, and of the whitish, yellowish, or speckled saxifrages which belong to group A. (see the preceding table.) The colours and scents of the Alpine flowers are hence to be attributed partly to the direct action of the environment on the individual plants, and partly to the selecting influence exerted by insects on the race. It is extremely interesting to note that, just as the vegetative part of the individual plant responds to the Alpine conditions in a fashion beneficial to itself, so also do the flowers; the heightened colour, the increased excretion of honey, and the stronger scents induced in each individual by the Alpine conditions bring more visitors to the flowers, and thus tend to atone for the shortness of the flowering season.

One additional point with reference to the flowers of Alpine plants is that, as compared with those in the lowlands, there is an increase in the number of flowers habitually self-fertilised. This increase takes place at the expense of the flowers which are capable of self-fertilisation, but are usually cross-fertilised. The number of exclusively cross-fertilised flowers remains relatively the same in the Alps and in the plains. This increase of self-fertilisation is possibly associated with the shortness of the active season and the necessity for forming seeds quickly. It is, however, significant that the increase in self-fertilisation takes place nearly exclusively in that class (Po. A.) which is normally (in the lowlands) visited least by Lepidoptera and humble bees, and is therefore least likely to profit by their relative abundance and most likely to suffer from the poverty in short-tongued bees.

iv. *Origin of the Alpine Flora.*—It is impossible to discuss, within the narrow limits of the present article, the origin of the Alpine flora, particularly as eminent authorities, such as Sir Joseph Hooker, Dr. Christ, and Mr. John Ball, have differed considerably in their views on this subject.

The first important fact is that many species of plants found in the higher parts of the Alps occur also in the Arctic regions, but are absent from the intervening low country. They afford examples of 'discontinuous distribution.' According to Dr. Christ's estimate there are 294 species of plants which live almost exclusively in the higher regions of the Alps, and of these 100 reappear in the Arctic regions. There is a second category of Alpine species—namely, those which do not occur in the Arctic regions, but are found on distant mountains, though they do not inhabit the plains separating the latter from the Alps. For example, Mr. John Ball calculated that 17 per cent. of the Alpine species occur in the Arctic regions, while as many as 25 per cent. reappear in the Altai mountains, in Asia. How are we to explain this sporadic appearance of plants in distant, isolated regions? We can no longer assume that they were created separately at the various spots in which they occur. It follows that they were evolved at some spot from which at some time they travelled to their present scattered quarters. It is impossible to assume that under present conditions the seeds were conveyed by the agency of wind or birds from one distant region to another, although intervening mountains might be regarded as stepping-stones; for we find that the number of identical species at widely separated spots is too great to permit of this explanation, and, furthermore, the agreement between the floras of different mountain chains is by no means proportional to their geographical proximity, even when their climates are closely alike.

It is found that some mountain plants reappear on the sea-shore, though absent from the country separating the mountains from the sea-shore. Though sea-shore plants have in general a wide distribution it is obviously impossible that the sea-shore should play more than a very limited part as a pathway for plants dwelling on the different mountain chains of the earth. Under present conditions, then, the existing plains form an impassable barrier between the Alps and the Arctic regions or distant mountain chains. In particular the climate in these plains is not suited to the high Alpine plants, which, furthermore, would be probably killed out by the competition of typical lowland forms. If these conclusions are correct we may assume that the plains did not always act as barriers, but that conditions reigned which permitted free communication between the extreme north and distant mountain chains. For the realisation of this scheme we must look to the Glacial Period, when the glaciers of the extreme north descended southwards, and the glaciers from the mountains stretched far north to meet them. For instance, during the Glacial Period in Europe the Scandinavian glaciers descended south as far as Germany, while the Alpine glaciers extended north into the same country. This condition of things would enable the Arctic and mountain forms to mingle in the lowlands. As the climate ameliorated the fixed flora would be either driven north or up the mountains till the present distribution of forms was the result. The majority of eminent botanists agree in regarding the Glacial Period as the key to the distribution of high Alpine forms, but differ as to the precise region of origin of the constituents. Mr. John Ball, however, was of opinion that for the explanation of the discontinuous distribution of mountain species it was necessary to look further back than the Glacial Period. In his opinion the mountains were centres of evolution of new species, which then streamed down into the plains. Against this view it may be urged that there is often clear evidence that high mountain forms (like Alpine species) in different parts of the world have been derived from lowland forms, whereas there is no evidence of the reverse process having taken place. Furthermore it is not found that the richness of the flora of a region is proportional to its possessions in the shape of mountains : Australia, for instance, poor as it is in mountains, is rich in endemic forms.

Amongst Alpine plants some are clearly derived from the Mediterranean-Oriental region, such as *Erica carnea, Crocus vernus, Colchicum alpinum.* These Mediterranean types are not numerous (only 48 species) in the Alps, but become more so in southern mountains.

In a previous section attention has been directed to the fact that the master key to the structure of Alpine plants lies in their need to guard against disproportinate loss of water. For plants inhabiting deserts and dry open steppes there is the same imperative necessity. Hence it is a matter of no surprise that certain steppe plants should have settled in the

Alps and have even given birth to Alpine species. Some species of *Saussurea*, and *Artemisia*, Edelweiss (*Gnaphalium leontopodium*), all seem to be steppe plants; in fact, the last named, and Alpine species of the first, are found on the steppes of Northern Asia. *Oxytropis* and *Astragalus* are typical genera inhabiting steppes and deserts, where they are represented by hundreds of species, though in the Alps each has only half a dozen species.

In addition to all the forms discussed above, and many ubiquitous forms found alike in the Alps and in the lowlands, there are a number of species which are found in the Alps but nowhere else. In the Alps there are (according to Dr. Christ) about 182 endemic species. These peculiarly Alpine plants exceed in beauty those which are common to the Alps and the Arctic regions. Of the beautiful gentians one alone, *Gentiana nivalis*, reappears in the Arctic regions. In the extreme north *Primula farinosa* alone represents the Alpine primulas. The same general rule holds good for the bright-coloured species of *Androsace*, *Soldanella*, *Campanula*, *Phyteuma*, and *Viola*, whose Alpine species do not reappear in the far north, or are only represented there by a single species. As might be anticipated from considerations set forth in iii, above, the beauty of many of the brightest Alpine flowers has been gained in the Alps themselves.

LIST OF BOOKS.

Among a very large number of books and articles the following are specially recommended :—

Climate.

G. *Berndt*. Der Föhn. Göttingen, 1886. (2nd edition. 1896.)
J. *Hann*. Handbuch der Klimatologie. Stuttgart, 1883 (2nd edition, 1898).
P. *Blumer-Zweifel*. Was ist Föhn? (article in the 'Jahrbuch' of the Swiss Alpine Club, published at Bern in 1895, vol. xxx. pp. 320-337.)

Botany.

John Ball. On the Origin of the European Flora (in the 'Proceedings of the Royal Geographical Society' for 1879).
John Ball. The Distribution of Plants on the South Side of the Alps. (Published in 1896 by the Linnean Society in vol. v. part 4 of the 2nd series of its botanical 'Transactions.')
A. W. *Bennett*. The Flora of the Alps. 2 vols. with 120 coloured plates. London, 1896.
G. *Bonnier*. Les Plantes de la Région Alpine et leurs Rapports avec le Climat ('Annales de Géographie,' 1895, pp. 393-415).
H. *Christ*. La Flore de la Suisse et ses Origines (Bâle and Geneva. German edition, 1879. French edition, 1883).
Loew. Blüten-biologische Floristik. Stuttgart, 1894.
H. *Müller*. Alpenblumen, ihre Befruchtung durch Insekten, und ihre Anpassungen an dieselben. Leipzig, 1881.
K. W. *von della Torre*. The Tourist's Guide to the Flora of the Alps. Translated by A. W. Bennett. London, 1886.
> Accompanied by A. Hartinger's 500 Plates of Alpine Plants. (German text and Plates appeared in 1882 and 1884 respectively; 2nd edition of the Plates completed in 1897; all published at Vienna by the German and Austrian Alpine Club.)

Art. XIV.—The Snow Region of the Alps.

Glaciers.—Avalanches.*

A large part of the heat which the sun sends to the earth is expended in converting water into vapour, and raising it into the atmosphere. As soon as any portion of the atmosphere becomes over-saturated with vapour, this is precipitated, at first in the form of cloud, and, if not re-absorbed, ultimately reaches the earth again as rain. Several causes, which it is beyond our limits to discuss, combine to lower the temperature of the air as it is raised above the earth's surface, and at a sufficient height it becomes so cold that whatever vapour is condensed takes the form of snow and sleet. In falling to the earth this is usually reconverted into water, but in high mountain districts, where the temperature of the surface is also low, the greater part of the aqueous vapour returned from the atmosphere retains the form of snow. When the air is calm, the snow of the High Alps consists of regular crystalline forms of exquisite beauty, being wonderfully varied modifications of a six-rayed star. When the air is disturbed, the snow assumes a new condition, which is that of small frozen pellets, little larger than a pin's head. It is this which forms that blinding snow-dust well known to those who have ever experienced the *tourmente*. The snow that falls on the exposed ridges and steep slopes does not long remain there. The larger portion is generally carried away by the wind; a further portion accumulates till the slope becomes too steep, when it slides down in an avalanche; and a small part is disposed of by melting and evaporation. The result is, that nearly the whole of the snow falling on high mountains is retained in the hollows, or on the more level parts of the surface. If these hollows and plateaux are below the level of perpetual snow, or, in other words, if they are so situated that the annual melting equals the quantity of fresh snow annually supplied, no accumulation can take place. A certain quantity of snow is gathered into these storehouses every winter, and is removed during the following summer, the same process being renewed year after year. This condition of things is seen in the Carpathians, the ranges of Central Spain, and many other European mountains, whose summits rise above the level of perpetual snow.

The case is otherwise when the winter snows are gathered in hollows and plateaux where the rate of melting is less than the annual supply. The first impression of a person speculating on the subject would be, that under such circumstances the accumulation would go on without limit, and that a layer of snow constantly increasing in thickness would be

---

* In giving a brief sketch of the present state of our knowledge of the phenomena of the snow region of the Alps, the writer (J. B.) involuntarily enters upon a discussion which has furnished abundant matter of controversy, now in great part set at rest. Those who desire fuller information may refer to the original writings of Rendu, Forbes, Agassiz, and Tyndall, or may satisfy themselves with an article in the *Edinburgh Review* for January 1861. For simple and lucid accounts of ice and its action the reader should refer to the late Prof. Tyndall's *The Forms of Water in Clouds and Rivers, Ice and Glaciers* (1872), and Prof. Bonney's *Ice-Work Present and Past* (1896)—both published in the 'International Scientific' Series. The standard work on Glaciers is now the *Handbuch der Gletscherkunde* (Stuttgart, 1885), by Prof. Heim, of Zürich: a very full summary in English was published by Mr. Tuckett in vol. xii. of the *Alpine Journal*.

formed on these parts of the surface. To understand what actually occurs, a little detail is necessary.

The higher region of the Alps, and other high mountains, is subjected to a constant alteration between heat and cold. In clear weather this takes place between each day and night; in clouded weather the intervals are longer. The sun shining upon the mass of snow-dust and minute crystals partially melts them, and ultimately fuses them together, till they form grains of larger size, which are frozen together in compact particles of ice during the next interval of cold. At first this process is confined to the uppermost layer of the snow, but as the alternate melting and congelation are frequently renewed, a similar change extends through the mass, which is gradually converted into that peculiar condition that has been called **névé**, or in German *Firn*. The longer the exposure of a layer of snow has lasted, the more complete is the change into névé; the sooner a fresh layer falls, the more imperfect will be the conversion of the older one.

A section of the upper strata of the névé, here and there exposed on the sides of a crevasse, shows successive layers whose upper surfaces are seen to be more near the condition of ice than the interior portions. In the lapse of years the névé increases layer by layer, one of them corresponding to every considerable fall of snow, until a considerable weight presses on the lower and older portions of the mass.

To understand what effects are produced by this pressure, we must bear in mind an important property of ice, to which the name *regelation* has been given. Two surfaces of ice, at or very near the melting-point, when brought into contact, freeze together so completely that no trace of their original separating surface remains. Adequate pressure applied to a mass of fragments of ice, by forcing them into positions where their surfaces come into contact, causes regelation, and the closer the contact the more completely will the separate portions be welded together.

Such is the change that is effected in the recesses where the Alpine snows are stored. Having been first brought to the condition of granular névé by the sun's action, these grains are more and more completely united in the deeper portions of the mass into nearly compact ice.

If the reservoirs of which we have spoken were closed basins of sufficient depth, they would simply become filled with stationary masses of ice; but, as a general rule, this is not the case. They partake of the general slope of the mountain, and each is connected with the lower level by a valley, glen, or ravine, through which the snow would speedily flow if it were converted into water. But, under adequate pressure, ice, and especially such imperfect ice as is formed from the névé, possesses a considerable degree of plasticity. It gives way in the direction of least resistance. A piece of ice compressed in a mould yields until it fills all the inequalities, and produces an accurate cast of the mould. The vast masses of névé that are piled in the upper valleys of the Alps yield in the same way to the pressure caused by their own weight, and gradually flow downwards through the channel of these valleys. In other words, they become **glaciers**.

We now see that the essential condition for the formation of a glacier is the existence of a reservoir large enough, and at a sufficient height, to accumulate such a mass of névé as will, by its weight, convert its own substance into ice, and force it to flow in whatever direction it encounters the least resistance. In moving onward the glacier conforms to the laws that regulate the motion of imperfect fluids. The resistance of the sides and the bed on which it moves retards the motion of the adjoining portions of the ice. The centre, therefore, moves faster than the sides, and the surface faster than the bottom. When the ice-stream flows through a bend in the valley, the point of most rapid motion is shifted from the centre towards the convex side of the curve. While the ice thus conforms to the laws of fluid motion, the internal changes by which it is enabled thus to comport itself are peculiar, and have no example among other bodies of which we have experience. The nature of the motion, involving constant changes in the relative positions of the particles, implies fracture, which must be frequently renewed; but this would speedily reduce the whole to a mass of incoherent fragments, if it were not for the property of regelation. At each step in the progress of the glacier this repairs the damage done to the continuity of the ice, and by the twofold process of *fracture and regelation* the glacier moves onward, constantly changing its form, yet in appearance an almost continuous mass of solid ice.

The rate of progress of a glacier depends upon various causes, but mainly on those which would regulate its motion if it were converted into water—viz. the dimensions of the reservoir, and the inclination of the slope down which it flows. It is also influenced by temperature: the nearer the ice is to its melting point, the more easily it yields, and the faster it moves. It is nearly certain that the cold of winter penetrates but to a slight depth into the interior of the glacier, and this accounts for the continuance of the motion in that season.

The above description applies to true glaciers, which, as we have seen, are rivers of ice flowing through definite channels. There are in the Alps a vast number of smaller accumulations of névé, gathered into the lesser' hollows and recesses of the surface, that give birth to minor glaciers, or *glaciers of the second order*, in which the phenomena of the true glaciers are imperfectly exhibited. In these the conversion of the névé into ice is incomplete, and the approach to the law of semi-fluid motion but slight. These secondary glaciers usually lie on steep declivities, and their downward motion, which is trifling as compared with that of the greater ice-streams, is mainly effected by sliding on the underlying surface of rock.

Returning to the description of the true glaciers, we have next to remark that although the ice of which they are composed is amenable to pressure, it is devoid of the other chief attribute of imperfect fluids or viscous bodies: it is but slightly capable of yielding to tension. When the general movement of the glacier tends to draw asunder adjoining portions of ice, this is unable to obey the strain, the mass is rent through, and in this manner are formed the **crevasses**. These are among the best known and most characteristic of glacier phenomena. They are most numerous and widest in summer, when the glacier moves most rapidly, and are partially or completely closed up in winter, when the onward flow of the ice is slackened. But the same causes recur year after year, subject to slight variation owing to the differences of seasons, and, as a general rule, crevasses reappear annually in the same places, though the ice in which the rent takes place may have been some hundreds of feet higher up the stream in the preceding season. Crevasses are at first narrow fissures, and are gradually enlarged by the onward motion of the glacier, increasing from a few inches to many feet in width, and sometimes reaching to a great depth. The positions in which crevasses usually oppose the most serious obstacle to the Alpine traveller, are those where the bed of the glacier suddenly changes its inclination from a gentle slope to a steeper declivity. The ice, as it bends over the convex surface, is rent by transverse crevasses of great depth and width, which often cross the entire breadth of the ice-stream, and these are repeated as each successive portion arrives at the same point, so that the result is to form a series of deep parallel trenches, divided by massive walls, or ramparts of ice, giving the glacier when seen from a distance the appearance of a gigantic staircase. It not unfrequently happens that, in the same places where the ice is thus rent by one set of parallel crevasses, another system of crevasses may be formed running transversely across the first. In this way the whole of the surface is cut up into isolated tower-shaped masses. When first formed the sides of crevasses are more or less vertical walls, with well-defined edges, but the exposed parts of the ice are rapidly attacked by the sun, and even by the air and by rain. In a short time the flat-topped ramparts and turrets have their upper edges eaten away till the broad rampart becomes a sharp ridge, and the tower a pointed pinnacle. This is the origin of those singular and beautiful forms that are often seen towards the lower part of an icefall in the greater glaciers, where the crevasses penetrate to a depth that must be reckoned by hundreds of feet.

A peculiar sort of crevasse, somewhat different in its origin from the rest, is best known by the German name *Bergschrund*. This arises along the line of separation between the fields of névé that partake more or less of the downward movement of the glacier, and the upper snow-slopes that remain attached to the rocky skeleton of the mountain. A continuous fissure, sometimes 20 or 30 feet in width, marks the separation, and interposes a formidable obstacle to the traveller who seeks to reach the higher peaks.

When the upper mountain slopes are covered by a considerable depth of névé, the crevasses naturally cut through the névé, and expose sections showing the outcrop of the successive beds of snow from which it was originally formed. When it is cut up by the intersection of transverse crevasses, the névé often appears in the form of huge square blocks. These blocks of creamy névé were known, Saussure tells us (§§ 1975 and 2054), in his time at Chamonix as ' séracs,' this being the name given to the compact white cheese obtained from 'petit lait,' or whey, and pressed together in square wooden rectangular boxes. But the name ' séracs' is nowadays commonly extended to all pinnacles or blocks, whether composed of névé or of ice, and particularly to those seen in an icefall.

A remarkable phenomenon, seen only on the greater glaciers, is that presented by the so called *moulins*. During the summer, when the sun acts with great force, the melted ice soon forms rivulets on the surface. In portions of the glacier intersected by crevasses the superficial water is quickly carried off; but where the ice is compact, these rivulets uniting together may accumulate until they form a considerable stream. Sooner or later this encounters a crevice, perhaps at first very small, which is enlarged by the action of falling water till a vertical shaft is formed in the ice, through which the stream pours in a waterfall that is lost to sight in the depths of the glacier. Another phenomenon is what are commonly called *glacier tables*, or ice cones capped by a great boulder which has protected that particular bit of ice from being melted by the sun's rays.

Among other apparent objections to the above given explanation of the origin of glaciers, it may occur to the reader that, as considerable pressure is necessary to account for the conversion of the névé into ice, the upper strata which have not undergone this pressure ought to continue in the state of névé, and that the upper surface of the glacier should consist of névé, and not of ice. This objection loses sight of the vast amount of *ablation*, or loss, which a glacier annually undergoes through the melting of the surface. By mounting high enough on each glacier we do find the upper surface formed of névé, but as it descends to a lower level a fresh slice of the surface is annually cut away by the sun's heat, and, taking a rough average, it is not too much to assert that the ice which we find on the surface in the middle or lower part of a glacier was 200 feet deep at the time when the same part lay one mile higher up the stream. For this and other reasons the writer (J. B.) is persuaded that the depth of the greater glaciers has hitherto been much underrated. If we possessed continuous series of observations on any of those glaciers, showing the annual rate of progress in successive parts of the stream, and the corresponding loss by ablation, we should be able to infer with great probability the thickness of the deposit in the reservoir whence it flows.

It is clear that the further a glacier flows towards the lower region, the greater will be the annual amount of ablation. At length it must reach a point where the amount of annual melting of the ice equals the amount borne down by the progress of the glacier, and at that point the latter must come to an end. The inequalities of the seasons may cause a slight oscillation in the length, especially when several successive seasons concur to produce the same effect. Abundant winter snow and cool summers cause the glaciers to advance, while opposite conditions cause a contrary result. The more considerable changes that have been occasionally recorded have been probably caused by local accidents.

During the summer months, as we have seen, the glacier is covered with streamlets produced by the melting of the surface; the sun is constantly eating away the edges and sides of the crevasses, and the air and the earth dissolve a portion of the under surface. The plenteous supply of water from all these sources finally makes its way to the rocky bed, where it passes on under the ice, and finally issues in a single stream from the foot of the glacier. Here the ice usually forms a dome-shaped arch, through which the stream flows out into the valley, and whose beautiful azure tints attract the notice of travellers.

The appearance of the surface of a glacier usually differs much from the previous conception formed by a visitor. Instead of the clear hues of ice, he finds it soiled by earth and other impurities, carried from the slopes of the adjoining mountains by violent winds. The surface is generally very uneven, for, even in the parts free from crevasses, the same ice over which the traveller walks was at some earlier period of its history rent by fissures, and has probably passed through the wild confusion of an icefall. Lower down, when pressure came into play, the broken members were welded together again so as to form a continuous mass, and the greater irregularities of the surface were removed; but many minor hillocks and depressions, unsuspected at a distance, preserve a record of the changes that have been undergone.

Besides the minor impurities that fleck the surface of the ice-stream, there are other more important foreign bodies borne down by it. The traveller who views it from some commanding station will almost always detect a fringe of blocks of stone, of various sizes, lying along both sides near the bank, and may usually trace one, two, or more lines of blocks descending from the upper end of the glacier, and marking a continuous trail along the course of the stream. The general name for these trains of blocks is **moraines**. In the ceaseless progress of decay which is eating away the solid materials of the mountains, blocks of stone, accompanied by finer gravel, constantly fall from the steep slopes above upon the surface of the ice. As this gradually advances it receives fresh contributions, and in this manner are accumulated the blocks and gravel along the sides of a glacier that are known as *lateral moraines*. As the glacier is wasted away by melting in the lower part of its course, a portion of the lateral moraine is stranded on the bank; a further portion finds its way to the glacier bed through the crevasses that usually abound near the sides; and, except under peculiar circumstances, a small portion only is carried down to the foot of the glacier. When two glaciers come together, each being provided with its lateral moraine, the consequence is that the two moraines that are brought together become joined and confounded into one in the centre of the united ice-stream. In this manner is formed a *medial moraine*. Being far from the edge of the glacier, it is much less exposed to destruction than the lateral moraine. It sometimes disappears from sight in an icefall, but as the crevasses, though deep, rarely penetrate through the entire thickness of the ice, the blocks of stone fall only to a certain depth, and in due time, when the upper ice is removed by ablation, they come again into view. In this way huge blocks of stone are borne down from the higher crests of the Alps to the lower valleys, with the edges still fresh, and without having suffered mechanical violence. Most of the greater glaciers are formed by the union of a number of smaller separate ice-streams. To the junction of each of these affluents belongs a separate medial moraine, which may often be traced for many miles from the point of junction to the foot of the glacier, disclosing the mineral composition of parts of the range difficult or impossible of access. When composed of large blocks, a medial moraine sometimes forms a ridge 30 or 40 feet in height, running along the middle of the glacier. The first impression is, that this ridge is formed of rocks piled one over the other; but it more commonly happens that each block rests upon ice, and that the reason why they form a ridge raised above the general level is that the blocks, and the gravel which accompanies them, protect the ice from ablation, though separate small stones conduct heat, and sink into the surface.

The mass of blocks and finer matter accumulated in front of a glacier forms the *terminal moraine*. Its extent depends very much more on the form of the ground in the place where the glacier comes to an end, than on the quantity of matter transported by the glacier. In the course of ages this would almost always suffice to produce a considerable mound, if the end of the glacier remained nearly at the same point, and if it did not often happen that the larger portion falls into the bed of the stream issuing from the glacier, and is there water-worn, reduced in size, and gradually carried onward through the valley.

Not less important than the transport of rocks on the upper surface of the glacier is the action of the under surface on the mineral materials with which it comes into contact. The motion of a glacier is mainly effected by means of the internal motion of the ice, by which one part is enabled to advance more rapidly than another, but in part the motion (as conjectured by Saussure) is accomplished by the sliding of the under surface of the ice upon its bed. The smaller particles of stone and sand that find their way under the ice are set into the surface, and, urged by the enormous weight of the glacier, become a most powerful graving tool, which wears away the surface of the hardest rocks. Blocks of stone falling from the moraines to the bottom of the glacier through crevasses are rapidly ground down in this gigantic mill, and the materials are reduced partly to small scored pebbles, and partly to an impalpable powder, finer than the finest mud. Every stream issuing from a glacier is at once recognised by its milky colour, derived from this minutely pulverised matter, which is often retained in suspension for a distance of 60 miles and more from its source. It is this glacier silt which has largely contributed to fill up the heads of the Alpine lakes, and no doubt a considerable quantity is carried directly to the sea through the Po, the Adige, and other rivers of the Eastern Alps.

By the process above described, every rock over which a glacier passes is worn in a peculiar manner. Not only are all projecting asperities removed, and reduced to the condition of uniform convex faces, but the surface is ground and polished in a way entirely different from the action of water or other known agents. The presence of fine striæ extending for a considerable distance, occasionally mingled with larger grooves, is one of the characteristic indications of glacial action. These have been studied with much attention of late years, since their importance as evidence of the former extension of the glaciers has been recognised by geologists. After much discussion, no difference remains among competent men of science as to the fact that the existing glaciers occupied a very much wider area than they now do, at a period geologically very recent. The exact limits of that area may not be settled, and there is room for discussion as to some of the results attributed to their action; but the fact that they played an important part as geological agents, not only in the Alps, but in other mountain countries where they do not now exist, is generally admitted.

The geological agency of glaciers is discussed in Art. XI. Many other interesting branches of enquiry connected with the glaciers remain untouched in the foregoing sketch. They are not only amongst the grandest and most impressive objects in nature, but at the same time amongst the most fertile in instruction to the student of her laws, while their influence on the climate and conditions of large portions of the earth is of vast importance to mankind in general.

To form an adequate idea of the part played by glaciers in the general economy of nature, let the reader consider for a moment the consequences that would arise in our continent if they were to disappear. All the greatest rivers would at once be reduced to insignificant streams, rising in rainy weather, and dwindling away in time of drought. The Danube nominally rises in Swabia, but its true source, which is the Inn, along with the Salza, the Drave, and its other chief tributaries, derives from the glaciers the streams that maintain the level of the river. The Rhine, the Rhône, the Po, and the Adige are fed almost exclusively by the Alpine glaciers, and it is these that maintain the abundant supplies of pure water that enable the Italian lakes to diffuse fertility throughout the valley of the Po.

The intimate structure of glacier ice has been much studied and discussed, and has revealed facts of new and unexpected interest. Those who feel an interest in the physics of the subject will not fail to read Professor Tyndall's important work, 'The Glaciers of the Alps' (1860, reprinted in 1896), or Professor Heim's work referred to at the opening of this Article.

The phenomena of glaciers may be studied in most parts of the Alpine chain, where the average height of the peaks approaches 11,000 English feet. Reckoning from west to east, the chief glacier districts are the Dauphiné Alps, the main range of the Graian Alps between the Roche Melon and the Little St. Bernard, the Vanoise group, the Grand Paradis group, the chain of Mont Blanc, the entire range of the Pennine Alps from the Great St. Bernard Pass to the Simplon, the Bernese Alps from the Diablerets to the Grimsel, the Sustenhorn group from the Titlis range to the Furka, the range of the Tödi, the Adula group, the Bernina group, the Ortler group, the Adamello range between the Val Camonica and the Val Rendena, the Oetzthal glaciers in the Tyrol, and lastly the snowy range extending from the Brenner Pass to the Heiligenbluter Tauern, and culminating in the Gross Glockner. There are a few small glaciers in the Maritime Alps (mainly in the Cima dei Gelas range), and one on Monte Viso (the true source of the Po), with some others in the Chambeyron group and in the Ambin group between the Mont Cenis Pass and Tunnel. In the Dolomites glaciers are few and far between. The Hohsand and Gries glaciers in the Lepontines are surprisingly extensive as compared with others in that district. Perhaps two of the most remarkable of small glaciers on minor peaks are the Blaugletscherli, at the N. foot of the Schwarzhorn, near Grindelwald (which has no névé), and the Glärnisch and Bächi glaciers (commonly called névés, though the former at least has a distinct icefall), on the Glärnisch, while on the still lower Säntis (8,216 ft.) there are at least two considerable masses of permanent névé. The largest single glacier is the Great Aletsch, draining the S. side of the Bernese Oberland group; it descends in one unbroken stream with a length of 15 miles and an average breadth of fully one mile, while its total area (excluding its feeders, which add 15½ square miles more) is no less than 50 square miles. Next in order of length and area (in the Alps, of course) come the Unteraar, the Viescher, and the Gorner glaciers, followed by the Mer de Glace and the Lower Grindelwald glacier; in the Eastern Alps the Gepatsch (area 8½ square miles, length 7 miles), Pasterze, and Gurgler glaciers are the largest (Richter reverses the order of the first and second named). The Lower Grindelwald glacier descended to the lowest level, having sunk to 3,225 ft. in 1818, though now, of course, its snout is far higher up. Professor Heim reckons that the total glacier surface (ice and névé) in the Alps is between 1,158 and 1,544 square miles; of this about half is in Switzerland, wherein the Vallais has nearly three times as much as its nearest rival, the Grisons, which is followed pretty closely by Bern. The same investigator tells us that there are about 1,155 glaciers in the Alps (though no doubt this is only a rough calculation). These are distributed as follows (see his work, p. 49):—

—	Large Glaciers	Small Glaciers	Total
1. Switzerland	138	333	471
2. Austria	71	391	462
3. France	25	119	144
4. Italy	15	63	78
	249	906	1,155

A few years ago a 'Commission Internationale des Glaciers' was formed to collect authentic information as to various questions relating to glaciers and their fluctuations in the whole world. Limiting ourselves to the Alps (which form the scope of this work) special mention should be made of the very elaborate and valuable annual reports as to changes in Alpine (mainly Swiss) glaciers published by Professor Forel (the first two appeared in the 'Echo des Alpes' of Geneva for 1881 and 1882, but since then in the 'Jahrbuch' of the Swiss Alpine Club). The results of the long-continued observations on the Rhône Glacier have not yet been published. But there exist several excellent monographs (generally with sketch maps) on various glaciers, among which we may name the following :—

'Miage,' by Professor Baretti ('Memorie della Reale Accademia delle Scienze di Torino,' second series, vol. xxxii. 1880); 'Brenva,' by Signor Marengo ('Bollettino' of the Italian Alpine Club for 1881, and see the 'Alpine Guide,' vol. i. p. 373); 'Glaciers of the Grand Paradis Group,' by Signor Druetti (same periodical for 1897); 'Lower Grindelwald,' by Professor Baltzer ('Denkschriften der schweiz. naturforschend. Gesellschaft,' vol. xxxiii. part 2, 1898); 'Pasterze,' by Herr Seeland ('Zeitschrift' of the German and Austrian Alpine Club from 1880 to 1893); and the 'Vernagtferner,' by Dr. Finsterwalder ('Wissenschaftliche Ergänzungshefte,' no. 1 of the 'Zeitschrift' of the German and Austrian Alpine Club, 1897).

For the Eastern Alps we have Professor Richter's classical writings—
'Die Gletscher der Ostalpen' (1888) and 'Urkunden über die Ausbrüche
d. Vernagt- und Gurglergletschers im 17. und 18. Jahrhundert' (Stuttgart,
1892), as well as his 'Geschichte der Schwankungen der Alpengletscher'
(a general article in vol. xxii. of the 'Zeitschrift' of the German and
Austrian Alpine Club, 1891). In 1898 Dr. Magnus Fritzsch issued at
Vienna a very handy and detailed list of all the cairns, posts, splashes of
red paint, &c., placed (up to 1896) on various Tyrolese glaciers, with notes
of the advance or retreat of each.

A word must be said as to the *lakes* which are formed not so much in a
glacier as between it and the stones on one or other of its sides. They
not unfrequently drain through a hole in the ice and cause great damage
to the valley below. The best known case is the Märjelen lake, near the
Great Aletsch Glacier, and not far from the Eggishorn Hôtel (its
history has been written by Mr. Gosset in vol. xxiii. (1887-8) of the
'Jahrbuch' of the Swiss Alpine Club). Another case is that of the Rutor
lake, in the Rutor group, between Aosta and the Little St. Bernard Pass
(for its history see the admirable historical article by Professor Baretti in
the 'Bollettino' of the Italian Alpine Club for 1880; see also the 'Alpine
Guide,' vol. i. p. 289). A third is that formed at the foot of the Crête Sèche
glacier, at the head of the Val de Bagnes, in 1894 (see M. Pioche's article
in vol. xxi. of the 'Annuaire' of the French Alpine Club, and the 'Alpine
Guide,' vol. i. p. 442) and 1898. A somewhat analogous phenomenon is
when, owing to special circumstances, water accumulates (a 'poche
d'eau') within a glacier, suddenly breaking loose and devastating the
valley beneath. The chief case is that of the bursting of such an accumulation in the Tête Rousse glacier, on the Aiguille du Goûter, which in
1892 practically destroyed St. Gervais les Bains (see M. Durier's article
in vol. xix. of the 'Annuaire' of the French Alpine Club, and the 'Alpine
Guide,' vol. i. p. 368). In the Val de Bagnes the Giétroz glacier has at
least twice in historical times (1595 and 1818) so blocked the narrow
valley that when the barrier was broken through the valley below suffered
tremendous damage; but this danger is now averted by an ingenious
device, described in vol. i. p. 442 of the 'Alpine Guide.'

Avalanches.—It is impossible to quit the snow region of the Alps
without a brief reference to *avalanches* (Germ. *Lauinen*).* These are of
different kinds, and very different in their effects, according as they
consist of snow, névé, or ice. The snow, which falls in prodigious
quantities on the slopes of Alpine valleys in winter, is little compact, and
when it accumulates to such a point as to begin to move, the disturbance
sometimes extends to a great distance, and a mass of snow sufficient to
overwhelm a village falls in the course of a few minutes. The chief
danger from these avalanches, which are very common in some valleys,

---

* The French name comes from 'ad vallem,' as they slide valleywards, while the German term
is said to be a form of the mediæval 'labina,' (which still survives in Romonsch as 'lavina'),
meaning that which slides. See an interesting note by Mr. Tuckett on these two words in vol. v.
of the *Alpine Journal*, pp. 346-9; the word 'lowinæ' appears as early as 1302, in two Latin documents relating to Morschach, above the Lake of Lucerne (*ibid.* xviii. 128). The standard work on
avalanches in Switzerland is Herr Coaz's *Die Lauinen der Schweizeralpen* (Bern, 1881), while
another book by Herr Elias Landolt, *Die Bäche, Schneelawinen und Steinschläge* (Zürich, 1887),
gives a most interesting account of the artificial means of defence devised against avalanches
floods, and the like.

and are called *Staublauinen* (dust avalanches), arises from the roofs giving way under the weight of the snow. So much air is contained in the snow that it is possible to breathe freely, and many persons have been delivered, or have been able to work their own way out, after being buried for many days and even weeks.

Far more formidable than the *Staublauinen* are those called in German Switzerland *Grundlauinen*. These usually occur during the spring, after the winter snow has become partially consolidated, and approaches the consistency of névé. When an unusual quantity has fallen in the preceding winter, the heat of the sun in spring sometimes causes the descent of very considerable masses in a semi-compact condition. The momentum gained in descending several hundreds or thousands of feet makes this description of avalanche very destructive in its effects. A broad passage is cleared through a pine forest as though the trees had been but stubble, and when it reaches inhabited places, which does not often occur, it either crushes the houses on which it falls, or buries them so completely as to make the work of extrication very difficult. In the higher valleys of the Alps these avalanches are very common in the spring, falling before the herdsmen go to the chalets on the 'Alps.' The remains are often to be seen throughout the summer, and not unfrequently serve to bridge over a torrent which works for itself a passage beneath the snow.

Comparatively small glaciers, lying on a steep rocky slope, have in a few rare instances been known to detach themselves partially from their beds, and to fall into some lower valley. Should this occur in the neighbourhood of inhabited places, the result is a catastrophe as formidable as that caused by the fall of portions of a mountain. The village of Randa was in 1819 all but completely destroyed by the blast of air occasioned by the fall of a portion of the Bies glacier; but the most recent and most terrible occurrence of this kind was the fall of an enormous portion of the Altels glacier on to the Gemmi path in 1895, when (as in 1782) several men and many cows perished (see the excellent account of this disaster published by Professor Heim at Zürich in 1895 under the title of 'Die Gletscherlawine an der Altels' as no. 98 of the 'Neujahrsblatt d. Zürcher. Naturforsch. Gesellschaft'). Smaller ice avalanches are of daily occurrence in the High Alps, in situations where a glacier reaches the edge of a steep rocky slope. In warm weather, when the movement of such a glacier is accelerated, blocks of ice frequently fall over the edge of the precipice, and in falling are broken into smaller fragments, each of which is, however, capable of doing severe injury. The guides, who are acquainted with the places exposed to the descent of such masses of ice, are very careful to avoid them, or else to pass very early in the day before the sun has set the ice in motion. Of this class are the avalanches that are seen and listened to with so much interest by travellers in the Bernese Oberland. They are apt to feel surprise that what appears to be no more than the fall of a little snow down the rocky face of the Jungfrau, or the Wetterhorn, should cause a roar that is impressive even at the distance of a couple of miles. They learn, on closer acquaintance, that what has appeared to be mere dust is caused by the fall of blocks of ice of very many tons weight, which are shattered into small fragments, each of them as formidable as a cannon ball.

A description of avalanche, which is rarely encountered except by mountaineers in the High Alps, arises where fresh snow rests upon steep slopes of ice or frozen névé. A trifling cause may set the loose snow in motion, and when this begins to slide it rarely ceases until the whole superficial stratum has reached the bottom of the slope. The danger is not so much that of being buried in the snow, as of being carried over precipices or into the bergschrund which often lies gaping at the foot of such a slope.

Art. XV.—Photography in the High Alps.*

This Article is devoted especially to the requirements of the Alpine aspirant who may desire to combine photography with his favourite pastime of climbing. Those who confine their attention to the subalpine districts hardly need further information than that to be found in the best class of the numerous existing text-books on the subject. Photography in the High Alps, which is certainly one of the most difficult branches of the art, cannot claim to have attained any great degree of popularity until the last twenty years; for although the camera had, previous to that period, been carried up sundry peaks and passes by some enterprising climbers, it must be confessed that their work was, with a few notable exceptions, of a somewhat inferior description. The rapid improvement made in the manufacture of dry plates between 1870 and 1880 was, without doubt, responsible for the real commencement of mountain photography, which may be said to have begun in 1879 with the extraordinarily beautiful series of views in the High Alps taken by the late Mr. W. F. Donkin, whose brilliant success naturally roused a spirit of emulation in others, and at the present time the camera is to be frequently found amongst the contents of the rucksack.

The climber should give a considerable amount of thought and consideration to the apparatus he intends to use, with especial reference to its size, weight, portability, strength, &c. It cannot be too strongly impressed on him that the frivolous form of photography, in which a mere button is pressed and the rest done by some other person who has probably never set eyes on a Swiss mountain, is altogether out of place amongst the snow fields and ice-clad peaks of the High Alps, where, if, in spite of the difficulties of transport, it be worth while to take a camera at all, it is surely worth while to take the proper amount of care in order to secure successful results, for it should always be remembered that a mountain rarely presents the same picture to the eye on separate visits. Whether the apparatus should take the form of a hand camera or a stand camera must, of course, depend largely on personal preference. The advantage would appear at first sight to be on the side of the hand camera. As regards weight, this certainly is the case, but the question of size and portability requires to be judged from a somewhat different point of view.

Of the hand *cameras* of the usual box form the quarter-plate and 5 in. × 4 in. sizes are the largest that can be conveniently carried up any

* This article is new and has been written by Mr. Sydney Spencer.

mountain of average difficulty ; whereas, under similar circumstances, a half-plate stand camera may be taken with perfect ease, the various parts constituting the latter being packed in the rucksack with greater comfort than the hand camera, whose cumbersome shape renders it a most awkward piece of luggage.

Moreover, although excellent enlargements and lantern slides can be obtained from quarter-plate negatives, the direct prints made from them produce an impression distinctly inferior to that given by half-plate prints of similar subjects.

Nevertheless many will, no doubt, give the preference to the hand camera, owing to the small amount of preparation required before using it. It is hardly necessary to point out that a multiplicity of complicated movements are a serious drawback to a hand camera intended for use in the mountains. It is obviously impossible to specify the numerous hand cameras now before the public, but amongst those which up to the present time (1899) have been well tried, and may be recommended for the High Alps, are the Frena (Beck), the Ross Twin Lens, the Primus (Butcher), the Newman and Guardia, the Key (Platinotype Co.), and the Xit (Shew), all of which are well constructed machines, and in the box form, excepting the last-named, which folds.

The chief points of each may be briefly set forth as follows :—

The Frena is a light camera possessing a magazine capable of carrying as many as forty films, the changing mechanism of which is, however, liable to upset by the inevitable bumping incidental to rock-climbing.

The Ross Twin Lens camera is also a fairly light machine, whose chief advantage lies in the fact that the photographer is able to see the exact picture he is taking.

The same result is obtained by an ingenious reflecting arrangement in the Primus No. 7 A hand camera, which is, in addition, fitted with double extension bellows, enabling lenses of varying foci to be used, an advantage which will be readily appreciated by Alpine photographers.

The Newman and Guardia Special Pattern B camera is a very beautifully constructed machine in all its parts, with which lenses of varying foci can also be used by means of its triple extension bellows, but it is, perhaps, open to the objection of being rather complicated and, in common with the last named camera, is somewhat heavy.

The ingenious dark slides and simplicity of manipulation are the most noticeable points of the Key camera, which has certainly proved as effective in practice as any of those named here.

The Xit camera stands by itself as a hand camera, and is, perhaps, the one which will recommend itself most to the climber, owing to its extraordinary lightness and portability. It can, indeed, be carried quite easily in the pocket, although this mode of carrying it is certainly not recommended. If fitted with the Xit extension back it may be used as an ordinary stand camera with all the advantages conferred by the use of lenses of varying foci.

All the cameras above mentioned possess in common the advantage of a rising front, which is indispensable for the mountains. The lenses used ought, of course, to be of a first-rate kind, and should have a focal length of about $5\frac{1}{2}$ inches.

As time exposures are often preferable, and even necessary for Alpine photography, it is advisable to make a rule of taking a tripod stand for use with the hand camera; for the trembling of the hands and the increased pulsation of the heart, caused by the exertions of climbing, render it impossible to hold the camera motionless for a sufficient length of time in the hands alone, while it is seldom easy to find a convenient object on which to place the camera.

A telescopic aluminium tripod of great lightness, with triangular legs made adjustable for uneven ground, has been recently brought out (Shew), and would probably meet the requirements of the case. Should the climber, however, desire to avoid the trouble of carrying a tripod, he can make use of a metal clip and screw by means of which the camera can be fastened to the head of the ice axe, which thus serves as the support to keep the camera steady.

A stand camera is undoubtedly more troublesome to manipulate than a hand camera, but, owing probably to the fact that it is used with greater care, it is on the whole more certain, and consequently more satisfactory in its results. If the apparatus be carried by a guide (who seldom regards it with a friendly eye) the climber should content himself with a half-plate camera, which is the largest size he can reasonably expect the guide to carry in addition to the other impedimenta necessary for a mountain expedition. If, however, the climber should be willing to bear the burden on his own shoulders, and have nothing else to carry, he could, if he wished, take the $7\frac{1}{2}$ in. × 5 in. size, but it is doubtful whether the slight enlargement in the size of the picture obtained fully compensates for the increased weight and dimensions of the whole apparatus.

The particular points to which attention should be given in selecting a stand camera may be enumerated as follows :—

The Body of the Camera.—It is important that this be of the best possible workmanship, made of thoroughly seasoned wood and metal bound (aluminium being used as far as possible), in order that it may withstand the variations and vagaries of mountain weather and the severe shocks which it is certain to encounter during its Alpine career. It will, of course, possess the usual advantages of a swing back and a rising front, the latter being quite indispensable. These movements should be easily adjustable, as nothing is more trying to the temper on a cold day than to have stiff movements to handle with half-frozen fingers; they should also not be of such a complicated nature as to be easily put out of order. An undetachable revolving adaptor, to hold the dark slide vertically or horizontally at will, is an improvement on the usual removable adaptor, and an aluminium turntable is of untold convenience. All thumbscrews should be made so that they cannot be removed. A small spirit level or a plumb indicator fixed on the camera will be found useful, and it is also advisable to take one or two extra focussing screens to replace possible breakages.

Lens.—The most serviceable for the mountaineer are the sets of interchangeable lenses now sold by various makers, which practically enable the photographer to include in his picture just as much as he wishes. For instance, the Set C of Zeiss convertible lenses, sold by Ross and Co., includes a 9-inch, an $11\frac{1}{2}$-inch, and a 14-inch single lens, the various combinations of which give 5¾-inch, 6¼-inch, and 7-inch focus, thus giving a range of foci varying from 5¾-inch to 14-inch. The lens mount is provided with an iris diaphragm and a movable ring marked with scales of apertures for the various focal lengths.

The yellow screen is a comparatively recent introduction into Alpine photography, of which the chief use is to give a correct rendering of colour values, and to diminish the sensitiveness of the plates to the violet and blue rays. It is intended more especially to be used with isochromatic plates, as its utility with ordinary plates is not very apparent. For mountain photography its chief advantages lie in the softening of shadows and the rendering of clouds and distant ranges, although, as far as the latter is concerned, it cannot be claimed that the same result may not be successfully obtained without the screen. Its use is distinctly beneficial in a hazy atmosphere. A primrose yellow screen is the most useful, of such a shade that about three times the usual exposure is necessary.

Shutter.—The climber may choose between two classes of shutter, the blind shutter and that used between the lenses. Of the former the Thornton-Pickard still holds its own for efficiency. Its best place is, perhaps, at the back of the lens, and fastened to the lens carrier, where it runs less risk of being damaged or of shaking the camera when set in motion. Of the between-lens shutters the Bausch-Lomb is probably the most popular at the present moment. The Goerz Sector Shutter may, however, prove the best for the climber, as all its working parts are covered in, being thus protected from injury. Both these shutters can be worked by a finger trigger instead of the pneumatic ball and tube.

A shutter is, of course, an absolute necessity for rapid plates, but where slow plates are invariably used it is not an altogether indispensable item in the outfit, as in this case the cap serves quite as well, and in any event should never be left behind.

Dark Slides or Changing Box.—For plates a changing box is recommended instead of the usual separate dark slides. The Burns-Shaw is probably the best for Alpine work, although it necessitates the use of a dark slide. It is a very solid light-tight wooden box to hold twelve plates, with two brass slides running in deep grooves at one end, through which the plates pass out of and into the changing box into and from the dark slide. The plates are protected from scratches by metal flanges, which bind them together in pairs. Of other changing boxes now in use the Adams, and the Newman & Guardia, neither of which requires the use of a separate dark slide, have both been well tried. In these the plates are changed by lifting them with the fingers from the back to the front of the box at the end enclosed by a soft leather bag. None of these appear to be wholly satisfactory for films, which are perhaps best used in dark slides specially made for them, of which the best pattern is, perhaps, that made by Shew. It is hardly necessary to emphasise the importance of having the sliding shutters of the plate holders, if these be used, fitted with the utmost accuracy, as the penetrative power of light on a high snow-field is very remarkable. For this reason it is also necessary to have the wood-work of these thin cameras and slides well painted with dead black *outside* as well as inside.

Tripod.—The ordinary camera legs, even if made fourfold, are, when closed, inconveniently long for mountain work, and in the descent of difficult and steep rocks may become a really serious source of danger. The prudent climber will, therefore, do well to be satisfied with a short set, measuring when folded twelve inches at the most, which can be easily carried in the side pocket of the rucksack. It is essential that the legs should be made sufficiently stout to possess the requisite rigidity in a high wind. They should also be provided with very sharp points, without which it is sometimes almost impossible to place the camera on the limited space of a rocky summit. On deep snow three small discs of cork or wood are most useful for preventing the legs from sinking.

The *focussing cloth*—the only remaining item of importance—should have along one end a running tape sewn down in the middle, by which means it can be tied securely to the camera.

A full discussion of the comparative merits of *glass plates* and *films* would require more space than these pages can afford, but it may be boldly asserted that, whenever it is possible to take them, glass plates are, in spite of their greater weight, much to be preferred. The wisest course, however, is to take a supply of both, as the lightness of films is an immense advantage when it is important to keep down the weight of the rucksack. Moderately slow plates are perhaps the best for Alpine photography—at any rate for a novice. After two or three years' experience the photographer will be able to please himself in the matter. With regard to the packing of the plates after exposure—a question of some importance to the climber, who is obliged so often to send his luggage unaccompanied from place to place—an excellent plan is to put them back, packed in pairs, face to face, in the original wrappings, into the same boxes from which they were first taken, and to place the latter in the middle of the suit-case or trunk, tightly packed all round with clothes. In this way they will run very slight risk of breakage during their travels. It is well to remember also—especially when using isochromatic plates—that hôtel dark rooms are often not quite light-tight, and that it is wise to remain in your darkened bedroom some time before deciding that you have shut out all the light and so rendered the room safe for handling extremely sensitive films. Otherwise the season's work may be found on development to be very disappointing. Many workers find the small portable *changing bags* useful and safe for this purpose. The replacing of the plates or films in the dark backs must all be done by the sense of touch, and hence it is necessary to be systematic in your proceedings, otherwise considerable confusion may occur. These bags are only suitable for plates up to half-plate size. They can be home-made of a double thickness of black twill. Of the type with eye-piece and ruby window the 'Shepherd' is a good example.

Probably the most convenient travelling *lamp* is one of a triangular form holding a night light, with sides of ruby fabric, not glass. Good patterns are Redding's and the 'Traveller.'

The exposures required do not on the whole differ very much from those necessary in the valleys and plains. The safest plan is to make use of an exposure meter, or one of the set tables of exposures calculated for ordinary use. A little curtailment of these will be necessary for most subjects, and even then there may perhaps have been slight over-exposure, which is a fault on the right side and can be corrected in development. For a picture in which there is nothing but brilliantly illuminated snow and ice the exposure must, however, be very much shortened, to avoid the risk of losing the half-tones, and for views of this kind it is better to have the sun as much as possible in front of the camera.

It is manifest that the climber labours under the great disadvantage of not always being able to pick and choose the time of day at which he would like to take his photograph, but as a general rule the early hours of the forenoon and the later hours of the afternoon are, in summer, the best for the lighting of the mountains, as the light is then more evenly diffused and the shadows less dense. In the concentrated glare of midday the contrast of light and shade are apt to be too violent, and there is inevitable risk of over-exposure as regards the snow, or hopeless under-exposure in the case of rocks in shadow.

During the first season of his photographic labours amongst the mountains the climber should develop his plates, or at least a portion of them, as soon as possible, in order to guide him in the matter of exposures. When he has gained sufficient experience he will probably prefer to postpone development until his return home, for the distractions of a climbing centre are decidedly unfavourable to the exercise of that amount of patience and care necessary for obtaining the best results. A detailed description of the developers, which must necessarily vary according to the speed of the plates and the different makes, is hardly necessary. Each probably possesses enthusiastic advocates who can put forward unanswerable arguments in favour of their pet developer.

With regard to the choice of subjects, so much depends on the æsthetic perception of the individual that it is almost impossible to give definite advice. One of the chief points to be kept in mind is a proper balance of proportion in the subject, to secure which a due amount of discrimination must be exercised in the choice of a lens of the correct focal length for the subject; for it is most important that the photograph should convey a true impression of the peak or mountain landscape as seen from the point at which it is taken. Too great an expanse of sky tends to dwarf the peaks, and the photographer must guard against the common fault of including too much in his picture.

Mountain views usually look best taken with the plate turned vertically, but to this rule there are necessarily exceptions, such as the views of Mont Blanc from the neighbouring summits, or such views as that of the great wall of peaks which overhang the Argentière Glacier. Panoramic views should be taken horizontally, but these are as a rule more useful than pictorial. Clouds add very much to the artistic effect of the picture, and the climber should never be persuaded to leave the camera behind on what may appear to be a hopeless day for photography, for during cloudy weather, or after a storm, he will probably secure some of his finest pictures.

If a foreground is to be included it must be good of its kind. A bad foreground may entirely spoil an otherwise satisfactory view, and should be left out altogether; or should this be impossible it will be better to leave the subject alone, unless the photograph is desired for merely topographical purposes.

PHOTOGRAPHY IN THE HIGH ALPS.

During the last few years, since the introduction by Mr. Dallmeyer of his *telephotographic lens*, the production of pictures of distant objects by this means has come a good deal to the fore. There is considerable difference of opinion as to the comparative advantages of photographing a distant object with an ordinary long-focus lens, with subsequent enlargement from the negative so obtained, and producing a large image direct by the use of a telephotographic lens. There is no question that higher degrees of magnification can be obtained by telephotography, as, in the case of an enlargement from an ordinary negative, the final degree of magnification is reached when the enlarged grain of the plate coating becomes unpleasantly visible. Many workers with telephotographic lenses have found great difficulty in obtaining satisfactory density in their negatives, but from results obtained by some photographers it seems likely that this failure was due to faults in manipulation, although no doubt highly magnified images often tend to be thinner than those less magnified. Probably the best telephotographic work has been done elsewhere than in the mountains, where the rays from the distant object have traversed an atmosphere of tolerably uniform density overlying land of uniform configuration or wide stretches of water. In the mountains it is far otherwise: the photographer is viewing his distant peak over deep valleys where practically no radiation reaches the upper part of the air, and over ridges of rock or snow from which the most intense heat is being reflected into the layer of air through which the light rays are passing. Hence the rays are bent and distorted, and a blurred image is produced. Moreover, owing to the longer exposure required with the telephotographic combination, the image produced by this is more apt to suffer from these conditions than is that produced by the ordinary lens. No one, however, can help recognising that from the point of view of topography, and for purposes of mountain exploration, this method is most valuable. On the other hand the artistic mind may fairly object to a foreground which is actually some three or four miles distant, but in which the windows of the houses are plainly visible.

Turning to the practical side of the question, we have to consider what modification of the ordinary camera and lens is necessary for this work. The camera must have a long extension bellows, opening to 17 or 20 inches in the half-plate size, for the degree of magnification depends with any given lens combination on the distance of the focussing screen from the negative lens. The negative lens which, attached to the back of the positive, forms the telephotographic combination may be either fitted to one of Dallmeyer's own Rapid Rectilinear lenses or to any similar lens of a good maker which will work at F/8. Zeiss and Voigtlander also make a similar negative combination. The angle of view included is about $12°-15°$.

The whole lens is probably best mounted for Alpine photography in aluminium, to save weight; if extreme magnification is desired a high-power negative lens combined with a portrait lens will be necessary, but this is too cumbersome and expensive for ordinary purposes.

When using this lens the rigidity of the camera and its stand must be carefully attended to. Owing to the camera being racked out to its full extent, and the exposure being somewhat prolonged, this is really a very great difficulty in Alpine telephotography. On a mountain ridge wind is rarely absent, and if a source of difficulty when using an ordinary lens, with a camera extended 9 inches, it is doubly so with this lens and an extension of 20 inches. Every plan for sheltering and anchoring the camera, with a string and stone, or by using an extra strut to the front, must be employed, and in buying a new camera it is well to avoid *too* light a pattern. Obviously with this high magnification any vibration becomes evident in the negative.

Accurate focussing, both by means of the rack and pinion on the lens and finally by the camera pinion, is necessary, and a focussing glass should be employed. The focussing should be done with the actual stop used.

In distant photography with this lens it is always wise to use an orange screen.

It is necessary to remember that, owing to the narrow angle embraced in these views, it is advisable to choose a point of view as nearly level with the object to be photographed as possible, otherwise the angle to which the camera must be tilted results in great distortion of the perspective. This to some extent limits the usefulness of the lens.

No precise rules can be laid down here as to the comparative length of exposure necessary when photographing an object with an ordinary rapid rectilinear lens, and with the same lens used with a negative lens to form a telephotographic combination, as this must depend upon the length of camera extension and the degree of stopping down that may be necessary. Full details for calculating the exposures at various degrees of extension are supplied in the instructions issued by the makers of these lenses, but it will usually be found that the exposure works out at a considerable multiple of that required with the positive lens. It will be seen that when a yellow screen is used the exposure will thus often extend to ten to fifteen seconds, and this explains why wind vibration is so troublesome and difficult to avoid. But snap-shot work has been done with this lens, and it is important to remember that under- rather than over-exposure is to be aimed at, and very prolonged and gradual development employed, until no further change in the plate can be seen. The time of development may easily extend to three-quarters of an hour. A developer strong in reducer and fairly well restrained should be employed. Most workers will probably find hydrokinon convenient for such long development, but many successful workers use pyrogallic acid and ammonia or soda. It is hardly needful to point out the importance of keeping the plate well protected from the red light during this long development.

In conclusion let us insist that, whatever the method employed may be, the photographer should above all endeavour to impress his work with an individuality of its own, and thereby show how much the artistic temperament can achieve with mechanical material. Finally, let him not be discouraged by failure in his early efforts, for he will do well to remember that in this, as in most pursuits, theory is but a signpost on the road to success, and that practice alone makes the master.

Further detailed information of a valuable nature on this subject will be found in a chapter by Mr. Clinton Dent in the Badminton volume on 'Mountaineering,' and also in a chapter by Captain Abney in the 'Barnet Book of Photography.'

APPENDICES.

APPENDIX a.

LIST OF BOOKS AND MAPS RELATING TO THE ALPS.

1. BOOKS.

[The following list is intended to include all the *more important books* relating to the Alps, but makes no pretensions to be a complete Alpine Bibliography. Works relating exclusively to the physical sciences, as well as articles in periodicals, are purposely excluded from it, while lists of Guide-books and Alpine Periodicals are more fitly given in the 'Preliminary Notes' to each of the volumes of the new edition of the 'Alpine Guide.'

The nearest approach to an exhaustive Alpine Bibliography (it is practically complete so far as regards Switzerland and the neighbouring districts) is the work entitled 'Landes- und Reisebeschreibungen,' by Herr A. Wäber, which was issued in 1899 at Bern as part iii. of the extensive 'Bibliographie der Schweizerischen Landeskunde,' published by the Swiss Government.]

Aeby, C., Fellenberg, E. v., and Gerwer, R. Das Hochgebirge von Grindelwald. Coblenz, 1865.
Allais, G. Le Alpi Occidentali nell' Antichità. Turin, 1891.
Almer's, Christian, Führerbuch, 1856-1894. A facsimile edition. London, 1896.
Alpenwirthschaft der Schweiz im Jahre 1864, Die. Bern, 1868.
Alpi che cingono l' Italia, Le. Part i. of vol. i. alone published. Turin, 1845.
Alpstatistik, Schweizerische. Solothurn.
 Now appearing in Parts, of which eight (by different authors) have as yet been issued, dealing respectively with the Cantons of Baselland (1894), Solothurn (1896), St. Gallen (1896), Nidwalden (1896), Uri (1898), Glarus (1898), Schwyz (1899), and Appenzell Inner Rhoden (1899).
Altmann, J. G. Versuch einer historischen und physischen Beschreibung der Helvetischen Eisbergen. Zürich, 1751.
Anderegg, Felix. Illustriertes Lehrbuch für das gesamte schweizerische Alpwirthschaft. 3 parts. Bern, 1897-8.
Arnod, P. A. Relation des Passages de tout le Circuit du Duché d'Aoste

venant des Provinces circonvoisines, avec une description sommaire des Montagnes, 1691-4.

MS. preserved in the State Archives at Turin, and only partially published. For further particulars see the new edition of the 'Alpine Guide,' vol. i. p. xiii.

Auldjo, J. Narrative of an Ascent to the Summit of Mont Blanc on the 8th and 9th of August, 1827. London, 1828.
Later editions in 1830 and 1856.

Baillie-Grohman, W. A. Tyrol and the Tyrolese: the People and the Land in their Social, Sporting, and Mountaineering Aspects. London, 1876. (2nd edition, 1877.)

Baillie-Grohman, W. A. Gaddings with a Primitive People. 2 vols. London, 1878.

Baillie-Grohman, W. A. Sport in the Alps. London, 1896.

Barth, Hermann von. Aus den nördlichen Kalkalpen. Gera, 1874.

Barth, L., and Pfaundler, L. Die Stubaier Gebirgsgruppe hypsometrisch und orographisch bearbeitet. Innsbruck, 1865.

Berlepsch, H. A. Die Alpen in Natur- und Lebensbildern. Leipzig, 1861. (5th edition, Jena, 1885.) English translation by Leslie Stephen. London, 1861.

Berlepsch, H. A. Schweizerkunde; Land und Volk übersichtlich vergleichend dargestellt. Brunswick, 1864. (2nd edition, 1875.)

Bernensium, Fontes Rerum. Bern's Geschichtsquellen. 7 vols. (with Index volume), extending to 1353. Bern, 1883-1893.

Bianchetti, Enrico. L' Ossola Inferiore: notizie storiche e documenti. 2 vols. (one of text and one of original documents.) Turin, 1878.

Biellese, Il. Milan, 1898.
Published by the Biella Section of the Italian Alpine Club on occasion of the Congress there in 1898.

Bonnefoy, J. A., and Perrin, A. Le Prieuré de Chamonix: documents relatifs au Prieuré et à la Vallée de Chamonix. 2 vols. Chambéry, 1879-1883.
See also *Perrin.*

Bonney, T. G. Outline Sketches in the High Alps of Dauphiné. London, 1865.

Bonney, T. G. The Alpine Regions of Switzerland and the Neighbouring Countries. London, 1868.

Bonstetten, Albert von. Superioris Germaniæ Confœderationis Descriptio.
The first description of Switzerland, written in 1479: the Latin and German texts have been well edited in vol. xiii., 1893, of the 'Quellen zur Schweizer Geschichte,' published at Basel.

Bordier, A. C. Voyage Pittoresque aux Glacières de Savoye. Fait en 1772. Geneva, 1773.

Bourcet, P. J. de. Mémoires Militaires sur les Frontières de la France, du Piémont, et de la Savoie, depuis l'Embouchure du Var jusqu'au Lac de Genève. Paris and Berlin, 1801.
Only partly by M. de Bourcet.

Bourrit, M. T. Description des Glacières, Glaciers, et Amas de Glace du Duché de Savoye. Geneva, 1773.
English translation by C. and F. Davy. 3 editions, 1775-6, at Norwich and Dublin.

Bourrit, M. T. Description des Alpes Pennines et Rhétiennes. 2 vols. Geneva, 1781.
In 1783 this work was reprinted at Geneva under the title of 'Nouvelle

Description des Vallées de Glace,' and again in 1785 in 3 vols. under the title of 'Nouvelle Description Générale et Particulière des Glacières, Vallées de Glace, et Glaciers qui forment la grande chaîne des Alpes de Suisse, d'Italie, et de Savoye.'

Bourrit, M. T. Descriptions des Cols ou Passages des Alpes. 2 vols. Geneva, 1803.

These three works are the most important of the number published by this author.

Brockedon, W. Illustrations of the Passes of the Alps by which Italy communicates with France, Switzerland, and Germany. 2 vols. London, 1828–9.

Brockedon, W. Journals of Excursions in the Alps: the Pennine, Graian, Cottian, Rhetian, Lepontian, and Bernese. London, 1833. (3rd edition in 1845.)

Burch, Lambert van der. Sabaudorum ducum principumque historiæ gentilitiæ. Leyden, 1599.

The Elzevir edition (Leyden, 1634) is entitled 'Sabaudiæ Respublica et Historia.'

Busk, Miss R. H. The Valleys of Tirol: their Traditions and Customs, and How to Visit them. London, 1874.

Campell, Ulrich. Rætiæ Alpestris Topographica Descriptio. Finished in 1572.

Campell, Ulrich. Historia Rætica. Finished by 1577.

These two important works were published at Basel as vols. vii. (1884), viii. (1887), and ix. (1890) of the 'Quellen zur Schweizer Geschichte.'

Carl von Oesterreich, Erzherzog. Ausgewählte Schriften. Vienna and Leipzig. Vol. iii. (1893) narrates the campaign of 1799 in Switzerland.

Chabrand, J. A., and Rochas d'Aiglun, A. de. Patois des Alpes Cottiennes (Briançonnais et Vallées Vaudoises) et en particulier du Queyras. Grenoble and Paris, 1877.

Christomannos, Th. Sulden-Trafoi: Schilderungen aus dem Ortlergebiete. Innsbruck, 1895.

Cole, Mrs. A Lady's Tour Round Monte Rosa. London, 1859.

Coleman, E. T. Scenes from the Snow Fields: being Illustrations from the Upper Ice-World of Mont Blanc. London, 1859.

Conway, Sir Martin. The Alps from End to End. London, 1895.

Coolidge, W. A. B. Swiss Travel and Swiss Guide-Books. London, 1889.

Contains a history of Swiss Guide-books, of Alpine Inns, and of Zermatt, with a list of Books of Swiss Travel.

Coxe, W. Travels in Switzerland and in the Country of the Grisons. 3 vols. London, 1801 (4th and best edition).

Cunningham, C. D., and Abney, W. de W. The Pioneers of the Alps. London, 1887. (2nd edition, 1888.)

Lives of Famous Guides.

Daudet, Alphonse. Tartarin sur les Alpes. Paris, 1885. (English translation, same date.)

Deluc, J. A., and Dentan, P. G. Relation de Différents Voyages dans les Alpes du Faucigny. Maestricht, 1776.

Dent, Clinton T. Above the Snow Line: Mountaineering Sketches between 1870 and 1880. London, 1885.

Dent, Clinton T., and others. Mountaineering. London, 1892.

In the 'Badminton Library.' German translation. Leipzig, 1893.

Desjardins, Ernest. Géographie de la Gaule Romaine. 4 vols. Paris, 1876–1893.

Desor, E. Excursions et Séjours dans les Glaciers et les Hautes Régions des Alpes de M. Agassiz et de ses compagnons de voyage. 2 Series. Neuchâtel and Paris, 1844 and 1845.
Dumas, Alexandre. Impressions de Voyage—Suisse. Paris, 1833 or 1834.
Durier, Charles. Le Mont Blanc. Paris, 1877. 4th edition, 1897.
Ebel, J. G. Schilderungen der Gebirgsvölker der Schweiz. 2 vols. Leipzig, 1798-1802.
Eckenstein, O., and Lorria, A. The Alpine Portfolio—The Pennine Alps from the Simplon to the Great St. Bernard. London, 1889.
Eckerth, W. Die Gebirgsgruppe des Monte Cristallo. Prague, 1887. (2nd edition, 1891.)
Edwards, Miss Amelia B. Untrodden Peaks and Unfrequented Valleys: A Midsummer Ramble in the Dolomites. London, 1873.
Egger, J. Geschichte Tirols. 3 vols. Innsbruck, 1872-1880.
Egli, Emil. Kirchengeschichte der Schweiz bis auf Karl den Grossen. Zürich, 1893.
Engelhardt, C. M. Naturschilderungen, Sittenzüge, und wissenschaftliche Bemerkungen aus den höchsten Schweizer-Alpen, besonders in Süd-Wallis und Graubünden. Paris, Strasburg, and Basel, 1840.
Engelhardt, C. M. Das Monte-Rosa und Matterhorn-(Mont Cervin)-Gebirg aus der Inseite seines Erhebungsbogen gen Nord; seine Ausläufer und Umgrenzung, besonders der Saasgrat mit dem Mischabeldom über dem Gletscherkrater von Fee. Paris and Strasburg, 1852.
Ferrand, Henri. Histoire du Mont Iseran. Grenoble, 1893.
Ferrand, Henri. La Frontière Franco-Italienne entre le Mont-Thabor et le Petit Saint Bernard. Grenoble, 1894.
Forbes, James D. Travels in the Alps of Savoy and other parts of the Pennine Chain. Edinburgh and London, 1843. (2nd edition, 1845.)
Forbes, James D. Norway and its Glaciers visited in 1851; followed by Journals of Excursions in the High Alps of Dauphiné, Berne, and Savoy. London, 1853.
Forbes, Sir John. A Physician's Holiday, or a Month in Switzerland in the Summer of 1848. London, 1849. (2nd edition, 1850.)
Freshfield, D. W. Across Country from Thonon to Trent: Rambles and Scrambles in Switzerland and the Tyrol. London, 1865 (privately printed).
Freshfield, D. W. Italian Alps: Sketches in the Mountains of Ticino, Lombardy, the Trentino, and Venetia. London, 1875.
Freshfield, Mrs. Henry. Alpine Byways, or Light Leaves gathered in 1859 and 1860. London, 1861.
Freshfield, Mrs. Henry. A Summer Tour in the Grisons and Italian Valleys of the Bernina. London, 1862.
Frey, Jacob. Die Alpen im Lichte verschiedener Zeitalter. Berlin, 1877.
Friedländer, Ludwig. Ueber die Entstehung und Entwickelung des Gefühls für das Romantische in der Natur. Leipzig, 1873.
Fröbel, Julius. Reise in die weniger bekannten Thäler auf der Nordseite der Penninischen Alpen. Berlin, 1840.
Fuchs, Josef. Hannibal's Alpenübergang. Vienna, 1897.
Furrer, Sigismund. Geschichte, Statistik, und Urkunden-Sammlung über Wallis. 2 vols. Sion, 1850-2.
Gay, Hilaire. Histoire du Vallais. 2 vols. Paris and Geneva, 1888-9.
Gelpke, E. F. Kirchengeschichte der Schweiz. 2 vols. Bern, 1856-1861.
Gelpke, E. F. Die Christliche Sagengeschichte der Schweiz. Bern, 1862.
George, H. B. The Oberland and its Glaciers: Explored and Illustrated with Ice-Axe and Camera. London, 1866.

LIST OF BOOKS AND MAPS RELATING TO THE ALPS.

Gesner, Conrad. Epistola ad Jacobum Avienum de Montium Admiratione. Zürich, 1541.
   Prefixed to Gesner's ' Libellus de lacte et operibus lactariis.'
Gesner, Conrad. Descriptio Montis Fracti sive Montis Pilati. Zürich, 1555.
Gilbert, Josiah. Cadore, or Titian's Country. London, 1869.
Gilbert, Josiah, and Churchill, G. C. The Dolomite Mountains. London, 1864. German translation, Klagenfurt, 1865.
Gioffredo, Pietro. Storia delle Alpi Marittime. Turin, 1839.
Girdlestone, A. G. The High Alps Without Guides. London, 1870.
Gnifetti, G. Nozioni Topografiche del Monte Rosa ed Ascensioni su di esso. 2nd edition. Novara, 1858.
Gremaud, J. Documents relatifs à l'Histoire du Vallais, A.D. 300-1431. 7 vols. Lausanne, 1875-1894.
Gröger, G., and Rabl, J. Die Entwickelung der Hochtouristik in den Oesterreichischen Alpen. Vienna, 1890.
Grohmann, Paul. Wanderungen in den Dolomiten. Vienna, 1877.
Gruner, G. S. Die Eisgebirge des Schweizerlandes. 3 vols. Bern, 1760.
Günther, R. Der Feldzug der Division Lecourbe im Schweizerischen Hochgebirge. Frauenfeld, 1896.
Güssfeldt, Paul. In den Hochalpen. Erlebnisse aus den Jahren 1859-1885. Berlin, 1886.
Güssfeldt, Paul. Der Montblanc. Berlin, 1894.
   French translation. Geneva, 1898.
Haller, Albrecht von. Die Alpen. Bern, 1732.
   This famous poem appeared in the first edition of the author's ' Gedichte ;' a convenient annotated edition of the ' Gedichte ' was edited by L. Hirzel at Frauenfeld in 1882.
Harpprecht, Th. Bergfahrten. Stuttgart, 1886.
Hartmann, Otto. Der Antheil der Russen am Feldzug von 1799 in der Schweiz. Zürich, 1892.
Hegetschweiler, Joh. Reisen in den Gebirgsstock zwischen Glarus und Graubünden in den Jahren 1819, 1820, und 1822. Zürich, 1825.
Herzog, H. Schweizerische Volksfeste, Sitten, und Gebräuche. Aarau, 1884.
Heusler, A. Rechtsquellen des Cantons Wallis. Basel, 1890.
Hinchliff, T. W. Summer Months among the Alps : with the Ascent of Monte Rosa. London, 1857.
Hirzel-Escher. Wanderungen in weniger besuchte Alpengegenden der Schweiz, und ihrer nächsten Umgebungen. Zürich, 1829.
Hoffmann, Georg. Wanderungen in der Gletscherwelt. Zürich, 1843.
Hudson, C., and Kennedy, E. S. Where there's a Will there's a Way : an Ascent of Mont Blanc by a New Route and Without Guides. London, 1856.
   2nd edition (1856) has also an account of the first ascent of Monte Rosa.
Hugi, F. J. Naturhistorische Alpenreise. Solothurn, 1830.
Hugi, F. J. Ueber das Wesen der Gletscher und Winterreise in das Eismeer. Stuttgart und Tübingen, 1842.
Idiotikon, Schweizerisches (Swiss-German Dialect Dictionary.)
   In course of publication since 1881 at Frauenfeld ; has now (April 1899) reached the letter ' P.'
Javelle, Emile. Souvenirs d'un Alpiniste. Lausanne, 1886. (3rd edition, 1897.)
King, S. W. The Italian Valleys of the Pennine Alps. London, 1858.
Kohlrusch, E. Schweizerisches Sagenbuch. Leipzig, 1854.

Laborde, J. B. de, and Zurlauben, F. A. de. Tableaux Topographiques, Pittoresques, Physiques, Historiques, Moraux, Politiques, Littéraires de la Suisse. Paris, 1777–80. 2 vols. of text and 2 more with the 278 Plates.
Latrobe, C. J. The Alpenstock ; or Sketches of Swiss Scenery and Manners, 1825-6. London, 1829. (2nd edition, 1839.)
Latrobe, C. J. The Pedestrian : a Summer's Ramble in the Tyrol. London, 1832.
Lechner, E. Piz Languard und die Bernina-Gruppe. Leipzig, 1858. (2nd edition, 1865.)
Lechner, E. Das Thal Bergell (Bregaglia) in Graubünden, mit Chiavenna. Leipzig, 1865. (2nd edition, 1874.)
Lendenfeld, R. von. Aus den Alpen : die Westalpen und die Ostalpen. 2 vols. Prague, Vienna, and Leipzig, 1896.
Leonhardi, G. Das Poschiavinothal. Leipzig, 1859.
Leonardi, G. Das Veltlin, nebst einer Beschreibung der Bäder von Bormio. Leipzig, 1860.
Lorria, A., and Martel, E. A. Le Massif de la Bernina. Zürich, 1894.
Löwl, Ferdinand. Aus dem Zillerthaler Hochgebirge. Gera, 1878.
Lurani, F. Le Montagne di Val Masino (Valtellina). Milan, 1883.
Lütolf, Alois. Sagen, Bräuche, und Legenden aus den Fünf Orten, Lucern, Uri, Schwyz, Unterwalden, und Zug. Lucerne, 1865.
Lütolf, Alois. Die Glaubensboten der Schweiz vor St. Gallus. Lucerne, 1871.
Main (Burnaby) Mrs. The High Alps in Winter. London, 1883.
Mathews, C. E. The Annals of Mont Blanc : a Monograph. London, 1898.
McCrackan, W. D. The Rise of the Swiss Republic. Boston (Mass.) and London, 1892.
Ménabréa, Léon. Des Origines Féodales dans les Alpes Occidentales. Turin, 1865.
Merian, Matthew, and Zeiller, Martin. Topographia Helvetiæ, Rhætiæ, et Valesiæ. Frankfort, 1642.
Meurer, Julius. Handbuch des Alpinen Sport. Vienna, Pesth, and Leipzig, 1882.
Meyer, J. R. and H. Reise auf den Jungfrau-Gletscher und Ersteigung seines Gipfels. Aarau, 1811.
See also *Zschokke.*
Miaskowski, August von. Die Schweizerische Allmend in ihrer geschichtlichen Entwickelung vom xiii. Jahrhundert bis zur Gegenwart. Leipzig, 1879.
Miaskowski, August von. Die Verfassung der Land-, Alpen-, und Forstwirthschaft der deutschen Schweiz in ihrer geschichtlichen Entwickelung vom xiii. Jahrhundert bis zur Gegenwart. Basel, 1878.
Michelet, J. La Montagne. Paris, 1868.
English translation, 1872.
Mohr, Th. and Conradin von. Codex Diplomaticus ad Historiam Ræticam. Coire, 1848–1858. 3 vols.
Vol. iv. (1863) forms vol. i. of the periodical ' Rätia.'
Montannel, De. La Topographie Militaire de la Frontière des Alpes. Grenoble, 1875.
Moor, Conradin von. Geschichte von Currätien und der Republik 'gemeiner drei Bünde ' (Graubünden). 2 vols. Coire, 1870–1.
A useful detailed chronological Index to the above appeared in 1873 at Coire under the title of 'Historisch-Chronologischer Wegweiser durch die Geschichte Currätiens und der Republik Graubünden.'

Moore, A. W. The Alps in 1864. A Private Journal. London, 1867 (privately printed) : a published edition is in preparation.
Mummery, A. F. My Climbs in the Alps and the Caucasus. London 1895.
Münster, Sebastian. Cosmographia. German edition at Basel, 1544, and Latin one at Basel in 1550.
Nüscheler, A. Die Gotteshäuser der Schweiz. 3 parts. Zürich, 1864-73.
Ober, P. L'Oberland Bernois sous les Rapports Historique, Scientifique, et Topographique. 2 vols. Berne, 1854.
Opérations Géodésiques et Astronomiques pour la Mesure d'un Arc du Parallèle Moyen. 2 vols. Milan, 1825-7.
Oesterreichisch-Ungarische Monarchie in Wort und Bild, Die. Vienna. Vol. vi. Oberoesterreich und Salzburg, 1889 ; vol. vii. Steiermark, 1890 ; vol. viii. Kärnten und Krain, 1891 ; vol. xiii. Tirol und Vorarlberg, 1893.
Pallioppi, Z. and E. Dizionari dels Idioms Romauntschs d'Engiadina ota e bassa, della Val Müstair, da Bravuogn, e Filisur, con particulera consideraziun del idiom d'Engiadina ota. Samaden, 1895.
Payer, Julius. Die Adamello-Presanella Alpen. Gotha, 1865.
Payer, Julius. Die Ortler-Alpen (Sulden-Gebiet u. Monte Cevedale). Gotha, 1867.
Payer, Julius. Die westlichen Ortler-Alpen (Trafoier Gebiet). Gotha, 1868.
Payer, Julius. Die südlichen Ortler-Alpen. Gotha, 1869.
Payer, Julius. Die centralen Ortler-Alpen (Martell, &c.) Gotha, 1872.
These five pamphlets form 'Ergänzungshefte' nos. 17, 18, 23, 27, and 31 to 'Petermann's Mittheilungen.'
Peaks, Passes, and Glaciers. 1st Series, edited by John Ball. London, 1859. 2nd Series, 2 vols., edited by E. S. Kennedy. London, 1862.
4 editions of 1st Series, all in 1859, 'Knapsack' edition, 1860, and partial French translation by Elise Dufour, Paris, 1862.
Perrin, A. Histoire de la Vallée et du Prieuré de Chamonix du 10ème au 18ème Siècle. Chambéry, 1887.
For the 'Documents' see under *Bonnefoy.*
Peyer, G. Geschichte des Reisens in der Schweiz : eine culturgeschichtliche Studie. Basel, 1885.
Pezay, Marquis de. Description des Vallées des Grandes Alpes : Dauphiné, Provence, Italie. Grenoble (in French) and Turin (in Italian), 1793.
The most convenient edition is that published in 1894 at Grenoble.
Planta, P. C. von. Die currätischen Herrschaften in der Feudalzeit. Bern, 1881.
Planta, P. C. von. Geschichte von Graubünden. Bern, 1892.
Rahn, J. R. Geschichte der bildenden Künste in der Schweiz von den ältesten Zeiten bis zum Schlusse des Mittelalters. Zürich, 1876.
Rahn, J. R. Kunst und Wanderstudien aus der Schweiz. Vienna, 1883.
The same author has also published (in the 'Anzeiger für Schweizerische Alterthumskunde') many lists of the artistic treasures to be found in several of the Swiss Cantons, *e.g.* Tessin.
Rambert, Eugène. Ascensions et Flâneries. 2 vols. Lausanne, 1888.
Rebmann, H. R. Ein Neuw, Lustig, Ernsthafft, Poetisch Gastmal und Gesprach zweyer Bergen, in der Löblichen Eydnossschafft, und im Berner Gebiet gelegen : Nemlich des Niesens und Stockhorns. Bern, 1606.
Enlarged edition, 1620.
Reding-Biberegg, R. von. Der Zug Suworoff's durch die Schweiz. With many plans. Stans, 1895.

Regesten der Archive in der Schweizerischen Eidgenossenschaft. 2 vols. Coire, 1848–54.
  Contains calendars of the muniments of many of the great Swiss monastic houses, *e.g.* Disentis, Einsiedeln, Interlaken, Pfävers.
Rey, R. Le Royaume de Cottius et la Province des Alpes Cottiennes d'Auguste à Dioclétien. Grenoble, 1898.
Richter, E. Die Erschliessung der Ostalpen. 3 vols. Berlin, 1893-4.
Rilliet, Albert. Les Origines de la Confédération Suisse : Histoire et Légende. Geneva and Bâle, 1868. (2nd edition, 1869.)
Rochas d'Aiglun, A. de. Les Vallées Vaudoises : Etude de Topographie et d'Histoire Militaires. Paris, 1881.
  See also under *Chabrand.*
Rohrdorf, Caspar. Reise über die Grindelwald-Viescher-Gletscher und Ersteigung des Gletschers des Jungfrau-Berges. Unternommen und beschrieben im August und September 1828. Bern, 1828.
Roman, J. Dictionnaire Topographique du Département des Hautes-Alpes.
Roman, J. Tableau Historique du Département des Hautes-Alpes. 2 vols.
Roman, J. Répertoire Archéologique du Département des Hautes-Alpes.
  These three splendid works were published at Paris in 1884, 1887-1890, and 1888 respectively.
Ruden, J. Familien-Statistik der löblichen Pfarrei von Zermatt. Ingenbohl, 1870.
Ruppen, P. J. Die Chronik des Thales Saas. Sion, 1851.
Ruthner, A. von. Aus den Tauern : Berg- und Gletscher-Reisen in den österreichischen Hochalpen. Vienna, 1864.
Ruthner, A. von. Aus Tirol : Berg- und Gletscher-Reisen in den österreichischen Hochalpen. Vienna, 1869.
Salève, Le. Geneva, 1899.
  Published by the Geneva Section of the Swiss Alpine Club.
Saussure, H. B. de. Voyages dans les Alpes. 4 vols. Neuchâtel and Geneva, 1779-1796.
  The 'Partie Pittoresque' of this work has appeared in several editions since 1834.
Schaubach, A. Deutsche Alpen. 5 vols. Jena, 1865-1871.
Scheuchzer, J. J. Helvetiæ Stoicheiographia, Orographia, et Oreographia. Zürich, 1716.
Scheuchzer, J. J. Itinera per Helvetiæ Alpinas Regiones facta annis 1702-1711. Collected edition. 4 vols. Leyden, 1723.
Schiller, F. von. Wilhelm Tell. 1804.
Schlagintweit, A. and H. Untersuchungen über die physikalische Geographie der Alpen. 2 Series. Leipzig, 1850 and 1854.
Schott, Albert. Die deutschen Colonien in Piemont. Stuttgart and Tübingen, 1842.
Sella, V., and Vallino, D. Monte Rosa e Gressoney. Biella, 1890.
Sererhard, N. Einfalte Delineation aller Gemeinden gemeiner dreien Bünden im Jahr 1742. Coire, 1872.
Simler, Josias. Vallesiæ Descriptio et de Alpibus Commentarius. Zürich, 1574.
  Handy Elzevir edition, Leyden, 1633.
Simony, F. Das Dachsteingebiet. Vienna, 1889-1896.
Sinigaglia, L. Climbing Reminiscences of the Dolomites. London, 1896.
Smith, Albert. The Story of Mont Blanc. London, 1853.
Sonklar, K. von. Die Oetzthaler Gebirgsgruppe, mit besonderer Rücksicht auf Orographie und Gletscherkunde. Gotha, 1860.

LIST OF BOOKS AND MAPS RELATING TO THE ALPS. cxlix

Sonklar, K. von. Die Gebirgsgruppe der Hohen-Tauern. Vienna, 1866.
Sonklar, K. von. Die Zillerthaler Alpen. Gotha, 1874.
  ' Ergänzungsheft ' no. 32 to Petermann's ' Mittheilungen.'
Sowerby, J. The Forest Cantons of Switzerland. London, 1892.
Sprecher, Fortunatus à. Pallas Rætica armata et togata. Basel, 1617.
  Also Elzevir edition, Leyden, 1633.
Stanyan, Abraham. An Account of Switzerland. Written in the Year 1714. London, 1714.
Stephen, Leslie. The Playground of Europe. London, 1871.
  Later editions (with some changes), 1894 and 1899.
Stubei: Thal und Gebirg, Land und Leute. Leipzig, 1891.
Studer, Bernard. Geschichte der physischen Geographie der Schweiz bis 1815. Bern and Zürich, 1863.
Studer, Gottlieb. Topographische Mittheilungen aus dem Alpengebirge. Bern and St. Gallen, 1844.
Studer, Gottlieb. Ueber Eis und Schnee. 3 vols with supplement (1883). Bern, 1869-1871.
  New editions of vol. i. (1896), vol. ii. (1898), and vol. iii. (1899.)
Studer, Gottlieb, Ulrich, M., and Weilenmann, J. J. Berg- und Gletscher-Fahrten. 2 Series. Zürich, 1859 and 1863.
Studer, Julius. Schweizer Ortsnamen : ein historisch-etymologischer Versuch. Zürich, 1896.
Stumpf, J. Gemeiner loblicher Eydgnosschaft Stetten, Landen, und Völckeren Chronicwirdiger Thaatenbeschreybung. Zürich, 1548.
  2nd edition, 1586 ; 3rd edition, 1606.
Symonds, J. A. and Margaret. Our Life in the Swiss Highlands. London and Edinburgh, 1892.
Tatarinoff, E. Die Entwickelung der Probstei Interlaken im xiii. Jahrhundert. Schaffhausen, 1892.
Theobald, G. Naturbilder aus den Rhätischen Alpen. Coire, 1860.
  2nd edition, 1862 ; 3rd edition, 1893.
Theobald, G. Das Bündner Oberland. Coire, 1861.
Tissot, Victor. La Suisse Inconnue. Paris, 1888. English translation, 1889.
Tobler, Ludwig. Schweizerische Volkslieder. 2 vols. Frauenfeld, 1882-4.
Töpffer, R. Voyages en Zigzag. 2 Series. Paris, 1844 and 1853.
Tscheinen, Moriz. Walliser-Sagen. Sion, 1872.
Tschudi, Ægidius. De priscâ ac verâ Alpinâ Rhætiâ, cum cætero Alpinarum gentium tractu descriptio. Basel, 1538 (also in German). 2nd edition, 1560.
  Probably the first published treatise exclusively devoted to the Alps.
Tschudi, Ægidius. Gallia Comata. Constance, 1758.
  Published long after the author's death in 1572.
Tuckett, F. F. Hochalpenstudien. 2 vols. Leipzig, 1873-74.
  Only collected edition of the author's Alpine articles.
Tuckett, Miss L. How we spent the Summer ; or a Voyage en Zigzag. London, 1864. 4th edition, 1871.
Tuckett, Miss L. Pictures in Tyrol and Elsewhere. From a Family Sketch-Book. London, 1867. 2nd edition, 1869.
Tuckett, Miss L. Zigzagging amongst Dolomites. London, 1871.
Türst, Conrad. De situ Confœderatorum descriptio, 1495-7.
  Latin and German texts printed in 1884, at Basel, in vol. vi. of the ' Quellen zur Schweizer Geschichte,' together with a reproduction of his map, the earliest map of Switzerland known to exist.

Tyndall, John. The Glaciers of the Alps. London, 1860.
    Reprinted in 1896.
Tyndall, John. Mountaineering in 1861. London, 1862.
Tyndall, John. Hours of Exercise in the Alps. London, 1871.
Tyndall, John. New Fragments. London, 1892.
Ulrich, M. Die Seitenthäler des Wallis und der Monte Rosa topographisch geschildert. Zürich, 1850. See also under *Studer,* G.
Umlauft, F. Die Alpen: Handbuch der gesammten Alpenkunde. Vienna, Pesth, and Leipzig, 1887.
    English translation, 1889.
Vacation Tourists and Notes of Travel in 1860. London, 1861.
    Has articles by J. J. Cowell on the Mont Iseran, by Leslie Stephen on the Allalinhorn, by F. V. Hawkins on an attempt on the Matterhorn, and by J. Tyndall on the Lauithor.
Vaccarone, L. Le Pertuis du Viso. Turin, 1881.
Vaccarone, L. Le Vie delle Alpi Occidentali negli antichi tempi. Turin, 1884.
Vaccarone, L. Statistica delle Prime Ascensioni nelle Alpi Occidentali. 3rd and best edition. Turin, 1890.
    Does *not* include the summits of the Pelvoux Group.
Vénéon, Jean (i.e. *Perrin, Félix*). In Memoriam Tschingel. Grenoble, 1892.
Venetz, L. Mémoire sur les Variations de la Température dans les Alpes de la Suisse.
    Most valuable essay, containing much information as to old glacier passes. It appeared at Zürich in 1833 in vol. i. part ii. of the 'Denkschriften der allgemeinen Schweizerischen Gesellschaft für die gesammten Naturwissenschaften.'
Vernaleken, Th. Alpensagen: Volksüberlieferungen aus der Schweiz, aus Vorarlberg, Kärnten, Steiermark, Salzburg, Ober- und Niederösterreich. Vienna, 1858.
Vischer, W. Die Sage von der Befreiung der Waldstätte nach ihrer allmäligen Ausbildung. Leipzig, 1867.
Wagner, J. J. Historia Naturalis Helvetiæ Curiosa. Zürich, 1680.
Wagner, R., and Salis, L. R. von. Rechtsquellen des Cantons Graubünden. 4 parts. Basel, 1887–1892.
Weilenmann, J. J. Aus der Firnenwelt. 3 vols. Leipzig, 1872–7.
Welden, L. von. Der Monte Rosa: eine topographische und naturhistorische Skizze, nebst einem Anhange der von Herrn Zumstein gemachten Reisen zur Ersteigung seiner Gipfel. Vienna, 1824.
Whymper, E. Scrambles amongst the Alps in the Years 1860–9. London, 1871.
    2nd edition, 1871; 3rd edition (abridged), 1880; 4th and definitive edition, 1893. German translation, Brunswick, 1872 (2nd edition, 1892); French translation, Paris, 1873.
Wills, Sir Alfred. Wanderings among the High Alps. London, 1856.
    2nd edition, 1858.
Wills, Sir Alfred. 'The Eagle's Nest' in the Valley of Sixt: a Summer Home among the Alps; together with some Excursions among the Great Alps. London, 1860.
Wilson, Claude. Mountaineering. London, 1893. In the 'All-England' Series.
Windham, W., and Martel, P. An Account of the Glacières or Ice Alps in Savoy. In two letters—one from an English gentleman to his friend at

Geneva; the other from Peter Martel, engineer, to the said English gentleman. London, 1744.
 The original French text of both letters, written in 1741-2, was printed by T. Dufour in the 'Echo des Alpes' for 1879.
Wirth, Max. Allgemeine Beschreibung und Statistik der Schweiz. 2 vols. in 6 parts. Zürich, 1870-3.
Wundt, Th. Die Besteigung des Cimone della Pala. Stuttgart, 1892.
Wundt, Th. Wanderungen in den Ampezzaner Dolomiten. Berlin, 1893.
Wundt, Th. Wanderbilder aus den Dolomiten. Berlin, 1894.
Wundt, Th. Das Matterhorn und seine Geschichte. Berlin, 1896.
Wundt, Th. Die Jungfrau und das Berner Oberland. Berlin, 1897.
Wyss, F. von. Abhandlungen zur Geschichte des schweizerischen öffentlichen Rechts. Zürich, 1892.
 Contains a remarkable history of Swiss 'communes' and of the 'free peasants' of Eastern Switzerland in the late Middle Ages.
Wyss, J. R. Idyllen, Volkssagen, Legenden, und Erzählungen aus der Schweiz. 2 Series. Bern and Leipzig, 1815 and 1822.
Wyss, J. R. Reise in das Berner Oberland. In 2 parts with 'Hand Atlas.' Bern, 1817.
 French edition published at the same time.
Wyss, J. R., and Huber, Ferd. Sammlung von Schweizer-Kuhreihen. Mit Melodien und alten Volksliedern. 4th and best edition. Bern, 1826.
Zingerle, I. V. Sagen, Märchen, und Gebräuche aus Tirol. Innsbruck, 1859.
Zingerle, I. V., and Inama-Sternegg, K. Th. von. Die tirolischen Weisthümer. 4 vols. Vienna, 1875-1888.
Zschokke, H. Reise auf die Eisgebirge des Kantons Bern und Ersteigung ihrer höchsten Gipfel im Sommer 1812. Aarau, 1813.
 This pamphlet, compiled from information given by the Meyers, should be carefully compared with R. Meyer's original narrative, printed in the 'Alpenrosen' for 1852 (issued at Aarau and Thun).
Zsigmondy, Emil. Die Gefahren der Alpen. Leipzig, 1885.
 French translation, Neuchâtel, 1886.
Zsigmondy, Emil. Im Hochgebirge. Leipzig, 1889.

2. MAPS.

A. *Austrian Alps.*

i. *Government Maps.*—The best map is the 'Specialkarte der österreichisch-ungarischen Monarchie.' In all 763 sheets. Scale $\frac{1}{75000}$. Surveyed 1869-1885 (by 1874 most of the Alpine regions complete); published 1874-1888, while a later revised edition ('Reambulirung') is also appearing.

ii. *Special Maps.*—The 'k.u.k. Militär-geographisches Institut' has also issued 11 sheets of 'Topographische Detailkarten.' Sheet 5 is devoted to the Ampezzo and Sexten Dolomites; sheet 7, to the Langkofel and Rosengarten groups, or the N.W. Dolomites; sheet 8, to the Stubai Alps; sheet 9, to those of the Oetzthal; sheet 10, to the Pala group; and sheet 11, to the Adamello, Presanella, and Brenta districts, all these sheets being on a scale of $\frac{1}{50000}$.

 Another set of district maps is that issued by the German and Austrian Alpine Club on a scale of $\frac{1}{50000}$; these now include all the chief districts of the Austrian Alps, save the Dolomites (in preparation), the 4 sheets representing the Oetzthal and Stubai regions being particularly clear and beautiful, while the Ortler map is perhaps the most useful to English travellers.

B. *French Alps.*

i. *Government Maps.*—Carte de l'Etat Major. 258 sheets (1833-1876). Scale, $\frac{1}{80000}$. (The best edition is that lithographed, and kept up to date; it is known as the 'Type 1889.')
    Carte de la Frontière des Alpes (in 3 colours). 72 sheets. (*c.* 1875.) Scale, $\frac{1}{80000}$. *No longer sold to the public.*
    Carte du Service Vicinal. *c.* 600 sheets. Scale, $\frac{1}{100000}$. Legible, but very untrustworthy as to names and heights.

ii. *Special Maps.*—See vol. i. of the new edition of the 'Alpine Guide,' pp. xxxvii–xxxix.

C. *Italian Alps.*

i. *Government Maps.*—Carta Topografica del Regno d'Italia. 277 sheets. Scale, $\frac{1}{100000}$. Surveyed 1879-1891; published (so far as regards the Alpine regions) 1884-1897.
    Tavolette rilevate per la construzione della Carta del Regno d' Italia. (Surveyed 1880-4, published 1882-1892.) Scale, $\frac{1}{50000}$. Accurate, but very illegible. *No longer sold to the public*, as is no doubt also the case with the clearer $\frac{1}{25000}$ edition (surveyed 1884-1892).

ii. *Special Maps.*—See the new edition of vol. i. of the 'Alpine Guide,' pp. xxxvii–xxxviii.

D. *Swiss Alps.*

A very complete list (extending to over 700 pages) of all Swiss Maps of any kind (general or special), wherever they appeared, was published (for the Federal Topographical Bureau) by Professor Graf, at Bern, in 1896, under the general title of 'Literatur der Landesvermessung.'

i. *Government Maps.*—The *Dufour* Map (25 sheets, 1845-1864, scale $\frac{1}{100000}$—its history was published at Bern in 1896) has now been superseded by the publication, after careful revision, of the original large scale survey ($\frac{1}{50000}$ for the mountain districts, $\frac{1}{25000}$ for the plains); this is known as the 'Topographischer Atlas der Schweiz,' or *Siegfried Atlas*, and extends to 589 sheets, in course of issue (all the mountain sheets are now published) since 1870. It is extremely clear, and most accurate, being undoubtedly the most splendid representation of a mountain land ever yet published.
    The best small-scale map (unofficial) of the Swiss Alps is that issued in 1897 by L. Ravenstein, of Frankfort (2 sheets on a scale of $\frac{1}{250000}$).

ii. *Special Maps.*—The Siegfried map quite does away in Switzerland with the need for large-scale Special Maps, especially as the Federal Topographical Bureau issues combinations of sheets or parts of sheets, so as to form most convenient District Maps. See the new edition of vol. i. of the 'Alpine Guide,' p. xxxix, and also the notes on maps in the 'Preliminary Notes' of the new edition of vol. ii. (in preparation) of the same work.

APPENDIX b.

A GLOSSARY OF ALPINE TERMS.

[It is to be hoped that one day some well qualified person will take in hand the compilation of a complete Alpine Glossary, for which there are already abundant printed materials (sometimes hidden carefully away in local pamphlets or periodicals), that may be supplemented to almost any extent by personal investigation in the valleys of the Alps. The present Glossary aims only at including the principal *technical* and *patois* terms—slang excluded—that may puzzle an English traveller or reader. Many of the examples given can be found in the new edition of vol. i. of the 'Alpine Guide,' others in the *later* volumes of that work.]

Aigue. A stream (*aqua*).
Allmend. Land owned in common, whether arable, meadow, pasture, or forest.
Alm. The Tyrolese term for an 'alp' or mountain pasture. See Art. X. 3.
Alp. A mountain pasture used in summer. See Art. X. 3.
Alpbuch. The official register in which everything relating to a particular 'alp' is entered.
Alpenhorn. A long curved horn of wood, originally used by the 'Älpler,' but now mainly employed to amuse tourists.
Alpenschatzung. The estimate of the number of cows that can be supported on an 'alp.' See **Stoss.**
Alpenstock. The long wooden pole used by Alpine travellers and by hunters in the Tyrol, though of recent years on high mountains it has been superseded by the ice-axe.
Alpfahrt. The annual journey of the cows up to the 'alp' in June.
Älpler. A man employed on an 'alp' during the summer.
Amait (Italian). A small plain in the mountains, *e.g.* Col de l'Amait di Viso.
Amont, d'. The 'upper' pastures or huts as opposed to those 'd'aval.'
Anken. Butter.
Arête. A rock or snow ridge, generally a more or less sharp ridge.
Avalanche. Snow or ice which slides or falls by its own weight towards the valley ('ad vallem'). See 'Alpine Journal,' vol. v. p. 349.
Baisse, Bassa, and **Basse.** A local term in the French and Italian Alps for a low pass, *e.g.* Baisse de St. Véran, Bassa di Druos, Basse du Gerbier.
Baita. A hut (of wood or stones) on an 'alp,' built under the shelter of a boulder.
Balm and **Balme.** A cave.
Bannwald. A forest which is put under 'bann,' *i.e.* where no trees can be felled under very severe penalties, often because the forest shelters a village from avalanches; hence applied to the wildest portions of a forest.
Bänz (Bernese Oberland). Patois word for a sheep.
Baracca, Baraccone, and **Baraque.** Small stone hut.
Bec, Becca, Becco. A pointed summit, like the beak of a bird.
Beisass. Strictly speaking a Swiss who lives in a 'commune' other than his own; loosely applied to all such dwellers, whether Swiss or foreigners. See Art. X. 2.

Bergerie (Viso and Vaudois Valleys). A local term strictly meaning a sheep chalet on a mountain pasture; but also more generally applied to any cheese chalet.
Bergfall and **Bergrutsch**. A landslip.
Bergrecht. See **Kuhrecht**.
Bergschrund. A particular kind of crevasse—namely, that which occurs where the steep upper névé or icy slope of a peak touches the more level ice or snow-field at its foot.
Bise. A cold wind, generally blowing from the N.
Blatten. Smooth rock slabs lying at a great incline.
Bocca and **Bocchetta** (Italian). A narrow 'mouth' or pass, *e.g.* Bocca di Brenta.
Brenta. A wooden barrel-shaped vessel (carried on a man's back) used in Switzerland for bringing the milk home from the mountain pastures or from the stable below; a smaller vessel of the same kind is called a 'Bräntli.' Cf. 'Brenta,' used in the Sarca valley (Adamello district) for a shallow vessel employed for soup, and by analogy for a stagnant tarn in a dolomite glen (Freshfield's 'Italian Alps,' p. 378).
Brec or **Bric** (Viso and Vaudois Valleys district). A rock peak especially if fissured and pointed, *e.g.* Brec de Chambeyron, Bric Bouchet.
Brèche. A narrow or well defined gap in a rock ridge.
Buhl. A hillock.
Burgergemeinde. A 'commune' composed solely of the burghers, to the exclusion of mere 'residents,' &c. See Art. X. 2.
Caire (Maritime Alps). A peak.
Canale (Venetian Alps). A valley, generally a main valley.
Casera. A hut on a mountain pasture, especially the hut wherein the cheeses are stored.
Casse. A slope covered with small stones, the result of the wearing away or weathering of the rocks above, *e.g.* Casse des Oules; also a saucepan, or a hollow in the earth which holds water like a saucepan, *e.g.* Grande Casse.
Cengia or **Sengia**. A narrow ledge on a rock wall. See **Vire**.
Chalanche or **Cialancia**. A bare avalanche-swept slope of stones.
Chalet. A hut on the mountain pastures, especially one used for milk and cheese purposes in summer; by extension, any dwelling-house in the valley below. The word should have no accent.
Chiot. A small rocky plain, and any hut upon it.
Cima, Cîme, or **Cimon**. A mountain peak, *e.g.* Cima Tosa, Cîme du Vallon, Cimon della Pala.
Clapier or **Clappey**. A slope of stones fallen from above, or due to the weathering of the rocks above, *i.e.* screes (Cumberland term).
Clot. A small plain on a mountain-side, *e.g.* Clot des Cavales.
Cluse. A narrow rocky defile.
Col or **Colle**. Generally a pass (*e.g.* Col du Géant); in certain parts of the Italian Alps a hill (*e.g.* Col Vicentino). Possibly both meanings come from 'collis,' a hillock as opposed to a 'mons' or mountain; but perhaps 'Col' in the sense of a pass comes from 'collum,' a neck.
Collerin. A small gully or 'couloir,' *e.g.* Col du Collerin.
Colonnes coiffées. Earth pillars (see this word), as they are capped by a great boulder.
Colour and **Colouret**. A gully or 'couloir,' and a small gully, *e.g.* Col del Colour del Porco, and the two Colourets on the Col de la Galise.
Combe. A glen, especially a side glen, and a narrow glen, *e.g.* Combe de Malaval.
Commune. The association (based originally on common ownership of land,

and later on political considerations) of the inhabitants in a village, or some particular bit of a large valley, or in a small valley.

Conca. A high mountain hollow or basin. See **Kar**.

Corniche. Used in two senses: (1) a narrow ledge of *rock*; (2) an overhanging crest of *snow* on a ridge.

Couloir. A steep gully in the mountain-side; it is often filled with ice, snow, or stones.

Coupé (Cogne). A narrow gap or 'cut' in a ridge.

Crampons. An iron frame fastened underneath the boot by leather straps, and furnished with several sharp points. They are much used in the Eastern Alps, in order to avoid step-cutting on slopes of hard snow, or even ice, but are useless on rocks.

Crevasse. A crack or rent in a glacier, due to the straining of the ice on its downward flow.

Croda (Dolomites). Rock; 'croda morta' is 'disaggregated rock, loosened by weathering' (Ball's 'Eastern Alps,' p. 526).

Crot. A deep mountain hollow, *e.g.* Crot del Ciaussiné.

Crozzon. A very steep and massive rock peak, *e.g.* Crozzon di Brenta.

Dirt Bands. Transverse curved bands of fine mud or débris, which mark the line of depression (into which they have been washed by little rills) between the ridges which in an icefall run between the crevasses, but sink, through the action of the sun, when the crevasses are closed up at the base of the icefall.

Dirt Cones. Hillocks of ice on a glacier, which have been protected from the action of the sun by the thick layer of sand, &c., on them, and which therefore form miniature mountains.

Draye (Cottian Alps). A small cattle track along the mountain-side, formed originally by the dragging or sliding of a log of wood along the slope.

Earth pillars. Pillars of earth, standing out from the mountain-side, each capped by a great boulder which has prevented the earth of which they are composed from being weathered away by rain, &c.

Egg. A hillock. The word 'Egg' has nothing to do with 'Eck.'

Eglise. The church hamlet of a 'commune.'

Emd. The second crop of grass, or 'aftermath.'

Enge. A narrow passage along a rock wall or slope, *e.g.* the two 'Enges' near Grindelwald.

Erratic blocks. Boulders of one kind of stone which are now found stranded on rock of a different formation, having been carried thither by an ancient glacier and left there (sometimes very delicately poised) when the ice disappeared. When they are very delicately poised they are also called 'blocs perchés' (see below).

Etret and **Etroit.** A narrow defile in a valley.

Fenêtre and **Finestra.** A narrow gap or 'window' in a mountain ridge, *e.g.* Fenêtre de Saleinaz.

Ferner. The Tyrolese term for glaciers.

Firn. The accumulation of hard snow which has descended from the steep upper mountain slopes, and which on its further downward course will be consolidated by pressure into ice, and so form a 'glacier,' *i.e.* the raw materials of a glacier, *e.g.* the Jungfraufirn.

First (E. Switzerland). A ridge.

Fluh. A steep or precipitous rock cliff, especially if clean cut.

Föhn. A stormy hot and dry wind which rushes over the Alps from S. to N., *not* probably due to the heated desert of the Sahara, but to the suction of the air from the valleys on the N. slopes of the Alps, so that masses of air come from the S. to restore the equilibrium. See 'Alpine Journal,' vol. xiii. p. 274.

Forca, Forcella, Forchetta, Forclaz, Furka, &c. A fork-shaped depression in a mountain ridge.

Frazione (Italian). One of the hamlets that make up a 'commune.'

Fruitier. A cheesemaker. See **Senn.**

Gaden. A room.

Gand. Any kind of heap of stones or land covered with such.

Gandeck or **Gandegg.** A lateral moraine.

Gaumer. The man or lad who actually drives out and guards the cows on an 'alp.'

Gemeinde. See **Commune** and Art. X. 2.

Genossame. A guild or corporation of persons which owns certain lands in common, and which does not include all members of the Commune; also the rights of a member of such a corporation.

Gerechtigkeit. The right (generally 'real'—see Art. X. 3) of user over lands owned in common.

Geröll. Slope of loose small stones, or 'screes.'

Ghicet (Graian Alps). A deep-cut pass over a lateral ridge, *e.g.* Ghicet d'Ala. Cf. 'wicket.'

Gias. Properly the enclosed space or 'corral' on an 'alp' within which the cattle (in the S. valleys of the Maritime Alps only goats and sheep) are penned at night or for milking purposes; also the huts near by.

Giogo. See **Joch.**

Glacier Remanié. A second and lower glacier (*e.g.* the Schwarzwald glacier at the N. foot of the Wetterhorn), formed by the breaking away of fragments from a glacier above, these fragments being then pressed together, and thus reforming a glacier.

Glacier Table. A flat slab of rock lifted up on a pillar of ice produced by the non-melting of the ice, which is thus protected from the action of the sun's rays. The table generally leans towards the S., as the sun melts the ice on that side more quickly than on the N. side.

Glacière. Originally this word meant the 'Firn' or 'névé' as opposed to the ice of a glacier; now it is generally confined to caves with masses of ice which never melt (*e.g.* the Schafloch, in the Justisthal, above the Lake of Thun).

Glissade. Sliding down a snow slope, voluntarily or involuntarily.

Gola. A very narrow ravine.

Graben. A ravine torn in the mountain-side.

Grund. The level bit of a valley near the stream, as opposed to the slopes above.

Guffer. A heap of gravel, particularly when it forms a central moraine.

Gütsch. A hillock.

Guxe. A wild storm (blizzard or 'tourmente') in the mountains.

Gwachte. A snow drift; also an overhanging crest of snow.

Hanging Glacier. A glacier lying on a very steep slope, so that the spectator wonders how it can 'hang' there.

Heisse Platte. An exposed rock face in an icefall, over which fragments of ice, &c., frequently fall, *e.g.* that above the Grindelwald Eismeer.

Hintersass. A non-Swiss person living in a 'Commune' where he has no rights either as Swiss, Cantonal, or Communal burgher.

Hof. A homestead and its meadows, enclosed within a ring fence.

Hubel. A hillock.

Icefall. The dislocation of a glacier when descending over steep rocks from a higher to a lower level; the ice is then broken up into chasms and pinnacles, which are consolidated into one mass again, when the lower level is reached.

Jas. The French patois form of 'Gias,' *e.g.* Jas du Seigneur.

Joch. A broad pass, or 'yoke' (the Italian 'giogo'), *e.g.* Domjoch.

Jodeln. Shouting in a high falsetto in rhythm but without uttering any words.

A GLOSSARY OF ALPINE TERMS.

Kar. The Tyrolese term originally for a bowl or cup; and by analogy for a mountain hollow or basin, open on one side, a 'Kessel' being enclosed on all sides. See the 'Zeitschrift' of the German Alpine Club, vol. i. pp. 305-9.

Karrenfeld. A limestone plateau, with many fissures through which the water drains away.

Kees. A Tyrolese term for a glacier; it is said to come from an old German word, meaning 'frost' ('Jahrbuch' of the Austrian Alpine Club, vol. ii. p. 402).

Klus. See **Cluse.**

Krinne. A deep cut in a mountain ridge, *e.g.* the two near Grindelwald.

Kuhrecht. The right of a man to pasture one cow on the 'alp' in summer; also used in the sense of 'Stoss.'

Läger. One of the divisions into which an 'alp' is divided horizontally, so that the cows may shift their quarters in order to get fresh grass, *e.g.* Ober Läger, Mittel Läger, Unter Läger.

Lapiaz. See **Karrenfeld.**

Lau or **Laus.** A lake. *Lauzet*, a small lake.

Lauine. An avalanche. See 'Alpine Journal,' vol. v. pp. 346-9.

Lauze. Slate, *e.g.* Col de la Lauze.

Lei or **Lex.** A meadow enclosed by hills, *e.g.* Lex Blanche (Allée Blanche).

Limmi (Gadmenthal). A pass, *e.g.* Triftlimmi.

Lombarda. The wind which blows over the Mont Cenis from Lombardy.

Lücke. A gap or pass in a mountain ridge, *e.g.* Gamchilücke.

Maiensäss. The pastures used in spring before the cows go up to the 'alp.'

Maita. A small mountain plain. See **Amait.**

Malga. A cheese and milk hut.

Mandra. A herd of cattle; hence **Mandron** and **Margheria**, the huts erected for their use.

'Marmites des Géants.' See **Potholes.**

Massif. A mountain 'mass,' or group.

Mayens and **Monti.** See **Maiensäss.** 'Mayens' seems to be also used in the sense of 'Muanda.'

Montagne. Term often used in the French Alps for 'alp,' or mountain pasture.

Moos. A swamp.

Moraine. The stones and rocks that fall from the mountain-sides on to a glacier, and are often raised above its level, as the sun protects the ridge of ice beneath them from the rays of the sun. When two glaciers meet their *lateral* moraines unite to form a *medial* or central moraine; the stones unloaded at the snout of a glacier are called a *terminal* moraine, and those between a glacier and its rock bed are a *ground* moraine.

Motte. Clods of peat or turf.

Moulin. The funnel-shaped opening or shaft excavated (where at first there was but a crack) by the running streams on the surface of a glacier, which thus pierce the ice, and flow over the rock bed on which it rests. Hence the name 'Glacier Mills.'

Mourre. A mountain of which the summit resembles a 'nose,' *e.g.* le Mourre Froid (Dauphiné Alps).

Moutonnées, Roches. Rocks polished into smooth rounded masses (like the backs of sheep) by the action of a glacier moving above them.

Muanda and **Muande.** One of the sets of huts on an 'alp' from which the cows 'change' or shift to another.

Nant. A mountain torrent, *e.g.* the Bon Nant.

Névé. See **Firn.**

Niedergelassener. A 'settler' in a 'commune' wherein he has no rights. See **Beisass** and **Hintersass.**

Orrido. A wild and narrow gorge.
Ouille (Maurienne). Patois form of 'Aiguille,' *e.g.* Ouille de l'Arbéron.
Oule. A hollow in the ground like a kettle, *e.g.* Casse des Oules.
Pala (Dolomites). A mountain peak, *e.g.* Cimon della Pala. The derivation of the word is contested.
Paravas, Pelvas, Pelvo, or **Pelvoux.** A mountain, especially if rounded at the summit.
Parei. Patois form of 'paroi' (wall), *e.g.* Granta Parei.
Pas. Name sometimes given to a low pass (*e.g.* Pas du Bœuf), or to a difficult bit on a path (*e.g.* Pas d'Encel).
Perchés, Blocs. Erratic blocks (see above) which are delicately poised on a mountain-side.
Pertuis. A tunnel through the rocks, *e.g.* the Pertuis du Viso or tunnel under the Col de la Traversette.
Peyron. A huge boulder.
Pickel. Ice axe.
Pieve (Italian). The church hamlet, where is the parish church ('ecclesia plebana'), *e.g.* Pieve di Ledro.
Piolet. Ice axe.
Piz (E. Switzerland). A mountain peak, *e.g.* Piz Bernina.
Plan. A small plain or level shelf on a mountain-side, *e.g.* Plan des Dames.
Platten. See **Blatten.**
Potholes. In the bed of a mountain torrent, or at the bottom of a glacier 'moulin,' a stone is whirled round and round by the stream, and so scours out a hollow or 'pothole.' The holes are sometimes called 'marmites des géants,' *e.g.* in the Gletschergarten at Lucerne.
Primesti. The Ticino word for 'Maiensässen,' which see.
Puy. An isolated eminence on a side ridge.
Ramasse. A wooden sledge (sometimes with a rough seat or chair on it) used formerly on the descent from the Mont Cenis to Lanslebourg (and now at Allevard—see the 'Alpine Guide,' vol. i. p. 128 of the 1898 edition), by which travellers and their luggage, as well as wood, &c., are swiftly conveyed down the steep mountain-side to the village below. See a seventeenth-century description in the 'Rivista Mensile' of the Italian Alpine Club, vol. iv. p. 52. Sledges of this kind ('Holzschlitten') are still used in winter at Grindelwald for bringing down wood from the forests; and have been taken (for the convenience of ladies) in winter over the Mönchjoch and the Strahlegg.
Rechtsame. The right of user (generally 'real') on the 'Allmend.' See Art. X. 3.
Red Snow. This phenomenon (especially frequent in early summer) is due to the presence of a minute plant, one of a group of freshwater *algæ*, and now known as 'Chlamydococcus nivalis;' it is pink in the state of germination, but later becomes deep crimson.
Rimaye. A bergschrund. Desor (i. p. 333) in 1844 proposed to give this meaning to the word, which in the 'Suisse Romande' signifies a great crevasse. Littré says that it is a Savoyard word, coming from the Low Latin 'rima' ('fente'—'rima' is used in this sense by Simler in 1574), and this from 'ringor,' meaning 's'ouvrir.'
Rinne and **Runse.** A narrow gully down which water trickles, or small stones fall, *e.g.* the Schneerunse on the Tödi.
Roësa, Roise, or **Ruise.** A word which in the Aostan patois signifies a 'glacier:' it is the true explanation of the names Monte Rosa, Roisebanque, and Reuse d'Arolla.
Rua. See **Frazione.**

A GLOSSARY OF ALPINE TERMS.   clix

Rucksack. The form of loose bag preferred by the Tyrolese. See Art. VI. 2. The word should have no " on the u.
Rüti. A 'clearing' in a forest or 'backwoods,' by which a bit of meadow or pasture land is won. Hence 'Rütli,' a small clearing.
Sagna. A marshy spot, *e.g.* Sagna del Colle.
Sand Cones. See **Dirt Cones.**
Sattel. A broad and well defined pass or 'saddle,' *e.g.* Roththalsattel.
Scharte. The Tyrolese term for a 'fenêtre,' or narrow gap in a ridge, *e.g.* Tabarettascharte.
Scheidegg. A ridge 'dividing' two valleys.
Schrund. A crevasse.
Schwendi. See **Rüti**: the verb is still used to mean the clearing away in spring, on a mountain pasture, of the rubbish which has fallen on it since the preceding summer.
Screes. See **Geröll.**
Sella. See **Sattel.**
Senn. A cheese-maker.
Sennhütte. The hut wherein dwells a cheese-maker in summer on the 'alp.'
Séracs. A stage in the process of cheese-making—viz. the cheese made from 'petit lait' or whey ('serum'). Saussure (§§ 1975 and 2054) tells us that this cheese is compressed into cubes in rectangular boxes, and that these so resembled the creamy blocks of névé cut into squares by the crevasses formed in their downward course that the natives of Chamonix applied this cheese term to this particular state of the névé. Nowadays the term 'séracs' is generally (though inaccurately) used of the ice pinnacles formed in the icefall of a glacier.
Serra. A narrow defile (*serret*) in a valley; also an elongated mountain range (*serre*).
Sex. A rock (*saxum*), *e.g.* Notre Dame du Sex. Probably identical with the forms 'Scesa' and 'Scez.'
Seybuch. See **Alpbuch.** 'Seyen' is the Bernese Oberland term for the determining how many cows an 'alp' can support during the summer.
Snow Line. The point at which the melting of the snow in summer is exactly balanced by the fall of snow in winter; it varies considerably according to the steepness of the mountain slope, its exposure, &c.
Speck. Bacon.
Speicher. A hut on the 'alp' in which cheeses are stored before being taken down to the valley: it generally stands on six low stone pillars, so as to keep the mice out.
Staffel. One of the horizontal strips into which the 'alp' is divided, so that cows by shifting their quarters may obtain constant supplies of fresh grass during the summer.
Steigeisen. See **Crampons.**
Stoss. The amount of pasture required to support one cow for the summer on the 'alp.'
Striations. The deeply graven lines on rock slabs, especially those which have formed the bed of a glacier; they are caused by the boulders or stones that are imprisoned between the ice and rock, and act as graving tools.
Stube. The 'keeping-room,' 'stove' room, or main room in an Alpine dwelling-house: and thus 'Gaststube' is the best room given up to 'consommateurs' or guests.
Stuhlung. The estimate of the number of cows that can be supported by an 'alp' during the summer.

Stutz. A mountain slope along which a steeply mounting path is carried, *e.g.* Sandigenstutz, Lungenstutz.

Sust. A shelter in general (under an overhanging boulder, or a hut), but especially applied to a hut for customs officials, *e.g.* Susten, in the Rhône valley. The French form is 'souste' and the Italian 'susta.'

Talancia. A very steep slope of snow or ice that never melts; more particularly the strip of snow or ice in a steep couloir or gully.

Thalweg. The bed of a stream in the mountain valley; the stream has eaten its way through the slopes above it, and thus its bed seems to resemble a 'valley path.'

Tobel. A deep-cut ravine in the mountain-side, like a 'Graben.'

Toumple or **Temple.** Properly the deepest part of a river bed; then any deep hollow or gulf. It is masculine, so that, though the word occurs in Dauphiné, it is doubtful if it explains the name of the 'Col de la Temple.'

Tourmente. A blizzard in the mountains. See **Guxe.**

Tsanté. A patois word meaning a gently inclined slope (*e.g.* Tsanteleina) as opposed to a great wall, 'granta parei.' See vol. i. p. 275 of the new edition of the 'Alpine Guide.'

Ueberhang. An overhanging bit of snow, or 'corniche;' also applied to overhanging rocks.

Uja. Patois form of 'Aiguille,' used in the Graian Alps, *e.g.* Uja di Mondrone.

Vanoise. The wind which blows over the Mont Cenis from the Vanoise glaciers, in Savoy.

Vastera (Maritime Alps). An enclosed space or 'corral' for the cows at night. In the S. valleys of the Maritime Alps the word 'gias' (which otherwise has the same meaning as 'Vastera') signifies such enclosed spaces for goats and sheep only. See the 'Bollettino' of the Italian Alpine Club for 1897, p. 223 n.

Vedretta, or **Vadret.** The term applied to a glacier in the eastern portion of the Swiss, &c., Alps (Engadine, Valtellina, and Val di Fassa).

Verglas. A thin film of ice on smooth, inclined rock slabs; it is due to the freezing in the night of a trickle of water.

Villa (Italian). The chief or 'church' hamlet of a 'commune,' *e.g.* Villa di Lozio.

Vire. A rock ledge on a wall which often enables that wall to be traversed, or helps the traveller to turn some obstacle on the ridge above.

Voralp and **Vorsass.** Originally the mountain slopes between the dwelling-houses in an Alpine valley and the 'alp' or mountain pasture proper were owned in common; now this portion is generally owned by individuals. In either case these words mean the pasture grazed by the cows in spring before they go up to the 'alp' proper. See **Maiensäss.**

Wang. A steep *grass* slope as opposed to 'Wand,' which is of *rock*, *e.g.* the Maienwang, between the Grimsel Pass and the Rhône Glacier Hôtel. See G. Studer's 'Das Panorama von Bern,' p. 19 n.

Weiler. A hamlet of a 'commune.' Like Frazione and Rua.

Wildheu. Properly the grass or hay gathered by the first comer on mountain slopes far from any mountain pasture, and so visited only by the poorer natives who have not enough hay and no means of buying more. The word also applies to the grass or hay got above a frequented mountain pasture, which in this case is a perquisite of the 'Aelpler' who take the trouble to bring it down, and can *not* be taken by any one else.

Zieger. The cheese made from whey, which is known in French-speaking districts as 'séracs.'

INDEX.

ABLATION, cxxvi
Accidents, xli–xliii
Adamello, lxvii, lxxii
Aelpler, lxiv–lxv
Aletsch glacier, Great, cxxix–cxxx
Algäu, lxxx
Allmend, lv, lviii
Alluvium, ancient, lxxxv
Alm, lviii
Almer, Christian, lvii
'Alpargatas,' xlvi
Alpfahrt, lxiii
Alpregister, lix
Alps, Central, xx; Eastern, xxii, cxxxi; Western, xix
'Alps,' lvii–lxv, cvi–cvii; regulations, lix
Altels avalanche, cxxxii
Annuals, cxii
Arctic regions, cxix–cxxi
Arves, Aiguilles d', lxxxiii
Avalanches, cxxxi–cxxxiii

BÄCHI glacier, cxxix
Bagnes, Val de, cxxxi
Bees, cxvi–cxviii
Beisässen, lv
Belalp, lxi
Bérarde, La, liv
Bergschrund, cxxv
Bies glacier, cxxxii
Binnenthal, lxix
Birds, c
Blackenalp, lxi
Blanc, Mont, xxiv, lxxii, lxxxix, cix, cxxxviii
Blaugletscherli, cxxix
Books, List of, cxl
Boots, xxxiv
Bosco, xxviii
Bouquetins, xcix
Bread, xl
Brenva glacier, cxxx

Brienz, lv, lxxix
'Bündner Schiefer,' lxxiii
Burgergemeinden, lvi
Burglauenen, lvi
Butterflies, cii, cxvii–cxviii

CALFEISENTHAL, lxv
Canaria, Val, lxxvi
Carriages, xxv
Cenis, 'alps' on, lxv
'Chaises à porteurs,' xxv
Chalets, lxiv–lxv
Chamois, xcix; hunting, xxxii, lv
Chamonix, xlvi, cix
Cheese, xl, lxiii–lxiv, cxxv
Chestnuts, cv
Church town, liii
Citizenship, lvi
Climate, ciii sqq., cviii sqq.
Clothing, xxxiii
Club huts, l–li
Clubs, Alpine, xxxvii note, xlvii, l–li
Communes, lv–lvi
Coniferous trees, cv
Crampons, xxxvi
Crête Sèche lake, cxxxi
Crevasses, cxxiv–cxxv
Crystalline rocks, lxvii
Custom houses, xvi

DANGERS in the Alps, xxxvii, xl sqq.
Davos, xxviii
Deciduous trees, civ
Diablerets, lxxxiii
Dietary, xxxi, xl
Difficulties in the Alps, xxxvii
Diligences, xxiv
Dolomites, lxix, lxxvii, xcvi note, cxxix

EGGS, xl
Einsiedeln, lxii

k

clxii INTRODUCTION.

Einwohnergemeinden, lvi
Emmenthal, lxii, lxiv
Engstlenalp, lxi-lxii
Ennetmärchtalp, lxi
Equipment, xxxiii
Erratic boulders, lxxxi-lxxxiii, xciii-xciv
Expenses of a journey, xxx
Extrapost, xxv

FEE, lxi
Fersina glen, xxix
Festivals in the Alps, lxiv-lxv
Firn, cxxiii
Firs, cvi
Flowers, cvi-cvii, cxv *sqq.*
Flysch, lxxix-lxxx
Föhn wind, cx
Forests, lv, lvii, cvi, cxxxiii
Formazza, Val, xxviii
Fruitier, lxiv
Furka Pass, lxxviii

GEMEINDE, lv
Gemmi Pass, cxxxii
Geology, lxvi *sqq.*
Gepatsch glacier, cxxx
German colonies, xxviii
Gervais, St., cxxxi
Giétroz glacier, cxxxi
Glacial Age, xciii-xcvi, cxxviii; region, cvii
Glaciers, xxxviii, cvii, cxxiii *sqq.*, cxxxii; motion of, cxxiii-cxxiv, cxxvi, cxxviii, cxxx-cxxxi
Glärnisch glacier, cxxix
Glarus, lxxxi, lxxxviii
Gleckstein, lxiii
Gletscheralp, lix, lxiii
Glossary of Alpine terms, cliii
Gorner glacier, cxxx
Gotthard Pass, St.; lxxii-lxxiii
Goûter, Aig. du, cxxxi
Gries glacier, cxxix ; Pass, lxxviii
Grindelwald, xxxv-xxxvi, xlvi, lii note, liv, lvi-lxiii, lxxix, cxxix ; Lower glacier, cxxx
Grödenerthal, liv
Grundlauinen, cxxxii
Gruyère, lxiv
Guides, xxxv, xliv *sqq.*
Gurgler glacier, cxxx-cxxxi
Gydisdorf, liv

HABKERNTHAL, lxxxi-lxxxii
Hasleberg, lxii
'Herrschaft, Auf der,' lvii

Hintersässen, lv
Hohsand glacier, cxxix
Homesteads, lv, lvii
Horses, xxv
Humidity of the air, cx

IBEX, xcix
Ice axes, xxxv
Icefalls, cxxv
Inconveniences of Alpine travelling, xxxii, xxxviii
Inns, xxx-xxxi, xlviii-l
Interlaken, monastery of, liv, lvii-lviii note, lx

'JODELN,' lxv
Jungfrau, xxiv, lxxxviii, cxxxii

KUHRECHTE, lx, lxii, lxiv
Kuhreihen, lxv
Kuhstösse, lix-lxi

LADIN, xxix
Läger, lxiii
Lakes in the Alps, lxxxiv, xcii, xciv, cii, cxxviii-cxxix, cxxxi
Lämmergeier, ci
Languages in the Alps, xxviii *sqq.*
Larch, cvi
Lauterbrunnen, lix, lxi, lxxix, xcix
Letters, xvii
Life in an Alpine valley, lii *sqq.*
Litanies, lxv
Luggage, xvi-xvii
Lukmanier Pass, lxxii, lxxvi, lxxviii

MACUGNAGA, lix
Maiensäss, lvii
Majolica, lxxx
Maloja Pass, xcii
Man in the Alps of old, lxxxiv, xcvi
Maps, cli
Märjelen lake, cxxxi
Marmots, c
Matterhorn, xxiv, lxvii
Mayens, lvii
Measures, xvii
Megglisalp, lviii
Meije, lxxii
Meiringen, lxi-lxii
Mer de Glace, cxxx
Mettenberg, lxiii
Miage glacier, cxxx
Milk, xl, lxiii-lxiv, cxxv
Money, xvi

INDEX.

Monzonite, lxxvii
Moraines, lxxxv, cxxvii–cxxviii
Morschach, cxxxii note
Moulins, cxxv
Mountaineering, xxxvii *sqq.* ; dangers of, xl ; difficulties of, xxxvii ; inconveniences of, xxxviii ; solitary, xliv ; winter, xxviii : without guides, xliv
Mules, xxv
Mürren, lx
Music, lxv

NAGELFLUH, lxx, lxxxiv, xcv
Névé, xxxviii, cxxiii, cxxv, cxxix
Nufenen Pass, lxxiv, lxxvi, lxxviii

OBERSAXEN, xxviii
Olive trees, ciii
Ormonts glen, lxxxi–lxxxii
Oxford, lvi note

PARADIS glaciers, Grand, cxxx
Passports, xv
Pasterze glacier, cxxx
Pastures, lvii–lxv, cvi–cvii
Pedestrians, xxxii *sqq.*
'Pensions,' xxx
Perennials, cxii
Pfander, lxiv
Photography, cxxxiii
Pines, cvi
Plan of journey, xxvi
Polenta, xl
Pontresina, lxi
Poor relief, lv–lvi
Porters, xlv
Post offices, xvii
Prayers on the 'alps,' lxv
Precautions for health, xl
Pressure of the air, cviii
Provisions, tinned, xxxi, l
Pyrenees, xlvi, cxvi

RAILWAYS, xviii, xxiv, xxxi
Randa, cxxxii
'Ranz des Vaches,' lxv
'Rauchwacke,' lxxvi, lxxxvii
Regelation, cxxiii
Reschen Scheideck, xcii
Rheinwald, xxviii
Rhône glacier, cxxx
Riding, xxv
Rigi, lxx, lxxxiv, lxxxviii
Rivers in the Alps, cxxviii–cxxix
Rofel alp, lix

Romonsch, xxix
Rope, xxxvi, xli–xliii
Rousse, Tête, glacier, cxxxi
Routes from London to the Alps, xviii
Rucksack, xxxv
Rutor lake, cxxxi

SAAS, lxi
Safien, xxviii
Salles, Pointe de, xciii
Sämbtiseralp, lviii
Sandalp, lxii
Säntis, lviii, cxxix
Sauris glen, xxix
Scaglia, lxxx
Scheideggalp, lix, lxi, lxiii
'Schistes lustrées,' lxxiii
Schrattenkalk, lxxx
Schonegg, lvii
Scopi, lxxiv, lxxviii
Season for travelling in the Alps, xxvii–xxviii
Senn, lxiv
Séracs, cxxv
Sette Comuni, xxix
Settlements in the Alps, early, lxii–lxiv
Seybuch, lix
Sgrischus lake, cii
Sickness, mountain, xxxix
Silt, lxxxv, cxxviii
Slavonic, xxix
Snow Line, cxxii
Speer, lxx, lxxxiv
Staffel, lxiii
Staublauinen, cxxxii
Steamers, xxiv
Steigeisen, xxxv
Steinalp, lxii
Steinbocks, xcix
Striations, cxxviii

TABLES, glacier, cxxvi
Telegraphs, xvii
Telephones, xvii
Telephotography, cxxxix
Théodule Pass, St., cviii–cix, cxi
Time, xviii
Tourmentes, xliii, cxxii
Tonalite, lxvii, lxxii

UNSPUNNEN, lvii
Unteraar glacier, cxxx
Urnerboden, lxi

VALLEY, Life in an Alpine, lii *sqq.*
Valleys, kinds of Alpine, xci–xcii

Vals, xxviii
Vegetation in the Alps, ciii *sqq.*, cx *sqq.*
Vernagt glacier, cxxx–cxxxi
Verrucano, lxxv
Viescher glacier, cxxx
Villages, origin of Alpine, liii–liv
Vines, civ
Viso, Monte, lxvii, cxxix
'Voralp,' lvii
'Vorsass,' lvii

WALKING, xxiv, xxxii, xxxvii
Weights, xvii–xviii

Weissenfluh family, von, lxii
Wendelin, St., lxv
Wengernalp, lix, lxi
Wetterhorn, lxiii, cxxxii
'Wildheu,' lxiii
Winds, cx
Wine, xxxi, civ
Winter, xxviii, xxxvi, lii, cxxiv

ZÄSENBERG, lix, lxiii
Zermatt, lxi, cii
Zoology, xcviii

PRINTED BY
SPOTTISWOODE AND CO., NEW-STREET SQUARE
LONDON

www.ingramcontent.com/pod-product-compliance
Lightning Source LLC
Chambersburg PA
CBHW030256170426
43202CB00009B/764